LAWRENCE WELK

An American Institution

LAWRENCE WELK

An American Institution

William K. Schwienher

Nelson-Hall nh Chicago

Library of Congress Cataloging in Publication Data

Schwienher, William K 1916–
    Lawrence Welk—an American institution.

    Bibliography: p.
    Includes index.
    1. Welk, Lawrence, 1903– 2. Conductors
(Music) —United States—Biography. I. Title.
ML422.W33S4   785.4'1'0924   [B]   80–10739
ISBN 0–88220–737–6

Manufactured in the United States of America

10 9 8 7 6 5 4 3 2 1

Contents

Acknowledgments

My gratitude goes to all the members of the Lawrence Welk organization who granted interviews as recorded in these pages;

... especially to Lawrence Welk himself for his long and patient conversations, his willingness to cooperate in gathering the voluminous data for this book, and especially for his friendly help and encouragement;

... to Ted R. Lennon for supplying pertinent business data;

... to Welk's personal secretaries, Lois Lamont, Laurie Rector, and Barbara Curtiss, for their gracious assistance;

... to Margaret Heron who patiently furnished research files, personal scrapbooks, and photographs;

... to Bernice McGeehan for her helpful ideas and contacts;

... to Dr. Martin J. Maloney of Northwestern University, who originally suggested a research study on Lawrence Welk;

... and finally to my wife, Gloria, for her invaluable suggestions and ideas in the preparation of the final manuscript of this book.

Introduction

Much social concern exists today over the popular arts media—television, radio, motion pictures, and print—and how they incessantly impinge upon people's minds. Indeed they have become part of our way of life. Young people in our universities in record numbers are studying the psychological and sociological impact of the media upon modern life.

Television in particular is capturing the eye of critics and viewers alike. They are becoming increasingly concerned over its influence upon a passive audience. Remarkably, though, much of the critical thinking of the average person is quite negative. He will condemn television for its obvious faults—depressing the tastes of its audience, corrupting people's morals through violence and sex, or promoting audience passivity. However, the average person is able to do little to contribute to its betterment. He can only shrug his shoulders and allow for the fact that television has simply emancipated our culture, loosened the bonds of moral restraint, and given the masses strong doses of what they most enjoy—"bread and circuses."

Some negative aspects of television may be discussed in

the following pages. However, on the whole, this book will not approach television in a negatively critical manner. Rather it will present a sociopsychological study of one television program—"The Lawrence Welk Show"—inspired by these two remarkable facts: It has outlasted all other TV productions, and it has made broadcasting history by its wholesome appeal to millions of Americans.

It might at first seem ridiculous to propose a study based on the phenomenon of Lawrence Welk. Here is a man with only a few years of formal education, with little or no training with the "greats" in his own field of music and entertainment, and with no specialized preparation in musical entertainment. Yet, when he stepped into the television world in the early 1950s, he began one of the most successful broadcasting careers in history. Television critics have been clearly puzzled at his success and offer a variety of explanations for it. Music critics tend to dismiss him as a popular entertainer rather than a skilled artist. Never before in broadcasting history has any musical variety show claimed an uninterrupted twenty-six years of national television with consistently marketable ratings. It might seem that this farm boy from North Dakota had more instinctive knowledge of what American audiences were looking for in musical entertainment than the television experts in Hollywood. He not only succeeded in breaking into network television but has been enthusiastically renewed by his sponsors each year. Both these accomplishments were completely contrary to what television producers, network executives, and critics had either predicted or anticipated. He has been called "old hat," "square," and "repetitive." His homespun thinking reflects his Germanic idiom of speech. Yet his ratings have always been good, and advertising people insist that, though these ratings may decline for a while, they show good survival power. One must assume he has been doing something right to have survived such remarkable television exposure. One critic says his success is credited to his wholesomeness, while another lampoons him mercilessly for the same reason. Some have even suggested that Welk's big money interests have bought him a place on television. Others have said it is his hidden psychological appeal by which the rank and file of millions of little people can relate to his Horatio Alger story of rags to riches. Doubtless Welk has become a symbol of contradiction in the world of broadcasting.

Whatever explanation any individual critic might offer for Welk's success as a television entertainer and musician, it does seem clear that many elements have entered into his remarkable success story. Only a complete analysis of this man's career and the record of his present accomplishments can offer the curious intellectual the answers to these questions:

1. How does one account for Welk's continued success?
2. Why do some respond to a charisma in him while others find him a tiresome tradition of the past?
3. Is he popular with only the over-fifties?
4. Can his popularity continue with the American television audience?

By inductive reasoning echoing the old dictum "You can't argue with success," this book will demonstrate something apart from the usual overnight success story. Rather it will unfold a well-calculated career plan to achieve and maintain that level of popularity mandatory for national television.

Quite obviously the world has known many great stars who reached their plateaus during their own generation only to find truth in the old adage that passing years mean passing fame. Yet here is a personality who broke this tradition and managed to keep a solid footing on a consistently high pedestal for more than three decades, challenging the fickle and ever-changing tastes of American audiences.

Another objective of this book is to throw further light on the status of American broadcasting, showing why one musical variety show dating from 1952 to the present has achieved enduring popularity while many others have been cancelled after only one season or less. By almost every standard of television broadcasting, the Welk show can be considered successful. It spans exactly twenty-eight years from its first local broadcasts on KTLA in Los Angeles in 1952, through its acceptance by the American Broadcasting Company in 1955 as a summer network replacement, until the 1979–80 season at this writing. Its weekly audience is estimated in excess of 15 million people or 10 million homes.

This analysis focuses primarily upon the person of Welk himself. Every facet of his background and his present organization will be covered: his personal life; his basic philosophy; quoted opinions and interviews of those closest to him; sponsors and audiences who have admired him; critics and former employees who have either condemned him or praised him; his business empire and its impact upon the world of music and television; what unique lessons television itself has learned from Welk as from no other; and finally projections for tomorrow given by Welk himself as well as those of highest rank in his organization.

My association with Lawrence Welk began when I promoted six annual performances of his orchestra in Saint Louis's Kiel Auditorium from 1964 through 1969. I based my doctoral dissertation in broadcasting from Northwestern University on the Welk organization (1969–70). From 1970 to the present, Welk has graciously granted me numerous interviews and personal conversations pertaining to himself and his organization. The present book is a collage of the thousands of facts and experiences I have gathered over these years, both for my research and for the personal satisfaction I have gained from my study of this unique man and his organization.

1
"My Mother Loves Him"

Approval from the American Heartland

What does the average person think of when you mention an "American Institution"? Names of great statesmen like Lincoln, Washington, or Jefferson immediately flash upon one's mind. Prominent politicians who transcended the realm of partisanship or self-aggrandizement to inspire and lead a nation in time of difficulty like a Dwight D. Eisenhower or a John F. Kennedy could be considered American institutions. Great thinkers, writers, educators, or actors like John Wayne, Bob Hope, Will Rogers, Susan B. Anthony, Billy Graham, Martin Luther King were able to build upon their own great careers to offer Americans an ideal, a hope, or an inspiration. These are only a few examples of those who through their remarkable personalities, drive, and enthusiasm profoundly influenced the lives of Americans and who will doubtless be so permanently enshrined in the hearts of generations to come that they will never be forgotten. They are American institutions. They most clearly epitomize American ideals of dedication to God and country, tireless work, individual thinking, and love of their fellowmen that

1

have characterized all truly great Americans since the founding of our republic.

One such institution is Lawrence Welk. This book is not intended to promote his name as such, nor to represent him in press agent style as one who needs this acclaim. He is already considered an American institution by millions of his devoted fans, and little can be said by anyone to enhance their esteem of him. However, this book will attempt to gather the available data and chronicle the important events in the life of this remarkable man. It is a task so monumental that no single volume could contain all the pertinent facts. However, there is one single thread that is woven throughout Welk's life that can be used like a mirror in which to view a much deeper perspective of the man—that he is an American institution.

One of the first glimpses into how the career and personality of Lawrence Welk began to click with the American people can be seen in a story which he himself told me early in 1979. The incident took place soon after he began his coast-to-coast television broadcasts in 1955, when he was appearing at his first concert in Minneapolis:

> The Dodge dealers met us at the airport with twenty-one convertibles! Alice Lon and I were in the front convertible, and a police escort took us through the city to our hotel. You would think the president of the United States had come to town! We waved to everyone on the sidewalks, and it was just like a ticker tape parade for returning heroes. The crowd was so thick I couldn't get out of the car; when we got to the hotel, the lobby was so jammed that the police had to make a path for me to get up to my room. We couldn't even get back down again for lunch before the show, so they had to send up a sandwich to our rooms. Well, when we finally reached the place for our concert, we found the place packed with a sellout crowd of fourteen thousand people. Before this I had never played to more than a thousand people, and if we managed to crowd four or five hun-

dred people into a ballroom we considered it a good night. We really didn't have anything that resembled a Hollywood musical-variety show, and you can't imagine how embarrassed I felt in this huge auditorium with only a seventeen-piece band. But I went out anyway and started playing, and the audience applauded enthusiastically for every number we did. It was a remarkable experience which proved that once the audience is with you, almost anything you do goes over big.

But I just felt uneasy over the fact that so many people had come to hear us and many had paid five dollars and expected to see a big show. I felt uncomfortable until the end of the show when the people began to stand in line for autographs. After I had been signing programs for some time, I heard an announcement on the public address: "Lawrence Welk wanted on the phone." I asked to be excused and said I would be right back. I surely didn't want to lose any of those fans since it was the first experience in my life signing autographs. When I went backstage, I found it was my manager Sam Lutz who called me just to give me a little rest! I said: "Sam, how could you do that to these people? Do you think I could rest knowing this? Remember, nobody in my life ever asked me for an autograph!" When I went back, one man I'll always remember came up and shook my hand. I knew he was a working person by the callouses on his hands, and I also noticed his slightly worn shirt. He said: "Mr. Welk, I came from 500 miles beyond Grand Forks. When I got here, I had to pay five dollars to get in." I began to tremble at the thought when he added, "I'd just like to have you know that this is the best five dollars I've ever spent in my life." That really did something for me. It was my first experience of the overwhelming power of television. That night I stayed on and autographed, though I was so tired the line seemed to never end. Each time I looked up there seemed to be another twenty people. But I decided to stay with them until I signed the program of everyone who waited; and you know, I was there until two o'clock in the morning! The streets were by then deserted and everyone had left except one couple, Mr. and

Mrs. Gay Hinthorn, now old friends of mine, who were thoughtful enough to walk me to my hotel room. This was my first big adjustment from the world of the dance band to the world of television entertainment.

Incidents like this had begun to attract the attention of columnists and promoters of television shows as far back as 1955. Walter Winchell said in December of that year: "Lawrence Welk is more than a television personality. He is an American Institution, as all the polls indicate—including the Winchell Poll—and as documented by Mr. and Mrs. America and all the ships at sea."[1] This statement, coupled with the fact that Lawrence Welk had achieved first place in the Walter Winchell Nationwide TV Poll, stimulated Welk's promoters—Sam Lutz and Don Fedderson—to emphasize his image as "an American Institution."

One of the deeply significant indicators of Welk's appeal, right up to this day, is a constantly recurring remark to Lutz and other Welk associates: "My mother still follows that show religiously." Lutz says, "Even people who wish to disclaim any personal allegiance to the show will spontaneously remark that their mothers or grandmothers are such long-time, ardent fans that they still today arrange their Saturday nights so they'll not miss the Welk Show."

"You can't fool the public," Lutz maintains. "They read sincerity in Welk's face. His number-one objective is to please his public. This is evident in his selection of lyrics. If any portion of a song is the slightest bit suggestive, it is dropped. He is sensitive to his audience's wishes and is careful not to offend their tastes."

Lutz tells about the first time Welk took his show to Madison Square Garden in New York in 1957:

I went to New York two weeks ahead of the engagement to check on how ticket sales and arrangements were shaping up. At the Garden's box office was a long line of elderly people waiting for tickets. I walked over to a window just

*"Lawrence Welk is more than a
Television personality. He is...*

"an

American

Institution!

*"... as all the Polls indicate ... including
the Winchell Poll ... and as documented by
'Mr. and Mrs. America and all the ships at sea'".*

—WALTER WINCHELL

First *Place*
WALTER **WINCHELL**
NATIONWIDE **T.V. POLL**

GABBE, LUTZ, HELLER & LOEB | **DON FEDDERSON PRODUCTIONS**
Personal Managers for Lawrence Welk. | *Television Consultants for Lawrence Welk.*

5

Walter Winchell's accolade of Welk in December 1955 was a boon to Welk's promoters.

opening and handed the ticket agent my card showing I was Welk's manager, and he said, "You know, I've been with Madison Square Garden for thirty-five years, and I've never seen so many old people waiting in line for tickets! There was a man just here who was ninety-four years old. He picked up two tickets and said to me, 'Mister, let me tell you my problem. I can't see and I can't hear; so you've got to put me close to the stage!' "

There are twenty thousand seats in Madison Square Garden, and Lutz maintains that every time Welk has played there over the past twenty-five years he has sold out in advance of the show. Lutz went on to explain:

One of Lawrence's strongest assets is that he is an honest, straightforward man who calls a spade a spade. It is this sincerity that comes across on the TV screen which has marked him as a man of high credibility with the American people. Even in recommending the sponsor's products, when he says he takes Geritol and it has done him a lot of good, people tend to take his endorsement to heart.

It's surprising the number of people, especially critics, who have a totally new reaction toward Welk once they see him perform in person. A number of newspaper critics told me over the phone they would not review Welk's show when it came to their city. Yet when we would arrive, I'd tell them to just do us the favor of seeing the show, and they could write anything they wished about it. Invariably they would see me later and say, "Sam, I wouldn't believe it. To see this man operate and to witness the way the audience reacts to him is a totally new experience."

Honestly, I can't recall a single bad review we ever received from them. Oh, yes, they stressed the simple, folksy style of his show, but almost unanimously these critics were completely converted by the magnetism of his showmanship when they saw him perform in person.

With audiences, it's much the same. I've dealt with other performers like Sinatra and Liberace who were mobbed by aggressive fans, but with Welk, whenever the crowd became pushy, I would simply ask the people to step back and they did. They have a tremendous respect, a kind of reverence for him that's awesome.

I remarked to Lutz, "I've noticed that many of the people who work for Welk have that same respect." Lutz replied:

That's true. The closer you get to know him, the greater your respect for him. It was this power he had over an audience that I saw during World War II at Gardner General Hospital in Chicago. Soldiers, sailors, nuns, rabbis, whomever he played for, were simply captivated by his charm. I remember this vividly when I first persuaded him to leave Chicago and come to California in 1951 and booked him in the Aragon Ballroom at Pacific Ocean Park in Santa Monica. One evening the place was jammed with almost five thousand people on the floor. For about the first thirty minutes, the music played but nobody seemed to be very responsive. Then Lawrence came in and remarked that the place was dead. He went directly to the bandstand for his first appearance in the show. It took exactly three minutes, and the whole house was turned on like it was New Year's Eve. By just picking up his accordion he was able to involve a whole audience emotionally. This is a charisma, a personal magnetism, a kind of showmanship you don't often find in ordinary bandleaders that brings out from an orchestra the kind of music which electrifies people. All you can say is his sincere enthusiasm, his love of performance, his deep and personal concern over the people who are there to see him become so contagious that his audience can't help but react with similar enthusiasm.[2]

Grand Marshal of the
Eighty-Third Annual Tournament of Roses Parade

One bit of national news to come out of Pasadena, California, that delighted his friends and amazed his rivals in show business was the announcement in September, 1971, by the Associated Press that the 1972 New Year's Tournament of Roses Parade was to be marshaled by Lawrence

Welk. He would join a long list of illustrious and distinguished grand marshals who were chosen from many professions and from all parts of the world precisely because they were close to the hearts of Americans. The news release stated:

> Lawrence Welk, who has become a tradition in his own time, is the Grand Marshal of the 83rd Annual Tournament of Roses that is termed "Joy of Music." For years he has been the event's greatest booster. Almost annually since his famed Champagne Music Makers first appeared on national TV, the popular maestro has hosted the Rose Queen and Court on his television show. . . . Just as the Tournament of Roses has become a part of the American scene, the life of Lawrence Welk is truly the story of America's free enterprise system, and the opportunity it afforded citizens to avail themselves of natural talents to achieve personal goals and ambitions.[3]

Russ Leadabrand in the *Pasadena Star-News* of September 10, 1971, wrote:

> There is probably no person in the U.S. who encapsulates America's "Joy of Music" more than Mr. Welk and the choice of him by the Tournament was not only appropriate, but fitting and wise. We are harkening back to the old days when some of the choices of Tournament marshals were particularly inspired. Who can forget the year that Shirley Temple was grand marshal? Not me. I think that Lawrence Welk fits perfectly into the scheme of things, come New Year's morning. There will be bubbles all over Colorado Boulevard, and there will be champagne on everyone's breakfast table. The keynote of January, 1972, will be "wunnerful, wunnerful."[4]

As Welk and his wife, Fern, sat in their convertible leading the Tournament of Roses Parade that New Year's Day of 1972 waving fondly to Americans across the country, doubtless there were long thoughts in their minds of the irony of events that had taken place only four months before, when

ABC had terminated his contract. For it was at that time that Welk had made the difficult but farsighted decision *not* to allow the ax of a television network to end his show. Strangely he found his new syndicated show was being broadcast on many more stations than it ever had been on the ABC network. Here again he showed his first concern for his audience. His decision to form his own network was based upon the overwhelming mandate of more than a million letters of protest over the cancellation of his show.

It was this kind of devotion to the American people that the directors of the Tournament of Roses recognized in Welk. For in choosing recipients each year for the honor of grand marshal, they especially emphasized the criteria of permanence and warmth in the hearts of Americans. When receiving the honor, Welk's answer to Virgil White, president of the Tournament of Roses, was characteristically simple and direct: "This is one of the finest things that has ever happened to me. For many years I have admired Pasadena's gift of beauty to the world. I shall do everything possible to make the 1972 Tournament of Roses the best in history."

As with every other job he ever undertook, Welk did just that. The 1972 parade was like another colorful Welk show of gigantic proportions, with 60 floats, 21 bands, 180 silver-adorned equestrian units, and 2,500 colorfully uniformed musicians. Americans will never forget the theme of that parade—"The Joy of Music."

A Listener's Observation

A remarkable letter was written recently by a listener of the Welk television show, Charles E. Whitmarsh of North Liberty, Indiana:

> Dear Mr. Welk: There are times when I wonder if you fully realize what a national institution your great show has become over the years, or how attached to it your long-time regular viewers have become. Let me explain. Your show is so good it has built up a steady clientele. It has been on the

air so long that many of your viewers certainly have seen almost one thousand weekly shows with many, many more yet to come. You speak correctly of your Musical Family, meaning those who perform on the show in one way or another. However, it is just as correct to speak of your Viewing Family, meaning those on the receiving side of the TV picture. . . . If you see people a thousand times on a regular weekly basis, there is no way to think of them as strangers. They are "family" not as blood relatives but "family" in the sense of a household united by a common interest—your show. . . . Millions of us, your viewers, see the people on your show every week and their names are every bit as familiar to us as the names of our blood relatives. Truly you have a nationwide Viewing Family, instead of an audience of strangers.

Salute from the Young

If there is one group of people with whom Welk is thought to enjoy little rapport, it is the youth of our country. It's a byword among television executives and advertising people that he serves the over-fifty segment of society, but woefully lacks attraction for the younger set. True as this may seem in the commercial world of TV ratings and audience demographics, there are a few startling facts I've uncovered that might indicate a substantial and growing trend in the opposite direction.

Recently I arrived with Welk at a bank building in San Diego where he was to make a radio appearance at a phone-in talk show. We parked near the drive-in teller, and before we could walk into the building several young people employed in the bank recognized Welk and came rushing out to greet us. They flocked around him, asked for autographs, and shook his hand. They spoke highly of his show and displayed such respect for him personally that it was hard to believe they weren't his fans. As I waited in an adjoining room during his broadcast, at least half a dozen people, all about in their early twenties, came in and sat down to wait to see him and speak to him. One said to me, "If I'd pass up this chance of shaking hands with Lawrence Welk, my mother would never forgive me." Another remarked, "My grandmother loves him so much, she won't believe it when I bring her his autograph." Still another said: "My mother would never miss his show. She thinks he's wonderful."

It had only been a few hours earlier that day when Welk visited a local TV station in San Diego for an early morning "Sun Up" show which was produced exclusively by young people. They mentioned how flattered they were by his acceptance of the invitation to appear on their show, and they stressed that it was the first time the reserved seats had all been taken within twenty-four hours of the announcement of a guest's appearance. To the enjoyment of everyone in the studio as well as in the TV audience, Welk seemed to radiate so much joy and happiness that he looked like one of these young people himself. He danced and sang and played his accordion more like a twenty-six year old than a man of seventy-seven.

One particular outside activity that Welk accepted recently was to attend "A Night in Vienna," which was held at Balboa Park in San Diego. The big attraction for him was the fact that this musical program of Johann Strauss's waltzes was to be performed by a symphony orchestra of high school students. Though he must turn down hundreds of such invitations, he accepted this one because he felt he might have something to offer these young people. He did. After his presence at the dance was announced on the public address system, the director came down to our table and offered Welk his baton with the invitation to direct the young orchestra in *Tales from the Vienna Woods*. An uncanny and awesome attention was given him by these young musicians. While they were playing, their director leaned over and remarked to those at our table: "This group has never been so mesmerized by any director. Mr. Welk is literally pulling the music out of them. It's probably the best performance they've ever done of this Strauss number." No doubt they performed beautifully, as attested to by the thunderous applause from the hundreds who were both dancing and listening in this large ballroom. But Welk was in his glory on two counts: It was the kind of music he was thoroughly familiar with and enjoyed to the fullest, and he was directing promising young musicians, in whom he has an all-absorbing interest. When the number was over, the entire orchestra spontaneously rose to its feet and applauded the guest conductor.

From these several incidents it would appear that young people may not particularly like Welk's music—as expressed by their frequent remark, "My mother loves him." However, they definitely relate to him personally. His enthusiasm for youth is so strong and so contagious that they instinctively look up to him as a father or teacher. As a youth-oriented individual, Welk has his heart set on improving the opportunities, the education, and the development of the youth of our country.

Welk's Producer

Don Fedderson has been a prominent Hollywood television producer for thirty years; his name has been identified, not only with Lawrence Welk, but with "My Three Sons," "Family Affair," and "To Rome With Love." Fedderson, as a producer who knows the inner workings of a show, capsulized the Welk phenomenon when he was asked what he thought about Welk's being called an American institution:

Yes, I believe that title would be quite accurate. We haven't had many in the entertainment world, and only a few are alive today. He has such a place of high respect that when he talks on almost any subject—patriotism, religion, family life—people will listen just because it is Lawrence Welk speaking. He may be called a "square," but he stands for the good old-fashioned American way of hard work, honesty, patriotism, and all the rest of the homespun virtues which the less skeptical people admit have made America what it is. People may laugh, but they know deep down inside that this kind of man is the true American and that we need many more like him.

Fedderson then related a remarkable incident that occurred after they had sold the show to the Grant Advertising Agency in 1955 for the Dodge account:

> The first reaction of Lawrence was, "Maybe we can get a nice looking announcer now to act as MC for the show." He could hardly comprehend that we had already sold *him* as the MC since we all knew that the personality of Welk projected a charm, an honesty, and a sincerity which would benefit the show. He also had an instinct for knowing the kind of music people wanted. Our biggest problem was on Madison Avenue—to try to persuade the executives of the Grant Advertising Agency and the network that Lawrence Welk would succeed on television over a Glenn Miller or a Tommy Dorsey or a Guy Lombardo. It was this man's personality which proved the biggest drawing card in Los Angeles, a city we felt was a fair melting pot for the country.

I pointed out to Fedderson that, during only thirteen weeks on network television, Welk went from practically no rating to the first substantial rating ever achieved by an ABC network program, with the possible exception of the "Walt Disney Show." He remarked, "I feel sure that 70 percent of the success of the Welk Show is due to the personality of Welk himself. He would probably deny it, of course, because he has never really changed from being the same humble man he was before his success."

I then asked Fedderson what he considered was the psychological explanation of Welk's appeal to the mass audiences of America. This was his answer:

> It really isn't very different from any other good television program. I believe a show that is going to be successful on television must be able to furnish 10 to 16 million families

(this means 30 to 50 million people right in their homes) with characters and personalities with whom they can relate. A motion picture, by contrast, needs only do this for a relatively small yet strong minority of say 4 to 5 million. A television show, coming as it does right into the home, is in an extremely precarious position. If people don't like the characters or cannot relate to them, it is very easy for them to turn it off or look at something else. It is the genuineness, the credibility and the actuality which television creates through its characters and situations which enables people to relate in such a way that they can escape from the doldrums of their everyday existence. They want, for example, to be the kind of father Fred MacMurray was in "My Three Sons." This is the first requirement we always look for in any script or television cast: Can the average person relate to it and find a certain psychological "escape"? If he can, then the show will be welcomed into millions of homes and followed by many more millions of avid viewers. This may give you a small hint why many television shows are short-lived, and why good television scripts and casts are so difficult to find.

I interrupted with the question, "Do you believe these same norms of success apply to Lawrence Welk?", and he replied:

Though he is anything but a dramatic character, people readily relate to him as an ideal father, an ideal husband, an ideal friend, besides one who knows as well as anyone what the American public wants in the way of music. Often they are carried away by his music without their realizing, for example, that they are moving their foot to the beat of the music. They even relate to his accent, though they might joke about it or even ridicule him for it. It is a great compliment to Welk that so many cartoons and jokes are made about him and his show. Once he made a slip in reading the cue cards and said, "This is my cup of dish." He wanted to do the segment over, but we insisted it would spoil the psychological identification which such a slip would bring

about in so many of his viewers who might laugh, but who
would readily relate to such a mistake.

When I asked Fedderson if he agreed with the statement
about Welk that he is a present-day Major Bowes, he
answered:

> Yes, I agree that he does much for his talent. He is always
> looking for young people to appear on his show, and when
> he finds them he bolsters their confidence in a way that few
> MCs have ever done. Yet, he is even more than a Major
> Bowes. He is also the "last of the Pied Pipers"! This is
> what the Dodge dealers of southern California found out
> and is the principal reason he was put on national television
> in the first place. He instills confidence in his viewers by
> projecting an image of sincerity and honesty [so] that they
> buy the products he recommends. We know of actual in-
> stances of people buying Dodge automobiles who couldn't
> even drive, just because Lawrence Welk recommended them.

I then commented that millions of viewers consider the
Welk Show an inspiration to them, and asked, "What kind
of a model does the Welk Show offer TV?" Fedderson answered:

> It provides no magic formula for other shows to follow.
> Whatever happened did so only because of Lawrence Welk
> ... and his instinctive feel for what his people want in the
> way of entertainment. I cannot think of one other star in the
> whole entertainment industry who could do it. There just
> isn't anyone else with these qualities, or for that matter who
> has such an array of vociferous fans. One of the major rea-
> sons behind the success of "The Lawrence Welk Show" and
> its popularity among families is the "togetherness" which
> Lawrence has injected into his organization and is strongly
> projected to his viewers. Anyone who has ever seen the show
> on television or in a live performance would immediately
> have to agree that it is the feeling of "oneness" and strong
> moral responsibility with which his audience so readily
> identifies.[5]

TV Critics on Welk as an American Institution

What newspaper critics have said about Lawrence Welk over the past thirty years is covered in chapter 7. However, the notion of "An American Institution" keeps appearing so strongly in the decade 1970–80 that it deserves to be treated as a separate phenomenon as reflected by some of the best columnists and music critics across the country. Mimi Avens of the *St. Louis Post-Dispatch* (Sunday, May 18, 1975) states:

> Lawrence Welk is a band leader and accordion player. But that is not all. Just as Cher is the symbol of the would-be hip and Alice Cooper is the standard-bearer for the would-be flipped, Welk is the all-American, old-fashioned, down-home king of corn. His land is our land, the America one sees in soft-drink commercials—pretty girls and healthy kids on green lawns all helping, sharing, smiling. The 35 million people in Welk's television audience want to be reminded that there is more in America than divorce, drugs and danger. Weekly, Welk assures them there is.

Another TV columnist, Elston Brooks, in 1970 reminisced in the *Fort Worth Star Telegram* about how his parents were dragged from their TV set on a Tuesday night back in 1956 to go out dancing when "The Lawrence Welk Show" came to town:

> It was the night for the *$64,000 Question* which had welded people to their home screens. But 2000 of them jammed the Casino to dance this night 14 years ago. And the television-inspired popularity of one man had gotten them out of the house! Lawrence Welk, undisputed king of the Geritol Set and exponent extraordinary of the Businessman's Bounce, was playing his first one-nighter here, after his Saturday night TV show, offered as a summer replacement in July of 1955, had become the biggest thing on the tube. So what else is new? Here it is, the Spectacular Seventies. Man has walked on the moon, people have forgotten Hal March's isolation booth, and Welk still is the toast of the over-40 crowd with his Saturday night TV show.

A youthful columnist, P. J. Parton, in the *Sunday Herald-Leader* of Lexington, Kentucky, stated on September 6, 1970:

> An institution came to town Friday night in the form of the "establishment"—the Lawrence Welk Show was presented in Memorial Coliseum to a near capacity crowd largely composed of the over-30 group—neatly gloved, smoothly coiffed ladies and gentlemen, senior-citizen types who murmured to the strains of familiar tunes and swooned at the mellow tones of their favorite living room performers. You've read correctly—swooned—much like my generation did to Elvis and the Beatles. Since I am not a Lawrence Welk fan, I must admit I went to the performance with a youth-like negative approach. . . . Mr. Welk came, saw and conquered an already conquered audience who paid to hear his type of music and came away well satisfied. If I might be allowed a brief note, it did my heart good, made me want to dance myself to see our older citizens caught up and enthralled, freed of their cares and the problems outside the Coliseum with their own children and grandchildren, many of whom are our University of Kentucky students caught in the ever-increasing pressures of living today. If more of my age group could have viewed the enjoyment, the enthusiasm of this audience, they might have come away as I did, thanking Mr. Lawrence Welk and his troupe of entertainers for stopping by our city.

Jon Marlowe in the *Miami News* (March 11, 1977) states:

> With another show to do tonight (in Miami), Lawrence Welk and his 50-member musical family will reach over 16,000 people here today. "There are only three acts in the entertainment world that sell out this quickly and do business like this," says the Lakeland Civic Center manager—"Frank Sinatra, Elvis Presley and Lawrence Welk." There's no question about it. He is an American Institution.

Helen Smith, writing in the *Atlanta Constitution* (March 12, 1975) about the Welk Mystique says:

They came by the busloads from Macon and Albany, from South Carolina and North Carolina. They came by the thousands in cars until every seat was filled at Civic Center. They came in wheelchairs, on canes and walkers . . . and their faces were beaming. They were the Geritol groupies converging on their idol, Lawrence Welk, and his family of 45 gosh-almighty wholesome and attractive "children," as Welk refers to his performers. . . . In fact, love is just oozing out all over. The Welk mystique has taken over. When the champagne bubbles rise from the orchestra pit to fill the stage during the final number, the audience has gotten just what it came for—sweet love songs. (no kinky passions, no bleeding hearts stuff here), bouncy music, and the Welk smile and enthusiasm that makes his devoted fans feel as if he cared about each one of them.

Bill Potter, in reviewing Welk's first book *Wunnerful, Wunnerful* for the *Joplin* (Missouri) *Globe* (January 12, 1975) states:

This book uncovers the inner character of the man who has charmed America with his champagne music on television for more than 25 years and whose life span in the entertainment world has passed the 50-year mark. The basic simplicity of his honesty and humility provides a powerful profile of this prominent personality. Lawrence offers a viable three-point program for national unity and sums up his "dream" with this remark: "If we could effect these changes and trust in God, we could change the world." Any Welk fan will find this book brings both tears and smiles to the reader who appreciates the man who has truly become a legend in his own time.

Marvin Kitman, writing in the *New York Times*, May 6, 1971, states:

The other day I read in the press releases that, owing to the impressive demand on the part of both television stations and sponsors, the producers of the Lawrence Welk Show will begin syndicating the program next season despite its being cancelled by ABC. It just goes to show you can't keep a good program off the air. Sometimes I think ABC, bottlers of the champagne music since 1955, never appreciated the major contribution to American culture that Welk made every Saturday night.

Gerald Nachman in the *New York Daily News* (January 19, 1973) writes:

Like his songs, Lawrence Welk is now a standard, an institution who has withstood the cruel ravages of criticism, parody, the clock and pop music fads. With the Yankees, with Norman Rockwell, and "White Christmas" he prevails. The Lawrence Welk Show isn't just the oldest living TV musicale in history, it's older than TV itself, than radio, the oldest form of entertainment other than back porch swings and campfire songs. It is Paleozoic show biz. Since watching the program is like viewing stereopticon slides in the parlor by gaslight, there's nothing else to do with this gentle artifact but clasp it to your heart and sigh wistfully. To say anything mean would be to belt grandma. In a way, Welk is a public service show, true alternative programming, TV not just for shut-ins but for anyone who feels shut out of the racy, rat-a-tat TV world and can't keep up with Dean Martin, Mannix or Kung Fu.

Bill Fiset writes in the *Oakland Tribune* of January 9, 1975:

And in Santa Barbara we have one Anthony Defina, concerned citizen, currently sending mailing to newspaper editors pointing out the grave condition in which the country finds itself and suggesting we all become aware of the need of electing a President next year "who can give hope, restore confidence and bring the country together again—a person of the highest integrity, a man with understanding. In my estimation one individual meets the qualifications—a well-informed, astute business man—Lawrence Welk." Not a bad idea, but if he were president, who would lead the orchestra?

Humor over Welk

One of the strongest indications of Welk's place in the hearts of Americans is shown by the endless cartoons, jokes, and witty remarks about him that have found their way into the popular culture of America. For example, it is no setback for Welk himself that a syndicated cartoonist would take up his bubble motif and use it for a joke. Bubbles proved to be one of the trademarks of his show as far back as 1958 in Pittsburgh when a local radio announcer suggested that his music had a bubbly, lightsome quality and his orchestra could well be called "Champagne Music Makers." Another cartoonist depicts a used-TV salesman saying to a prospective customer, "This one belonged to a little old lady who listened to Lawrence Welk!" These quips are a source of great amusement to Welk himself, and he laughs over them like anyone else.

Another syndicated cartoon, "Side Glances" by Gill Fox, recently depicted an elderly man being nursed back to health by his attentive wife who assured him: "You've got lots to live for, Henry! Think of the Lawrence Welk reruns!"

Welk's office personnel have made a whole collection of cartoons which are framed and displayed just so everyone can get a good laugh. Ann Landers's column of March 25, 1975, had advice for nine top celebrities; she told Lawrence Welk, "Let 'em make fun of your 'ah-one, ah-two' and 'I think you're wunnerful,' and *you* keep laughing all the way to the bank."

Endless Welk cartoons have appeared in the American press, particularly in the early years of the television show on ABC from 1955 to 1965: bubbles were shown emerging from TV sets or children were shown making bubbles just to produce a little realism to go along with the Welk show! Actually, most of the gibes only contributed to the light-hearted acceptance of Welk as a part of the American scene,

a Saturday night institution everyone watched for a pleasant break from the cares of life. However, by 1970 one television critic, Larry Rummel, writing in the *Phoenix Gazette* (December 4, 1970) commented that time was when every comedian out for a laugh had a Lawrence Welk joke tucked away in his routine:

> Apparently the Welk joke has fallen from favor these days. I can't remember when I heard the last one but it was a long time ago. What happened, of course, was Welk simply outlasted those who went for laughs at his expense. His television show is now in its 16th season and apparently shows no sign of old age. One of the reasons, I think, for Welk's success is the maestro is not content to fill his season-long commitment to ABC-TV and then sit back on his laurels, waiting for the next premiere week. Welk takes his musicians out on a string of personal appearances throughout the country . . . thus he has an ear cocked to what people want to hear.

Perhaps the most significant tongue-in-cheek, half-humorous, half-serious column ever to appear on Welk was written by syndicated columnist John Keasler in August, 1975, for newspapers across the country. It was captioned, "Ford should have picked Lawrence Welk." Keasler stated:

> It is too bad Lawrence Welk wasn't picked as Vice-President. It would have been a wise choice for many reasons, the chief of which is that Lawrence Welk has never done anything wrong. . . . My feeling is that we here in Middle America are sick unto death of controversy. My further feeling is that we here in Middle America need to relax. . . . Also, Lawrence Welk would have come in with ready-made charisma. He does not have to hire a lot of press agents to get charisma. An Associated Press story about Welk said, "California's three greatest tourist attractions are Disneyland, Forest Lawn Cemetery, and Lawrence Welk." That's charisma. And yet, strangely enough, scintillating as both

are, the personalities of Gerald Ford and Lawrence Welk do
not clash but complement each other.[6]

Why a legend? An institution?

The good-humored banter that "Welk never goes away"
may well be true. *Billboard* and *Variety* keep reporting that
his stage shows are consistent sellouts throughout the country.
Critics, columnists, and fans insist he is a fixture in the
hearts of Americans. This book will document thousands of
such testimonials. But the thinking person will still ask:
Why has he become a legend in his own time . . . an American Institution?

The answer might well hearken back to another great
entertainment figure, that grand old man of motion pictures,
the late Louis B. Mayer, once production chief of Metro-
Goldwyn-Mayer. He is recognized as the most influential
movie executive of three decades, who discovered and made
careers for scores of all-time greats of the movie world. The
phenomenal success of MGM stemmed from Mayer's simple
philosophy: "Humor, charm and prettiness are essential
elements of the movie formula for successful family entertainment."[7] Just before his death in 1957, *High Society*—
a remake of the 1940 production *The Philadelphia Story*—
became the apotheosis of the charm and prettiness that
formed the distinctive style of Metro-Goldwyn-Mayer.

Most people who remember the days of the great spectacles
in motion pictures agree that there will always be a nostalgia
for those happy years of entertainment, as evidenced by
MGM's recent productions, *That's Entertainment* and *That's
Entertainment II*. And as Mayer left his own style permanently imprinted upon the movies of the thirties, forties, and
fifties, so has Welk left a similar imprint upon three decades
of television. It could be called an enduring nostalgia that,
like Welk, "never goes away." For the humor, the charm, and
the prettiness that Welk has always projected are just as
essential for television's success as for motion pictures.

According to most critics, today's television fare has highlighted two unacceptable extremes: Either violence and sex or the light, inane sitcoms, both of which have hypnotized today's audiences into an obsequious acceptance of one episode after another. However, there remains today that vast, silent majority of middle Americans who do prefer the wholesome and the uplifting in television entertainment. This audience is Welk's. It comes by the millions from every town and city, from every ethnic group, and from every walk of life. These people already know he's an American Institution. Those who don't know have yet to find out.

2
Lawrence Who?

A Biographical Sketch

Lawrence Welk was born on March 11, 1903, in a sod farmhouse near Strasburg, North Dakota, the sixth of eight children born to Ludwig Welk and the former Christina Schwahn. His parents were immigrants to the United States. They originally came from Alsace-Lorraine and had left it in 1878 after the Franco-Prussian War to settle in the Odessa region of the Russian Ukraine. Ludwig and Christina were married there and had one son, Anton, who died at the age of two. After his death, the couple immigrated to the United States and became homesteaders of a large tract of land three miles northwest of Strasburg, North Dakota. Here they reared eight children, all of them born in the original home built by Ludwig, which is still standing today.

Lawrence's earliest memories of his childhood were the strict discipline taught him by his parents, the daily tasks and religious duties which were of obligation to all, and the healthy respect he learned both for money and for a task well done. The family was poor, and there was a constant struggle to make ends meet financially. He shared a warm family life with his seven brothers and sisters, and he has nothing but loving memories of his gentle and pious mother and of his strong and demanding father. Lawrence was the shy, dreamy child who seemed always preoccupied with music. He was often ridiculed by his brothers and sisters as the "dumelhazen" of the family because he was lost in music, was very small, very shy and sensitive. He was ill a great deal during his early childhood and consequently was not sent to school until he was seven years old. Then he attended the small Catholic parish school of Saints Peter and Paul, taught by Ursuline nuns who had been sent over from Germany to do "missionary" work in rural areas of the United States. During the winter months the children stayed with the nuns at the convent and lived in a totally German environment. Even their classes were in German, so that young Lawrence never had a chance to learn the English language at all. He recalls that he was a fair student but was so shy that it was difficult for him to stand up in class and recite.

After the fourth grade his schooling was cut short by a violent attack of appendicitis. He woke up in the night writhing with pain, and he recalls that he was more worried over how he would be able to help with the threshing the next day than he was over his sickness. He feared all during that long night that he might not be able to drive the wagon, which was his asigned job, so he determined not to say a word to anyone about how badly he felt. By morning he was so sick he could hardly stand up, but somehow he forced himself to sit through breakfast. His mother finally discovered him rolling in a cornfield trying to assuage his pain and nausea. All he remembered after that was being taken in a buckboard wagon to a doctor in Strasburg who diagnosed a ruptured appendix and said an immediate operation would be necessary to save his life. He was rushed to a hospital in Bismarck in the only car in town, which was owned by John Klein, the father of Johnny Klein who until recently was a member of his band. Doctors there operated on him, but for weeks he hovered between life and death. At one point the whole family was summoned because the doctors were convinced that he would surely die soon. Though peritonitis had set in from the ruptured appendix, he somehow pulled through after a seven-week stay in the hospital. It was only the beginning of a much longer convalescence at home during which he was confined to bed with a drain in his side.

As he continued to improve, the family had to leave him alone in the house and go about their own duties. Meanwhile his mind lingered on the music he loved so much, and he even recalls "playing" on the keys of the accordion on his bed. As he grew better and stronger, he would strap the accordion on his back and play it by the hour, sometimes inside the house, sometimes sitting outside in the sun behind the barn. These were the days, he fondly recalls, that marked the beginning of his deep conviction that some day he must be a musician. He experienced a strange combination of being repelled by the butchering and the manure spreading of farm work plus an almost indomitable attraction to the accordion which has often made him wonder to this day whether it was his fear of becoming a farmer or his love of music that had the most influence on his decision!

After Lawrence had recovered fully and resumed all of his duties around the farm, there was the question of when he would be going back to school. On the plea that he was now a head taller than anybody else in the class—due to both his late start in school and his sickness—he came up with a typical boyish bit of rebellion: he just wasn't going to go back at all. Much to his surprise, the family agreed that perhaps he had enough education now to be a farmer, but they did not take into account his inner drives and ambitions toward music. While in his teens, he spent most of his spare time indulging his passion of playing the accordion. He simply drowned himself in music. He sent away for several cheap accordions, which he paid for by trapping animals and selling their hides, but he played them so hard they fell to pieces. It was about this time that a traveling musician named Tom Gutenberg came to Strasburg and brought with him the

first piano-type accordion Lawrence had ever seen. He was so
overwhelmed with Gutenberg's instrument that the idea of
having one for himself became an obsession. He priced one
in a mail-order catalog and discovered that he would have
to trap more animals than North Dakota could furnish if he
were ever to save up the grand total of $400. He admits that
he pondered for weeks, even months, over how he would
amass such a fortune. Finally he thought of a plan. He would
speak to his father and make a deal with him.

Considering the frugality of the Welk family's way of life,
this plan of Lawrence's was a masterpiece of audacity. Yet
like most plans he undertook in later life, it was both am-
bitious and practicable. He asked his father to buy him a
$400 accordion. In return he offered to work for four full
years on the farm and pay for the accordion by playing at
nearby weddings and parties. At first Ludwig brushed the
whole idea aside as preposterous. But finally he realized how
serious Lawrence was, and perhaps he recognized too that
there was something different about his youngest son. The
father agreed, and Lawrence admits that he spent an eternity
of waiting while the accordion was being shipped. Every day
he would go down to the railroad station to see if it had
arrived. The days and weeks seemed endless. When the
precious instrument was finally in his hands, Lawrence had
the thrill of his life. It was the beginning of his long and
great career as a musician. He played at every farm festival,
wedding, and name's day party in the countryside. He often
made $100 or more at three-day wedding parties which were
common among the Germans and Scandinavians. True to
his promise, he took his money home and gave it to his
father. It was a lesson, he believes, that was among the most
valuable of his life—to stick to his word no matter what difficulties he encountered. All during these years while Lawrence was doing his apprenticeship as a musician close to
the protective influence of his family, Ludwig had long and
serious talks with him on the dangers and pitfalls of a life

in the entertainment world. He feared for Lawrence's faith and morals in such a life, and made no apologies for warning him of the temptations that lay ahead. But finally, after receiving Lawrence's assurance that he would indeed be careful and faithful to what he had been taught at home and at church, Ludwig and Christina gave him their blessings, and he set out on his twenty-first birthday, March 11, 1924, to make a career for himself in the world of music.

While reminiscing on those days on the farm, Lawrence observed:

> My strongest asset in life has been that I was raised in a Christian family which believed in strict interpretation of the church's laws. I believe that our churches should give character training as well as spiritual guidance. If you don't think it was a strict observance of Catholicism, we would hitch up our horses on a Sunday morning at forty degrees below zero, and heat big stones in the fire to keep us warm over the three-mile trip to church. This was the strong training our religion gave us, besides of course fulfilling the obligation we felt to worship God on Sunday mornings by attendance at Holy Mass. I believe a person's chances of going straight after such religious training are so much better than if one's religious observance requires no sacrifices.

Thinking back on the good influence of his parents, Welk recalled:

> I think they taught us just to do a good job in whatever line of work we felt called to. What impressed me so much about my father was that he could get forty bushels of wheat an acre, though the farmer right next to us would get twenty, or another would get thirty. The thought went through my mind so often that this was all the same land, so what could be the reason for this difference of yield? Well, my parents used to walk through the fields on beautiful summer evenings holding one another's hand. Then they would return to tell us children we would have to pull more

weeds here, plough deeper in certain places, or even begin our ploughing earlier in the spring if we were to get the most out of our crops. This was the kind of lesson we were taught and one which made a lasting impression. They always tried to do just a little better job than someone else.

In their own particular ways, each member of my family was excellent in his own line of work. My sisters were fine housekeepers, and my brothers all excellent farmers. Perhaps they didn't have the same drive I had to succeed in my work; but of course I had been hindered from a music career and wanted it so badly that I tried so much harder to succeed. That deal, for example, that my father and I entered into when I was seventeen to buy me my first accordion with the understanding I would work for him for four years, gave me more motivation than you could imagine.

Going back to my days working with my father in his blacksmith shop, I remember him as a fine handyman who really enjoyed doing everything from shoeing horses to helping all our neighbors sharpen their ploughs. Of course I was only his helper and I'm sorry to say I got on his nerves a lot because I was such a clumsy kid doing that kind of work. I did help him a lot, but really didn't have much interest in what I was doing. From that experience dealing with my father who loved his work so much, I discovered that I would have to learn to do what I too liked. Sadly most people never find what they really want to do in life. Look at them when they go to work or come off their jobs—what long faces! For me, I just love to entertain people—for example those eighty- or ninety-year-old people who come to my restaurant. It's the same with the millions who see our TV show or who come to our shows in cities everywhere. Just to bring joy to them means a great deal to me.[1]

Lawrence commented further on his family members and their musical talents:

Yes, our family had excellent talent in such areas as rhythm and timing. They were all good dancers, and dancing made up a large portion of their relaxing hours. My father was a good natural musician and played his accordion beautifully. But my dancing talent probably comes from my mother, who was an exceptionally agile dancer. You saw me dancing those Viennese waltzes with that Russian lady the other night. Well, my mother was very much that kind of dancer, almost professional in her movements. Her personality was very ladylike, somewhat timid and unassertive, perhaps as we know Norma Zimmer. I have the idea that my own timidity and sensitive nature comes from my mother rather than my father. My father was much stronger, though not overbearing in his manner. He had rules for us children, and what I learned from him applies today to the exacting nature of television, which requires that firm rules must be followed. When the show is about to start, and the clock comes up to eight o'clock, if you're not right on the second, you're in trouble. This kind of work takes discipline, and I don't see how I could operate without it in my people. I believe the worst thing we have done in our schools is to soft-pedal the importance of discipline.

Lawrence was asked if he looks back over his days at home and thinks of his brothers and sisters. He said yes:

I always had a special fondness for my brother Louis or "Louie" as everyone called him. One time in church my brother Louie sat with some of his friends; and they began laughing at something which had happened in church. It was like kids often do—when one starts laughing, they all laugh and they can't stop. Well, Father Max, our parish priest, who was a very positive disciplinarian, told them to come up in front of the church and kneel down at the communion rail. It was a terrible humiliation for Louis, and of course he got a good spanking over that situation when he returned home.

Louis passed on some years ago. He was the unusual member of our family and loved to show off his strength by picking up a car. Indeed, he was the extrovert of the family and loved all kinds of sports, even boxing. We all loved him very much, and sadly he was the first one in the family to die, at an early age. My sister Barbara is quite old now, and she is confined to the hospital. However, my other three sisters are all living in the area around Strasburg, except Eva who lives in Aberdeen, South Dakota. My brother Mike, who is the youngest, looks after our family farm. He is very kind to visitors who stop to see my birthplace, the house where I lived until I was twenty-one. At one time we were thinking of taking my home and moving it to California. But of course the house was built by my father back in the 1890s, and it would be quite an ordeal to move it. Yes, looking back to those wonderful days at home, I remember only the happy times we all had together. There was discipline, but not the kind to make us afraid of our father. I would say that it was my good fortune to be born in a good Christian family which truly practiced their religion. My mother prayed constantly, and I never knew her ever to lose her temper or become out of sorts. The only frustration you could see her experience was maybe a little tear if something went wrong. Though my father was much stricter, he was not unbending or unreasonable as some people I found in the theater world after I left home. I've always felt that when a man lowers the boom on his family, he sometimes makes people so afraid of him that they can't act like human beings. It is a very sad thing when a child grows up fearing his parents. Their relationship cannot be normal.

When I was growing up in Strasburg, though I played my accordion at many celebrations around town, it was very seldom that I was allowed to go any distance from home. The first time I was allowed to leave I went to visit my married brother, John, in Ipswich, South Dakota. It was too far to drive in those years, so I took the train. As I was leaving I met some friends getting on the train who later asked me if I would play my accordion for them. And so I obliged by playing my polkas and waltzes and schottisches. I had played for what I had thought was a short time, when someone suggested, "Why don't we play some cards?" They asked me, and I said "No, I don't believe so," and I kept on playing my accordion. Finally one of the fellows blurted out: "Hold it. Hold it. It was good at the start to hear your accordion but I just can't take it any more!" It finally dawned on me the reason they wanted to play cards was so I would quit playing the accordion! That experience was a lesson for me not to be so naïve as to expect others to enjoy my playing as much as I do. Like all good things, even an accordion can get on people's nerves, and not all people actually like it. Then when I got to Ipswich almost the reverse happened to me. I played for a group of dancers from nine until twelve that night. Then they passed the hat and asked me to play for another hour. By one o'clock they were having so much fun they passed the hat again and asked if I'd play still another hour. I couldn't refuse. The next morning I attended ten o'clock mass with John and Theresa, and the priest had his sermon built around the "devil that had come to town" and had the people dancing right into the early hours of the Lord's day! Ironically, though, it turned out that the same priest had a dance in his church basement not many years later and wanted to hire my band to play for it! By that time, of course, the old rules about dancing on Sunday had been relaxed.

Finally I asked Lawrence if, after all those wonderful years at home with his good parents and brothers and sisters, he felt any personal regrets or guilt over the fact that he had left it all to embrace a totally new career in show business with glamor and success and notoriety. "No," he assured me.

I've never had any feeling of guilt at all. I visit home every year or so and keep up with my family and old friends in North Dakota. They watch my show very faithfully and are all interested in my activities. It may be a very simple way of life, but my family never lived any differently from the time my parents came to this country back in 1889. From that time until the depression in 1929 we may have been very poor at times, but we had good years when we received forty bushels an acre. Other years the prairie fires came and destroyed everything we had. Over those years we were able to save almost $30,000 which tided us over the terrible years of depression. We always had enough wheat to take to the

mill for our personal use. Then we always grew our own
vegetables and had enough cream from the cows so we could
sell it and buy whatever else we needed. We may have been
poor by today's standards, but we always got by and had
enough to eat. Most of all, though, we enjoyed a happiness
together which few people of greater means ever seem to
have. And things with my family are much the same today.

Oh, yes, my father did not quite approve of my music
career when I started. As a good father he had warned me of
the dangers to my faith and morals. But once he had my
assurance that I could be relied upon to be at mass and to
receive the Sacraments on a regular basis, he was satisfied.
In his later years my friends used to tell me how he would
stand outside the ballroom where I was playing, smoking his
cigarette, which he held in a long holder, and listen to the
band play with great enjoyment. He would talk to the
people and always made sure they knew it was his son's
band. And so he seemed very proud of the work I was doing,
as well as the success I found in my career.[2]

The new sights and sounds of the world outside were a
constant source of amazement to young Lawrence just embarking on his career. There were many things he had never
seen before and many ideas he had never heard of even at the
age of twenty-one. But he overcame his natural shyness and
personally arranged bookings for himself and his accordion
at any prospective entertainment spot he could find. He made
it a practice to find out which saints' days were being cele-
brated in different towns. To celebrate the day of the patron
saint of the parish church was an old Catholic custom
brought over from Europe. One of his major successes of
this period was in Hague, South Dakota. He arrived early
in the day and rented a small building for a dance hall. Then
he went around town putting up handbills announcing the
dance, and he even began canvassing for his customers by
approaching them on the street and inviting them to come to
the dance that evening. If anyone felt the price of one dollar per couple was too high, he would make a deal with them

and give them three tickets for the price of two, as long as they were buying them in advance. He kept this up all day, and when evening came the small hall was filled to capacity. It was his first lesson on how to make his own success by hard work.

He recalls that another of his great successes in these early years was at Satterwood Lake, South Dakota, when he was hired to play for a big Fourth of July celebration and had to hire some very capable musicians to play with him for the affair. Because the baseball game scheduled for the same holiday had to be called off due to rain, everyone crowded into the dance pavilion. Welk recalled:

> Since the band was such a big-sounding attraction, people swarmed to the ticket booth to pay their admissions. I not only established a great reputation for having a good-sounding band but made more money than I had ever made at one time before. After all my expenses were paid, I had $260 left, enough to complete payments on my car which I had bought a month before. Now I could return for a visit home driving a shiny new car that was all my own. My dear mother was proud of me, and my father could see for himself that his investment in his son's hopes was working out. Though the visit was short, it was a happy reunion with my family whom I had not seen for two long years.[3]

Back on the road again, Lawrence arranged for a booking at a county fair in Selby, South Dakota. After the performance and dance were over, he was approached by a genial Irishman named George T. Kelly who offered him a job with his traveling troupe of players, the Peerless Entertainers, for the unheard-of salary of forty dollars a week. Welk was so astonished at the offer that he stood aghast with his mouth open unable to say a word. Kelly concluded that Welk must not be satisfied with the offer and offered to split the take 50–50; Lawrence said "ja" so fast and wrung Kelly's hand so hard that Kelly nearly backed down from his offer. Welk considers his association with Kelly one of the finest he ever made in his life. He learned not only about show business but a great deal more about human nature from this amiable Irishman.

The Peerless Entertainers worked throughout the winter months, first presenting their little routine in which Kelly played the part of "Ole the Swede" and Welk, in an inspired bit of miscasting, played a Spaniard! He was dressed in short black satin pants with a fringed bolero and red sash, and nobody was ever the wiser since he never opened his mouth! Kelly did all the talking. After the performances, the room was cleared and Lawrence would play his accordion for the dance that followed. It was literally a two-man show. Kelly phoned ahead to make the bookings. When they arrived in town they put up handbills, set up seating, sold tickets, put on the show, played for the dance, and then cleaned up the place afterwards. It was Kelly who taught Lawrence the real basics of show business: timing and pacing a show, how to get along with people, how to please the audience, and how to look for the best in others and really succeed in drawing it out of them. Kelly used to bill Lawrence as "America's Greatest Accordionist" and he feels that this drew out the best that was in him, though he knew very well it was a gross exaggeration. During the two years Lawrence performed with the Peerless Entertainers, from 1926 to 1928, he took English lessons from Mrs. Kelly, and he seriously set out to learn how to read music. He also developed more self-confidence and belief in himself and gave serious thought to what his future would be. All in all, George Kelly became Lawrence's first and greatest teacher in his show business career. Though their association was relatively short, their friendship was warm and cordial, lasting for many years until George Kelly's death in 1962.

The Kellys left for Poplar, Montana, and Lawrence, with four other musicians, headed south for the Mardi Gras in New Orleans. They were hoping to drive into a warmer climate, but banks of snow covered the road, and they had to follow a snowplow for many miles. The going was slow, and by four o'clock in the morning they were so exhausted they decided to stop at Yankton, South Dakota, for a much-needed rest. Being a true farmer, Lawrence was up with the dawn while the others were still sound asleep. With his customary eye for business, he decided to look around for some possible engagements to play in Yankton. There happened to be a new radio station in town—something of a novelty even as late as 1928—and Lawrence decided to call on the manager, Chandler Gurney (who later became United States senator from South Dakota). Gurney was willing enough to listen to the new orchestra in town, and so Lawrence lost no time dashing back to the hotel to alert the boys, who by now were all eating their breakfast in the dining room. They gulped down their bacon and eggs, made a straight line for radio station WNAX, and to everyone's amazement they made a hit with Gurney. He put them on the air immediately. Calls came in before the program was over complimenting the station and requesting special songs by the new band. Gurney was so pleased he signed up the band for a whole week. Later he extended it to two weeks; finally he kept the band on permanently. It was the first great step forward in Lawrence Welk's broadcasting career.

WNAX was an extraordinarily powerful station blanketing almost all of the upper midwestern states, and it was these first broadcasts that began making the name of Lawrence Welk known to tens of thousands. Now when he went out on dance engagements, people already knew his name from his broadcasts. At first he turned down offers because he still had in mind to travel south to New Orleans, but then he discovered that his refusals only increased the amount of money offered him. He therefore continued to play on the Yankton station for four years, and these broadcasts led to bigger and better dance bookings. Naturally it was the most successful period of his life up to that time, and it led to an unexpected complication, as Welk related:

I had a little personal problem back in those successful days in South Dakota. One particular girl I was going with in Aberdeen was as nice and attractive as anyone could be. But I hadn't been dating her for more than a few weeks when I found her mother was asking when we were going to get married. And to make things worse, this became a pattern—whenever I would start dating a girl, the mothers wanted to step in and rush us into marriage. That really scared me. I guess it might have been my home training and religious teachings about preparing properly for Christian marriage, but I wasn't about to be rushed into any such arrangement. In fact, what puzzled me most was that the mothers seemed to like me more than the girls![4]

Along with his success, a strange and unforeseen event occurred. It was his first serious setback. Though everyone in the band was being paid well, the whole group left him in one stroke. They accused him of being a "hick" orchestra leader, a poor musician, and one who couldn't even speak English and be understood by the people. They said they were leaving him because he was keeping them from succeeding. They told him he'd never make it in show business. Nothing could have been a more severe blow to Lawrence. He was almost paralyzed by the shock and totally discouraged besides. He had several engagements lined up, but no orchestra to play. This was a supreme test of ingenuity. All he could do was to try to hire a new but inexperienced band. Welk described the incident in his own words:

I felt sick and numb, and I kept hearing those blunt words: "You're the reason we've decided to leave. You can't even speak English. You're holding us all back. You'll never make it." It was the lowest moment of my life. A few days later I dropped into church for some quiet reflection and some of the hurt and bewilderment began to leave. As I looked up at the crucifix of Our Lord I was reminded of the humiliation and pain He had endured and suddenly my hurt seemed so small. I realized if we put our faith in another human being, we are often open to hurt and disappointment. The only one to trust completely is God, and once you learn not to bear any malice or bitterness in your heart, life will be much happier. I came out of church feeling much better. I made up my mind I would try to start all over again with a new band.

Strange to say, his reputation had grown so that everyone still accepted whatever he brought in as "The Lawrence Welk Orchestra." It was another of his great lessons of experience: the value of a good reputation gained through hard work. He worked day and night with his new musicians to whip them into shape, so that they eventually sounded better than his original group. For the first time he put his men on a straight salary instead of a percentage basis as before.

All in all, the days from 1927 to 1936 at Yankton, South Dakota, were happy days for Lawrence. In spite of the depression, he and his band did well financially. He was able to drive a new white Cord automobile, one of the better foreign cars available at that time. Later he invested in a Pierce Arrow car to carry the band instruments and put his surplus money into the stock market, which proved a shrewd idea for those days of depression. Dance engagements were plentiful; he worked very hard to improve his band; and his reputation as the foremost band of the upper Middle West was undisputed.

One of the great events of Lawrence's life occurred during those happy days at Yankton. There in the radio station's little auditorium sat a young student nurse named Fern Renner with a group of young ladies from Sacred Heart Hospital viewing this remarkable band during a broadcast. Lawrence's eye immediately caught the beautiful heart-shaped face with big brown eyes, but unfortunately the young lady was too busy with her studies, her work, and other duties to respond very favorably to this "good-time Charley" musician. He tried and tried, but to no avail. She just wasn't interested.

But not too long afterwards, Lawrence's tonsils suddenly flared up and needed some attention. He thought of a scheme he felt would work. He called on his friend, Dr. Abst, in whose home Fern had been staying while enrolled as a student at the hospital. The doctor agreed to operate, and Lawrence thought he would diplomatically suggest that Miss Renner be assigned to his case. But as luck would have it, someone else was on duty. By way of the "grapevine" Fern heard about his disappointment in not finding her and decided to at least pay him a little visit. To her astonishment, as often happens in tonsillectomy cases, the patient had begun to hemorrhage rather severely. Apparently this crisis seemed to call forth the heroic from Fern. From then on she had more time for Lawrence and nursed him back to health, and there seemed to be no question that they were meant for each other. Her real "hang-up" all along had been the problem of how she would ever introduce a traveling musician to her family. She admitted it was one of her great traumas at that time and was the reason why she kept putting off Lawrence with one excuse after the other.

For Lawrence and Fern, it was the beginning of a most difficult courtship. It was continually interrupted by Lawrence's travels and Fern's studies. After finishing her training at the hospital, she left for postgraduate studies in Dallas, Texas. Fern herself recounts:

> Before leaving for Dallas, while Lawrence and I were on a dinner date, he made the remark, "I was wondering if you would like to have a picture of me?" He was leaving the next day for Lake Placid, New York, and I replied nonchalantly, "O.K. if you happen to have one with you, but we'll perhaps never see each other again." "Don't say that," he replied. And so he left for Lake Placid and I went on to St. Paul's Hospital in Dallas. I was there barely a few days when I had a letter from him. He wrote, "I would surely like to ask you something, but I don't want to put it in writing." Well, I had to laugh because I knew what it was.

So I wrote back like a real dummy pretending not to know what he wanted to ask me. "I don't know what there is you couldn't ask me in writing," I wrote teasingly. Then as luck would have it I had to be in Denver on some business with the Phelps Medical Bureau, who had asked me to recommend some nurses for particular jobs. To my astonishment I noticed in the paper that Lawrence was playing at the famous Broadmoor Hotel in Colorado Springs. Well, I phoned the hotel immediately but received little help in locating Lawrence until finally the Chamber of Commerce discovered where the band was staying. When I succeeded in locating Lawrence he was so glad to hear from me that he came immediately to Denver, and I remember we met at the Brown Palace for lunch. Then he drove me up into the mountains for a ride. I always tell the children that I absolutely had no chance to refuse their father—if I hadn't accepted his proposal, he would have pushed me off the mountain![5]

It was there in the Colorado Rockies that they finally decided on marriage, after four years of waiting. It was indeed a momentous decision for both of them. For Fern it meant giving up her plans for further study in her field of medicine: she had planned to become a physician. Lawrence, too, was well aware of the difficulties of his work which took him from place to place, of how hard it would be to carry on a normal home life under such conditions, and of the lifelong commitment their Catholic faith attached to the state of marriage. But they loved each other and were willing to put aside their fears for the future. They were married on April 18, 1931, in Sioux City, Iowa, at 5:30 A.M. This unconventional hour was due once again to the demands of the orchestra business which required his being in Pittsburgh the next night. Fern recalled:

As soon as we were married I took to the road, which I didn't like at all. One of the most difficult aspects of this life, especially in those days of depression when you were lucky enough just to make a living, was that you couldn't afford to stay in the nicer places. Once when we played at Lake Delavan, Wisconsin, we were given room, board, and just so much money. The boys all stayed in a large open space back of the stage, and there was a little tiny room off the stage where Lawrence and I were expected to stay. The window was dirty, spider webs covered the wall, and the bed was full of lumps. Well, my background both from home and as a nurse was so spotless that I just couldn't live any other way. I guess I registered so much shock at this that Lawrence wanted to take me home. But I said, "No, I don't want to go home. I'll clean this place so you won't know it." The one thing I learned from working in a hospital is that a little soap and water can do miracles if you just use them. When we asked where the bathroom was, the manager replied, "Oh, there is no bathroom. When you need a bath, you have to go to the lake!" Well, it's all a matter of making up your mind, and once you do that you can put up with conditions like this for weeks if you have to. This was only an example of many places we had to stay which, to put it mildly, were far from first-class accommodations. But when the children came along, traveling with them did really make an almost impossible existence.[6]

The years that followed for the Lawrence Welk family were some of the most difficult that could be imagined. The depression was in full swing, and the entertainment business went into a deep slump. It required all the ingenuity and resourcefulness Lawrence could possibly call on to keep himself, his family, and his band going throughout these years. Though Yankton was his home base, he traveled everywhere from Phoenix, Arizona, to Pittsburgh, Pennsylvania, to try to survive financially. One tragic story he tells is of a long trip his band made to play at the El Mirador ballroom in Phoenix. "When we arrived we found the place locked and boarded up. The booking had been cancelled. In desperation I rounded up the twenty-two stockholders who owned the ballroom and made an impassioned plea to them to please open it long enough to give us a chance to play our way out of town. The stockholders resisted until I solemnly promised to repay them if they lost any money at all. They finally gave in, and the band opened at first to only a small house. But the crowd grew each night until the original booking was lengthened into a three-month stay, and due to our percentage agreement, we did very well financially. It was a turning point in my career, indeed the first real challenge when I felt I had to earn money just to fulfill my obligation to my family."

Their first child, Shirley, was born on April 29, 1932, in Dallas, Texas, while Lawrence was playing in Denver. After the little family was reunited they traveled through Texas doing one-night stands, then on to Denver hoping to find work; finally, they made their way back to their home base in Yankton.

After Lawrence tried a few misguided business ventures, such as the hotel and restaurant business, he finally decided to sponsor himself, just as all the big-name bands did. He founded the Honolulu Fruit Gum Company as his sponsor, and ended up in the chewing gum business. It was during these days of crossing and recrossing the middle western states in search of band engagements that he invented a sleeper bus, an ingenious idea that enabled his whole band to stretch out for a night's rest while they made their way to the next town. But a tragic accident happened. The bus careened off the road and into a ditch eighteen feet below, injuring a few of his band members. This dampened Lawrence's enthusiasm for night bus travel. He had nightmares for weeks afterwards worrying about the accident, and finally he went to a priest to discuss the situation. The priest convinced him that the accident could have happened to anyone and that playing music was probably God's mission in life for him. Lawrence was always deeply spiritual, and the priest's advice only strengthened his conviction of how God wanted service from him.

It was about this time that Lawrence definitely put his mind toward the then fantastic goal of playing the "big time." In 1937, he was successful in getting some engagements in such leading hotels as the Saint Paul in Saint Paul, Minnesota, the William Penn in Pittsburgh, and a few others. He was so successful in Pittsburgh that he was rebooked there beginning on New Year's Eve of 1938. The newspaper reviews were excellent, and one of the local radio station announcers, Phil David, christened the band with a new name, "The Champagne Musicmakers." Lois Best was the band's first "Champagne Lady." At last he seemed destined for the "big time." The Fredericks Brothers Agency, with whom he had recently been associated, succeeded in booking him at the famed Edgewater Beach Hotel in Chicago. It had been his dream since childhood to play at the Edgewater Beach. He heard those early bands like Danny Russo and his orchestra "playing from the beautiful Edgewater Beach Hotel in Chicago, where there is dancing under the stars on the shores of Lake Michigan."

The engagement at the Edgewater Beach Hotel put Lawrence into the orbit of the big-name bands. He realized that he would have to talk over the microphone as did the other great band leaders, instead of hiding behind his accordion with his big smile. Because of his heavy accent, he had been avoiding the problem. He and the manager of the hotel worked out a short speech of welcome for opening night, but the very anticipation worked Lawrence into a state of near panic. He had practiced the speech until it was letter perfect, but when he strode out on stage at the outdoor terrace ballroom to deliver it, a sudden summer cloudburst drove everyone off the dance floor. The entire orchestra left too, but not Lawrence. He had practiced that speech too long to stop for a little rain. He went right on delivering it to an empty dance floor while the rain drenched his new white suit and ran down his face like tears.

Welk's inauspicious beginning at the Edgewater Beach

almost led to his total falure on the hotel circuit. He was no
longer in his familiar territory of the small-town ballroom
and dance hall. He was now playing for a sophisticated type
of audience, and he was not at all sure how to please them.
Unfortunately, he made the mistake of playing every song
that every "song plugger" in Chicago offered him. He nearly
ruined his programs, and some influential patrons even urged
the management to fire him. Finally, he was able to contact
the complaining couples and in desperation asked for their
advice. They told him: "Play the songs we know. You've
been playing melodies we've never even heard before." Welk
thanked them and in a burst of inspiration offered the man
his baton to lead the band while he asked to dance with his
wife. The couple was delighted, and this was probably the
start of his custom of allowing his patrons to lead the band
while he danced with their partners.

Shortly after this experience at the Edgewater Beach,
Lawrence managed a booking at the Chicago Theater where
a popular Bette Davis movie was playing. A newspaper pho-
tographer snapped a picture of the crowds of people lined
up for the movie, and the photograph happened to clearly
show "The Lawrence Welk Band" across the bottom of the
marquee. When the photo reached the papers, it was a
triumph of promotion. The name of Lawrence Welk was
before the eyes of all Chicago. Through this publicity a
certain Eddie Weisfeldt, owner of the Riverside Theater in
Milwaukee, became aware of Lawrence's success and offered
him the unheard-of amount of $3,500 a week *if* he were will-
ing to act as master of ceremonies. Lawrence's own description of his Milwaukee offer bears repeating:

> A fellow came back to my dressing room from Milwaukee
> named Eddie Weisfeldt from the Riverside Theater. He
> liked the way I talked and said it would go over great in
> Milwaukee. His first offer was for $1,750 a week if I would
> announce every number. I said no to him because I didn't
> want to do the talking. So he told me, "Think it over, and

I'll be back in a half hour." When he came back, his first
words were: "Come to Milwaukee! I'll give you $3,500 a
week. Will you talk for that?" My answer was a definite
"Yes, I'll talk for that!" You know, in Milwaukee they
really liked the way I talked. I'd get up, and sometimes before I'd even say anything, they would start laughing![7]

Needless to say, this was the beginning of Welk's speaking
career. Though he made many embarrassing mistakes at the
outset, he has continued to talk and over the years has developed an easy and natural stage presence. The Riverside
Theater in Milwaukee really launched him on his career as
a big-name bandleader.

The late thirties and early forties were the nostalgic era
of the big-name bands of America. They were the years when
names like Glenn Miller, the Dorsey brothers, Benny Good-
man, Henry Busse, Kay Kyser, Dick Jurgens, Russ Morgan,
Orrin Tucker, and the greatest of all, Guy Lombardo and
Wayne King, became a part of American popular culture.
Radio had a great deal to do with their success, for they were
all heard coast to coast on the networks, and whenever a big
band performed, tour patrons by the thousands turned out
to dance to its music in ballrooms all the way from Jantzen
Beach in Portland, Oregon, to the Steel Pier in Atlantic City.

Lawrence Welk had just become an important bandleader
by the late thirties, and all during the forties, he held forth
in the great Trianon and Aragon ballrooms of Chicago. During these war years his band played numerous free concerts
and dances for the armed forces personnel at Gardner General Hospital in Chicago under the aegis of Sam Lutz, later
to become his personal manager in Hollywood. Sam, as
special services officer for the army, always knew he could
count on Lawrence for a free show any time he needed one.

One of Lawrence's principal motives in trying to establish himself in Chicago was that he realized his continual
traveling made it extremely difficult to maintain a satisfactory
home life. His and Fern's second child, Donna Lee, had been

born in Omaha, Nebraska, on February 13, 1937. Lawrence had performed at the Adolphus Hotel in Dallas, the Roosevelt in New Orleans, and the Peabody in Memphis for a few weeks at a time, but each trip away from home made it clearer to him that he was shirking one obligation he considered most serious, that to his family. In fact, he even considered giving up his music career entirely because he did not feel it furnished the best atmosphere in which to raise a family.

He decided that if he could play on a regular basis at the Trianon ballroom in Chicago, this might solve his problem. His booking agents, the Fredericks Brothers, were not optimistic but did manage to book him for a one-night stand at the Trianon. Andrew Karzas, then manager of the ballroom, was so impressed by the Welk band that he hired it on the spot for a six-week stand. And by the end of that period, the band had become so popular among Chicagoans that it was rehired over and over. The original engagement stretched into a nine-year stand with occasional breaks for road tours.

The next addition to Welk's family was the birth of his only son, Lawrence Leroy. He is often referred to as Lawrence, Jr., but his name is Lawrence Leroy Welk, and he goes by the name Larry to distinguish himself from his father, who is always simply Lawrence to friends and family alike. Welk's first real home life was a warm and happy one in the River Forest area just west of Chicago. The three children, Shirley, Donna, and Larry, were able for the first time to attend school on a continuing basis. Shirley remarks to this day that it was the only time of her life when she was able to attend any one school regularly over a period of years. Though Lawrence could never be called anything but a most loving husband and father, the task of raising the children of necessity fell upon Fern. She was really both mother and father to the children, and all who know the Welks say no one could have done the job more effectively. The closest friends of the family heartily agree that Fern was indeed the valiant woman who communicated to her children her own spirit of deep religious conviction coupled with a warmth and tenderness of the best of mothers. The difficult years on the road with young children, in and out of hotels, changes of schools, and living away from relatives and friends proved her strong love and devotion to her family. Lawrence adds:

> Fern has been another great influence in my life. She was as dedicated to the raising of our children as I was to my music career. We would have lost Donna if it hadn't been for Fern's around-the-clock nursing care of her. We were in Detroit, and Donna developed such a high fever that the doctor gave up, saying that Fern could do more than all the medicines in the world by just keeping ice packs on her day and night. Well, Fern being the great nurse that she is, brought her around almost miraculously.[8]

Fern's somewhat humorous reply to Lawrence's division of labor in their household was:

> The handling of the family sicknesses and crises must have seemed to Lawrence to be perfectly simple and natural to me because he was not there to be part of it. I can re-member times when I had all three children seriously ill at the same time with strep throats. I would be walking all night between the three beds, sponging them to bring down their fever, giving medication, and praying for them. Lawrence was understandably dependent upon me for every-thing pertaining to the health and the raising of the children since naturally he was gone much of the time.[9]

Today it is clear to anyone who knows Fern and her family that there could never have been the success story of Lawrence Welk if she had not been willing to contribute more than her share toward family stability. So strong was this dedication during these years that she preferred to stay out of the limelight.

It was also during these Chicago years that Lawrence hired

Lois Lamont as his private secretary. He discovered her while performing at Milwaukee's Riverside Theater in 1945, and a short time later she began working for him in Chicago. Of all of his employees, perhaps no one has been more loyal to him and more hardworking and devoted than Lois Lamont. Now, after thirty-five years, she is still employed by Welk in a somewhat less demanding role, as conscientious and devoted as ever. His friends always referred to Lois as "the ideal secretary," and Lawrence himself called her his "right hand." Few women could have stood the strain that Lois Lamont capably bore for over twenty-five years, one of diplomacy in handling people plus skill in managing endless detail jobs that come up in their large office on Wilshire Boulevard in Santa Monica, California. She also deserves to be given much of the credit for the business success of Lawrence Welk. Because of her recent illness, her sister, Laurie Rector, now fills the post of private secretary.

During the years 1940 to 1950, Lawrence's home base was Chicago, where he played more or less regularly at the Trianon ballroom. However, he did many short stints at Chicago's Aragon ballroom, as well as many out-of-town jobs that took him as far away as California and New York. On one of his trips to Saint Louis, he met a young accordionist named Myron Floren, who had made quite a name for himself with several bands in that city and had become well known through his radio appearances on Station KWK. It didn't take Lawrence long to make up his mind that he eventually wanted to hire Floren. However, it was not until a 1950 trip to Saint Louis that Welk became aware of how Myron's talents had blossomed. Welk was so impressed with the development of this man over not more than five years (which Myron attributed simply to eight hours' practice a day) that he hired him on the spot. However, when Welk returned to Chicago with his new accordionist, the owner of the Trianon was Bill Karzas instead of his brother Andrew. Bill Karzas took issue with Welk over the addition of

another accordionist, especially one who clearly would out-
shine Welk himself. It was just another disagreement with
the Karzas brothers, one of a long line of similar differences
that had built up over the years. Actually Lawrence had felt
deep dissatisfaction with his job at the Trianon. Over those
long ten years, he had received no increase in pay, and in
order to earn any extra money, he was obliged to travel long
distances from home. Lawrence's description of the situation was:

> Karzas would say to me: "Lawrence, always remember
> I'm your friend. Don't ever get too expensive." He paid
> $1,750 a week for nine years . . . for the entire band. Some-
> times I had to tell him that the cost of living is going up
> and so is union scale. He would say: "Lawrence, be my
> friend!" He would take me into his little office and open
> the receipt books. "Things aren't as great as everybody
> thinks, Lawrence," he would say, showing me the receipt
> books. "Look here," he would say, and show me Tuesday
> and Wednesday nights only, then quickly shut the book and
> never show me his Friday, Saturday, and Sunday receipts![10]

The managers of Chicago ballrooms and hotels invariably
offered Welk less money because they knew he both lived
and preferred to stay in the Chicago area. Still, the crowds
at the Trianon kept coming, and his popularity in the Windy
City never waned. Yet he honestly felt he would have to
begin looking elsewhere for a home base. Prolonged trips to
the West Coast only aggravated his home situation and
caused both himself and Fern tremendous disquiet of mind
over their growing family.

Fern recalls that Lawrence's real beginning in California
was in August of 1950, when he began an engagement at
the Saint Francis Hotel in San Francisco.

> We were still living at the time in River Forest, Illinois,
> near Chicago. That was our very happy home during the
> years when Lawrence played at the Aragon and Trianon

The complete Welk family in 1903, a few months after Lawrence was born. Left to right: Barbara; his father, Ludwig Welk; Louis; John; Agatha; his mother, Christina, holding Lawrence; and his sister Ann Mary. The home that Lawrence's father built is in the background. It is a sod house covered with siding, and it still stands on their farm near Strasburg, N.D.

Lawrence's first portrait. It was taken in 1924, just after he left home at the age of 21 to begin his musical career.

Welk's 1928 orchestra, which played on WNAX, in Yankton, S.D. This was his base of operations until 1936.

The Welk orchestra in 1930. They were playing at the famous Broadmoor Hotel in Colorado Springs.

The interior of the beautiful Trianon Ballroom in Chicago, where the Welk orchestra played during the years 1941-1951. (Photograph courtesy of Chicago Architectural Photographing Company.)

Lawrence Welk with his entire family in 1977. Front row (left to right): Lawrence; his daughter Donna; his wife, Fern; his daughter Shirley; and his daughter-in-law Tanya. Middle row: Shirley's youngest, Lisa; Donna's daughter, Christine; Lawrence Welk III and his brother Kevin; and Donna's youngest, David. Back row: Shirley's husband, Bob; sons David and Robbie; Donna's son Jimmie; Shirley's Jonathan; Donna's husband, James; and Larry Welk, Jr.

Crowds in the late forties and early fifties, like this one, were already asking for autographed pictures of the Welk band.

In the mid-1950s Welk produced a second ABC television show, called "Top Tunes and New Talent." The Lennon Sisters got their start here, and they also became one of the big attractions of the Saturday night show on ABC. Shown here with the entire band are Kathy, Dianne, Janet, and Peggy Lennon, and Champagne Lady Alice Lon (standing).

Welk's seventy-fifth birthday protrait was painted by artist Kalan Brunink, shown here with Lawrence.

The TV show featured a party to celebrate Welk's seventy-fifth birthday, March 11, 1978. The festivities were transmitted over all 225 stations throughout the United States.

A character study.

The Champagne Music Makers of the early 1950s. All of them started with Welk on his long television career, which lasted three decades.

Lawrence and the Champagne Music Makers in 1954, with Champagne Lady Alice Lon. Several of the Music Makers are still with Welk's organization.

This 1967 stage performance in St. Louis was one of the hundreds that Welk and his band made around the United States and Canada. Here Welk is introducing Kathy and Janet Lennon, who are holding hands with their brother-in-law Dick Cathcart (Peggy's husband). (Photograph courtesy of Arteaga Photos, St. Louis.)

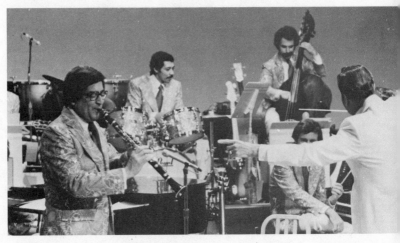

This is the kind of close-up that studio audiences see each week at Television City. Here Welk directs a feature number with his talented clarinetist, Henry Cuesta.

The groundbreaking ceremony for the Lawrence Welk Plaza in 1969 had Welk in overalls driving a mule and a plow. (Photograph courtesy of Larry Lee Photography, Los Angeles.)

Lawrence Welk's twenty-one-story office building in Santa Monica, Calif., houses his Teleklew offices. Adjoining it is the sixteen-story Champagne Towers Apartment Complex, which he also owns. These two buildings, known as the Lawrence Welk Plaza, will soon be joined by another high-rise office building. The three buildings will occupy the entire block on Ocean Avenue between Wilshire and Arizona.

Welk's system—early 1950s. Garth Andrews, Larry Hooper, Dick Dale, Rocky Rockwell, and Roberta Lynn were all young singers and musicians who started with Welk twenty-five years ago. He trained them in his own way, and Hooper and Dale are still members of his musical family.

Welk's system—1970s. David and Roger Otwell and Sheila and Sherry Aldridge have just completed their training under Welk. They are now regulars on the show.

Welk on the future: "At the present time my band would fall apart. The good Lord willing, if I am allowed to live a few years longer, that may be changed."

Welk's system: "It is the sharing with employees as persons that makes the working relationship family-like .... The relationship is somewhat like a father with his children." (Photograph courtesy of Tom Mareschal Photograph, Los Angeles.)

One of the 371 awards that Lawrence Welk has received, the "Entertainer of the Year Award" was presented to him by the American Guild of Variety Artists in 1976.

ballrooms in Chicago. The following October I joined Lawrence in San Francisco, and then I returned to Chicago while he remained in California. Lawrence flew home for Christmas that year and spent the holidays with me and the children in Chicago. I remember so well how the children prayed that the planes wouldn't be able to fly so their Dad could stay with them longer. But the sun finally did come out and the snowstorms stopped right on December thirty-first in time for his return to San Francisco for New Year's Eve. He played there through February of that year and was then booked at the Claremont Hotel in Berkeley, California.[11]

It was on a road trip in early 1951, when Lawrence was just finishing this engagement at the Claremont, that he decided to head for Texas to settle some possible bookings there. On the way to Texas he managed to stop off in Los Angeles and look up some old friends, among them "Pops" Sandrup, who headed the Aragon ballroom at Lick Pier in Santa Monica. Lawrence had played there years earlier, when it was a new and beautiful ballroom, but now it looked shabby and deserted. The whole area of Pacific Ocean Park, as it was called, was run down. After a little conversation with Sandrup, Lawrence offered to play another engagement at the ballroom. But Sandrup shook his head, saying it wasn't any use, that business was so bad they couldn't begin to pay Welk's price. Lawrence felt so sorry for him that he offered to play four weeks for union scale; further, he would split any profits 50-50. Naturally, Sandrup jumped at the offer, and Welk began another great episode of his career.

The Welk band started at the Aragon in Santa Monica and within a week the word got around. Crowds began to fill the place. The rough element that had taken over the pier and battered the property gradually disappeared, and the added profits made it possible to redecorate and refurbish the whole ballroom. A prominent television station in Los Angeles, KTLA, had been doing an occasional late-evening broadcast from the Aragon, and now through the good ser-

vices of Sam Lutz, Lawrence's old friend from Chicago, the
station agreed to telecast one appearance of the Welk band,
provided Lawrence would pay the extra salaries of the
musicians. It turned out to be one of the best investments
Lawrence ever made. Viewers began to call before the show
was over. They bombarded the station with requests for
more of the Welk orchestra; and KTLA immediately signed
it to a four-week run, with options for an extension. The
television career of Lawrence Welk had begun. It was August
21, 1951. Since that date he has never ceased to present
a weekly television show.

It looked as though the Welk family was destined for still
another move and would have to give up their delightful home
in River Forest. Fern recalls that everyone seemed sure she
would be opposed. Naturally she loved her home in River
Forest. It was the first time in their married life they had
ever been able to stay in one place for a prolonged period.
"Why don't we wait until you're sure it's the place to be before we make the decision to move? We have this nice home
in Chicago where grade school, high school, and college are
all within walking distance," she pleaded. "I only want to be
as sure as possible that it is the right move." Fern's reasoning was:

> You know the entertainment business is one of the most
> unstable in the world. When you're well settled and must
> suddenly pull up stakes and move your family across the
> country, it's terribly disrupting to the children, especially
> their schooling. I know that many families have found that
> sudden moves like this proved to be their worst mistake.
>
> So one Sunday I received a call from Lawrence and he put
> Klaus Lansberg, manager of Station KTLA, on the phone to
> talk to me. Lansberg assured me: "Your husband receives
> so much fan mail from his TV show that he is sure to be-
> come a sensation in Los Angeles. I can guarantee him a
> good job for a long time to come." I took my opportunity
> to make it clear to both of them that I was not against mov-
> ing, but only wanted to be sure it was the right move for

the children before we decided. If Lawrence was sure his work was going to be on the West Coast, I told them I would be most happy to move there.[12]

Meanwhile, Lawrence was continuing his appearances at the Santa Monica Aragon, seven nights a week until 2:00 A.M. Fern and the children were still in Chicago, and he was living alone at the William Tell Motel in Santa Monica. Due to loss of sleep, too much tension, and improper food, he finally collapsed on the bandstand and was rushed to Saint John's Hospital in Santa Monica, where he underwent gall bladder surgery. Fern flew to California to be with him as soon as she was able to find someone to stay with the children. He made a remarkable recovery, but the experience left him with a nervous stomach that to this day requires rigid self-discipline in the matter of diet.

It took months for Lawrence's complete recovery, but still he worked in dead earnest to completely rejuvenate the old crowd at the Aragon. He inaugurated teenage dance sessions and weekly dance contests. The Aragon was packed every night, at a time when all the other big-name bands were beginning to wane. The television shows were drawing a bigger and bigger audience on KTLA, for now he had the Dodge dealers of southern California sponsoring him. The future looked bright as more and more important men in the industry began to take notice of this local broadcast and as more and more Dodge dealers became interested in "the best salesman who ever worked for us."

From 1952 to 1955, Lawrence continued to be a top local television attraction in the Los Angeles area. After some loving persuasion, with the end of the school year of 1952, Fern agreed to move to California and reestablish their home once again, for Lawrence had the vision to see that his success on KTLA was only a first step toward a coast-to-coast show. Indeed, he would never stop talking about "that coast-to-coast hookup" to men like Jack Minor and Sam Lutz

and Don Fedderson. Though these men were themselves
thoroughly sold on the merit of his show, they had formidable
opposition from network officials in New York and from
Chrysler executives in Detroit. The job of selling both network and sponsor would take over a year to accomplish.

Welk's first broadcast on the ABC network took place on
July 2, 1955. At the start he was only a summer replacement
for the "Danny Thomas Show," but before the summer was
over the Welk Show was firmly established as a popular
favorite. It was re-signed for the regular 1955-56 season.
People all over the country responded just as the local audiences in Los Angeles had done, and Dodges were sold as
never before. Nielsen ratings went higher and higher each
month, and both the network and Welk's offices were deluged with fan mail. Three thousand letters a week poured
in. At this writing a remarkable record has been established
—the Welk Show has been broadcast for twenty-six successive seasons on national television (sixteen seasons on ABC,
ten by syndication), and during that time it has had only
two principal sponsors—The Dodge Division of Chrysler
Motor Corporation for the first eight years, and the J. B.
Williams Company (Geritol, Sominex, Rose Milk, Aqua
Velva, etc.) for the past twenty-one years.

For one year in the middle 1950s Lawrence produced a
second ABC television show on Wednesday evenings for the
Plymouth Division of Chrysler Motors. It featured much
youthful talent, as well as members of his regular band, and
was called "Top Tunes and New Talent." However, the
main focus of Welk's professional life continued to be the
Saturday night show, which reached and held a peak of
popularity unmatched by any other musical show in television history. It has been through this latter show that he
has become an American institution, having received a
unique kind of personal esteem from his fellow Americans.

Events in the life of Lawrence Welk over the twenty-five
years on national television may largely be characterized as

reaching a plateau. It was his life's ambition to bring his orchestra into the homes of millions of Americans by means of television. He admirably achieved this ambition. However, his mounting popularity, his ready acceptance by 50 million television viewers, and the faithfulness of the fans who never miss a single Saturday night's performance have to a large extent been the result of hard, determined work by both Welk and members of his organization. There have been a few important events—for example, his selection as grand marshal of the Tournament of Roses Parade of 1972, his twice being chosen to chair the National Cancer Crusade, and his hundreds of awards and trophies from almost every humanitarian organization in the country.[13] But mostly it has been Welk's constant television exposure, his stage appearances, his personal writings, and his person-to-person dealings with thousands each year that have made this man a legend in his own time.

One of Welk's notable personal qualities is his eagerness to improve himself whenever he reads some negative comments by a critic. It is safe to say that Welk is his own worst critic, and he has written dozens of letters to critics thanking them for their sometimes caustic remarks about him and promising to improve himself. When I myself undertook the task of researching Welk's life and organization, I was told by Welk to feel at perfect liberty to write whatever I wished, provided only that what I said was the truth!

Once when I noticed how courteous Welk's employees were to me though I had made many impositions upon their time and goodwill, I asked Lawrence, "Do you make a conscious effort to indoctrinate your employees and the members of your musical organization with courteous behavior?" "No, I never really instruct them to be that way," he said. "Early in my career I did speak to my band members and encouraged them to always speak in a friendly way to people, but I've never done this with my office employees or musical family. Basically, I feel that they learn pretty much from

the example of those in charge rather than from rigid in-
structions and orders." No statement could demonstrate more
accurately or reflect more clearly his own attitude of courtesy
and consideration of others.

This concern for people is brought out by Welk's frequent
remarks about his own retirement. "Why should I retire
when hundreds of people who work for me would be out
of jobs if I stopped working?" He never forgets people who
have done good work for him. Those who were instrumental
in starting him in his career—people like Sam Lutz, Don
Fedderson, Bert Carter, Jim Hobson and many others—are
constantly being thanked and given credit for small favors
they did for him many years ago. In fact, the very people
who have done favors for Lawrence Welk end up receiving
far more than they ever gave. He is the kind of person who
always returns a favor tenfold.

Another of Welk's qualities is that he tries never to dis-
appoint or inconvenience anyone. He is scrupulously prompt
and prefers to arrive at engagements about half an hour
ahead of time. When I have had the privilege of driving
him anywhere, he has always been waiting for me before the
appointed time. People who attend his road shows are always
gratified by Welk's willingness to sign autographs for them.
He stands for hours until everyone's program is signed.

It can be stated without qualification that Welk's success
has been predicated upon a projection of the kind of personality that sincerely tries to give his audiences what they
want, both in entertainment and in personal treatment. He
attributes the demise of the big bands to the fact that bands
began playing for themselves rather than for their patrons.
"They weren't critical of their own shortcomings," he said.
"This is what George T. Kelly taught me early in my career.
You have to please your people, or you won't stay in business very long."[14]

3

"As a Man Thinketh in His Heart . . . So Is He"

The Philosophy of Lawrence Welk

More than half a century ago, in 1924, Lawrence Welk emerged into a somewhat undefined milieu of popular music in rural, small-town, Midwest America. The people of his farm community of Strasburg, North Dakota, already had a well-established form of popular folk music, developed in Europe over the generations and brought to this country by immigrants, many of them still living. They also brought skills of performing on violin, piano, accordion, and guitar. Music was a part of their life, as it had been for hundreds of years. It contributed to their dances and social life on weekends, and during the week it cheered their long winters of confinement. Of course, Lawrence could not single-hand-edly change this music, but he did uplift and dignify it. His efforts, along with those of many of the "greats" who were his contemporaries—the Gershwins, Lombardos, Warings, Kings and many others—helped elevate popular music to a new plane of social acceptance.

A Sociological Phenomenon

Lawrence Welk is a remarkable sociological phenomenon in the world of music and broadcasting: a poor boy from a farm, with little formal education and only a good business sense, not only envisioned the American dream of success, but ended with a vast television enterprise of twenty-eight years' duration. Other musicians have also had remarkable success, of course, but almost none has had the exposure of Lawrence Welk in so many millions of American homes. If all the big bands of America were to total their bandstand audiences from 1930 through 1950, their combined listenership would not equal Welk's during a single thirteen-week television season. He succeeded in what his adversaries claimed he could never do: to bring into the homes of America the big-band sound, with familiar American songs and dances, and to present it all with his own farm boy personality. This record constitutes a chapter in the sociology of music.

TV's Problems

Further, it must be borne in mind that television, the medium Welk chose as his showcase, has stumbled into a thicket of the thorniest social problems of any of the mass media. Newspapers, books, movies, comic books have all had their share of problems. But television comes directly into the homes of people, to be viewed and absorbed by all ages and classes, sometimes against their wills, and so it has profoundly affected education, behavior, attitudes, morals, and values. The tastes of the television public are fickle. Often its most experienced producers seem woefully unable to predict the popularity of a show or an entertainer. Much is expected of television by the American public, almost too much. It has had its high moments of glory in the immediacy with which it has covered events that otherwise could never have been seen by so many. Yet, due to its constant need of new sights and sounds, it has fallen into a pit of mediocrity and in the estimation of one critic—Newton Minow, former FCC chairman—has become "a vast wasteland."

Welk and TV

When Lawrence Welk emerged into television in 1952, he must have been aware of its pitfalls—its excessive commercialization, its inadequate feedback, its cultural downgrading, its manipulation of the minds of its viewers, and its all-too-mediocre content. Lawrence Welk blithely took up his baton before the camera, determined that he would not degrade television, nor would television degrade him, as it had so many.

Further, Welk must have brought to television something unique. For he met the problems and challenges as few others have, and he met them through long preparation, first in his own mind and thoughts. This is the reason for the present chapter, entitled, "As a Man Thinketh in His Heart."

Lawrence Welk will never go down in history as a great original thinker. Yet he has much in common with many of the great thinkers of antiquity. He is disarmingly simple, but at times he is profoundly spiritual. Whatever he says, he means; and everyone who hears him understands exactly what he is saying. Though he is a businessman, a musician, and an entertainer by profession, he is above all else a deep, pragmatic thinker. His thoughts have found their way into millions of homes in America and Canada through television. He has gathered them into several books and smaller publications written over the past twenty years. Some of his thoughts have been recorded in the *Congressional Record* for September 16, 1968. Hundreds of people who have worked with him in the entertainment world have been influenced by his thinking. Over 6,000 newspaper and magazine feature articles have recounted stories of his life. But most of all, the phenomenon of his vast broadcasting enterprise, the largest musical broadcasting organization ever to grow up in America, is the direct result of his philosophy, his personality, his vision, and his dedicated efforts.

Without in any way minimizing the importance of material accomplishments, one must agree that the greater accomplishment is to be a person who is at peace with himself and whose wholesomeness diffuses peace, comfort and good will to the men and women with whom he associates. To do is one thing, but to be is another, and he who in the conquests of material objectives has neglected to be successful as a person will find his conquests illusory.[1]

The above quotation from Welk's book *Guidelines for Successful Living* has been demonstrated to me personally in so many ways through my association with him that I would have difficulty recounting all of them. I told him I knew of a fan of his who had recently suffered a broken hip and was in a Long Beach hospital. He immediately asked for her phone number, called her, and carried on a conversation for a half hour just to cheer her up. He often spends as much as an hour after a show signing autographs and saying a few friendly words to the people who have come to see him. In this connection he has often told me that it is a source of wonder to him, and even irritation, that so many musicians disregard their audiences. He feels that the performances of his band were important events to the people of the small rural communities of the upper Middle West. To some of them it meant a long trip on a Saturday night and an opportunity to dress up and enjoy themselves. He felt they deserved his best treatment. His efforts to sign autographs, to say a friendly word, or to play the kind of music they liked was his way of diffusing peace, comfort, and goodwill. It was his way to give of himself.

Playing for His Audience

Welk claims that his attitude of accommodating his audience, satisfying their wishes and tastes, was taught him early in his career by a close friend and associate, Tom Archer, who owned several ballrooms in the Midwest. Tom hired Welk to play in his ballrooms and they became close friends. "I would help Tom by playing my little orchestra for a low fee, and he in turn would give me work when I needed it," Welk recounted in a recent conversation.

> Those were difficult days back in the depression, but Tom was a very good businessman, and he taught me some of the best lessons of my early career. He worked hard to please his people, and he succeeded as few others in keeping his establishments going during the 1930s.
>
> Whenever I would work for him we would go out and eat after the show was over. This was mostly to discuss whether or not we went over with the audience that night. Did the people stay or go home early? Did we play enough of the kind of music they enjoyed? These were the questions we would ask ourselves. My association with Tom was my schooling on how to please an audience. This was my constant aim then, and it still is today. The times when we failed to do it, everyone suffered.

As a man of superior tact in dealing with others, Welk might be expected to have some opinions on the opposite behavior. He has often said that he considers rudeness and boisterous demands upon others as signs of emotional immaturity. He claims that people who behave in this manner do not consider themselves equal to others but rather that they are somehow better. "They are very insecure persons, and by openly treating others as inferiors, they are able to build up their own egos and conceal their own inferiority from themselves," he explained. This is the basis of his choice in hiring people. First he evaluates each person's talents, background, and personality to try to determine whether he or she will project a pleasing image to the television audience. He considers audience identification with the performer to be important to his fans and one of the essential ingredients in the success of his show.

Those of us who have observed his performers rehearsing all day at the CBS studio in Hollywood have never seen a display of temper or abusive conduct, even when they worked under trying conditions. Especially the musicians might be expected to act like prima donnas at tense moments if they had not been made to understand from the start of their employment that such behavior would definitely be out of place and not tolerated. As a result their friendly behavior toward one another easily projects itself to the audience. In fact, they are regarded by Welk as his "musical family"; as with all good families, there may arise small disagreements, but basically they pull together and help one another. It is no accident, therefore, that Welk's television audience senses cooperation, friendliness, and a spirit of loyalty among the members of his show.

"Let George Do It"

Each individual's personal responsibility in shaping his own destiny has been a frequently recurring subject of Welk's conversations with me. He firmly believes that either the individual takes the responsibility of shaping his own life, or others will shape it for him according to their whims. The person will then flounder aimlessly, a prey to the ambitions and selfishness of others. "Too many," says Welk, "rely upon others to shape their life, to think for them and ultimately to support them. 'Let George do it' as a motto has been replaced in recent years by 'Let Uncle Sam do it'." Lawrence Welk is a staunch believer in the American system of free enterprise which encourages the use of opportunities —through education, work, and personal initiative—to make one's contributions to the cause of humanity. He thinks the attitude of "Let someone else do it" is particularly harmful to our country since it means doing the least amount of work, falling back on others, and never developing one's own initiative and meeting one's own responsibilities.

Serving Others

Very recently, in speaking of his responsibilities to his own family and to his "musical family," Lawrence candidly admitted:

I feel that I haven't been the kind of father or grandfather I would have liked to be. I always feel I would like to spend a great deal more time with the children, like playing ball with them, visiting with them and getting to know them better. I would say that about 90 percent of my time has been taken up in the orchestra business, and one of the reasons is that so many depend upon me for their living. Another reason is that so many millions in our country receive their biggest enjoyment of the week just from listening to our show. If you could hear the spontaneous remarks I hear from people who watch our show, like: "Thank God for you and your orchestra, Lawrence. You'll never know how we look forward to your show." So you see, I feel we're doing something in which we are serving many, many people. This is basically my belief—not to live for myself but for others. The scriptural quotation which goes "Give and it will be given to you" [Luke 6:38] is the basis of my whole life.[2]

His own life exemplifies the above thinking. His dedication to responsibilities toward his family and his employees, to religious and humanitarian causes he has undertaken, and to his audiences is proof that he considers these moral obligations paramount. Even those who do not agree with his thinking admit that he is a man who sets goals for himself, and he never rests until he accomplishes them. He counsels young people who are working for him to set goals of professional excellence for themselves and never be satisfied until they are achieved. In fact it is almost impossible for anyone to work with Lawrence Welk and allow himself to slip into a pattern of mediocrity. His demanding example of high performance is enough to humiliate anyone who takes the road of least resistance.

Rewards of Work

There is no subject about which Welk is more ready and qualified to speak than the dignity and rewards of work. As most of the world knows, he began working on a farm as a young boy and there had his first experiences of the rewards of a job well done—perhaps the most important lesson of his life. The lesson was taught him by the example of his parents, who excelled in their respective skills of farmer, carpenter, builder, blacksmith, and provider; homemaker and mother. No wonder he could say in later life: "Without work man loses his vision, his confidence and his enthusiasm. His life becomes largely meaningless. . . . There is no other preventative or cure so effective for boredom and fatigue, or for many of our mental and emotional ills, as an honest day's work every working day of the year."[3]

The *Congressional Record* for September 16, 1968, contains a brief speech by Sen. Milton R. Young, given in the Senate of the United States, in which he outlines the life and accomplishments of Lawrence Welk. He stresses Welk's dedication to hard work and his perseverance in the face of trials and discouragements as the reasons for his great success. Whereupon he addresses the president: "Mr. President, I believe this speech by Lawrence Welk is an inspiration to all young Americans who have a desire to make good. I ask unanimous consent that it be printed in the Record." There being no objection, the speech was ordered to be printed in the *Record* as follows:

My Earliest Dreams

My earliest dreams were all about music—and it took a dream to start with—but in my wildest dreams I couldn't have envisioned our wonderful musical family of today.

I consider myself fortunate, indeed, to have been born to parents who were able to impart a Christian philosophy to their children. I am amazed I was able to make it, and it only shows how great the opportunities are in this good land—the land of free enterprise.

I believe our orchestra traveled more miles, played more "one nighters," endured more hardships, and it took us more years to gain recognition than any band in history. For 27 years we struggled, with very little success, then along came a miraculous new medium, TV. After 27 years we finally struck it rich—and the press called us an "overnight success."

Today we play for more people every Saturday night than we did in all those years of traveling from coast to coast, but it certainly didn't happen "overnight," and it didn't come about without lots of hard work.

Work has always been a very important part of my life, even from my early boyhood days back on the farm. I'm aware that this is a word that has declined in popularity in recent years, but I still feel that it is one of the basic, most vital ingredients of a good life.

There are so many good things which come about as a result of work, even when one works in the dark, as I have done at times. Something worthwhile is almost sure to develop as a result.

I had the good fortune and privilege of getting into the habit of working at an early age. Life was rough on our North Dakota farm, where I was born and spent the first 21 years of my life. Huge rocks had to be dug from the ground and moved before the land was fit for plowing—then there was the plowing itself and the pitching of hay, threshing, tending of animals and all the other back-breaking work that every farmer knows so well. This hard work gave me a tremendous advantage in life. The music business always seemed easy in comparison and when things didn't go well for me, I always had the fear of going back to the plow, the pitchfork and the rocks.

In our travels around the country, we are usually met at the airport by a group of newspaper, TV and radio reporters for interviews. The first question asked is almost always the same: "Mr. Welk, how do you account for the long-standing success of your orchestra?"

Of course, there is no single reason for our long life on TV, but I think I have narrowed it down to a few vital factors: First: I am most fortunate to have so many wonderful and talented people in my musical family, and to have the help of so many very able right-hand people. I have also been blessed with a devoted wife and family and have enjoyed an exceptionally happy home life. Finally, I believe my personal philosophy has been partly responsible for some of the good fortune which has come our way. This philosophy has actually been the guiding force in the operation of our orchestra. It's quite simple and is based largely on the principle of "earning your keep—giving value for value received." Well, why beat around the bush—the secret is "work."

The earth gives its fruits only to those who labor for them. To earn your bread by the sweat of your brow is a cold, hard reality. It applies to all, and without it, man loses his vision, his confidence and his enthusiasm. His life becomes largely meaningless. On the other hand, there is no preventative or cure so effective for boredom and fatigue or for the many of our mental and emotional ills as an honest day's work every working day of the year. There is no limit to the rich things that we may have—material, mental, spiritual—if we work hard enough to obtain them.

Know what you want, work for it and the earth will yield its treasures to you.

This is still the land of opportunity, perhaps more so now than ever before. Individual initiative is still the guiding force that makes our nation strong. Let us encourage it in every way possible. God's world is a beautiful world, rich beyond measure.

The terms for helping ourselves to this abundance are simple but ironclad. They are simple ways of life and among the most important of them are sincerity of purpose, honest effort, the desire to be useful, devotion to duty, just and compassionate relationship with our fellow man, faith in ourselves and in God—these are the coins to be placed in the till as prepayment.

Many sincere men are alarmed today about the increasing number of people who are looking for free buggy rides through life. I'm speaking of the free riders who live off the labors of others. They are the men and women who take the benefits of group activities, but who accept little or no responsibility for doing their share in creating the benefits they consume. In the world of nature we call them parasites. It is difficult to understand how these people can delude themselves into adopting as a way of life such a concept of social irresponsibility. If man realized the lack of justice of living off the efforts of others, there would probably be much less of it. Free buggy rides drain away the benefits earned for the group by its productive workers.

The fundamental law of life is that man must earn what he receives if he wishes to live with dignity, independence and security.

Man, of course, can live off the labors of others, but when he does, his personality disintegrates and decays, he becomes a parasite, a whining, frustrated weakling.

Let man, however, feel the challenge of creating his own life and of getting what he needs through his own labors and he becomes strong, virile and confident. He has found the way to dignity, independence and security—his life is his own.

I have tried to instill this type of philosophy in all the members of our musical family. The fact that they have responded generously, indeed, accounts for much of our success. This is why I am such a firm believer in the concept of "hard work" as a remedy for many of today's ills.

Our freedom did not come cheaply, and should not be taken lightly. American citizenship is a precious privilege and it carries with it certain responsibilities: To give a day's work for a day's wages, to make an honest effort to be self-supporting, to respect and obey the laws of the land.

I am in favor of greater emphasis on these ideals which helped to make our nation great—free enterprise, self-determination, personal initiative, individual responsibility.

I am convinced that work—hard work—is the answer if we are to return to these ideals and keep our country strong.

I feel that when people work with a happy and contented mind, they become immune to the diseases of hatred and discord.

I know that with God's blessing on our labors, we can accomplish miracles in the field of human relationships and in our fight for a better America and a better world.

This, I believe.[4]

As a corollary to his thinking on the subject of work, Welk has expressed his amazement on several occasions at people in show business who set goals for themselves but unfortunately act as if they had already reached them. "We cannot become skilled workers," he said, "unless at some time we face ourselves and make an accountancy of our abilities and deficiencies. This is the first step. . . . It would obviously be ridiculous for a man embarking on a business career to apply for a job as president of a large corporation. Yet there are a surprising number of people, particularly those with show business ambition, who seem to think they can 'start at the top.' What is called overnight success, I have found in most cases, is something that happens only after years of struggle and hard work."

The Mystique of the Present Moment

Another basic principle of Welk's thinking concerns his use of time in the rigorous demands of broadcasting and show business; it might be called the "mystique of the present moment." He follows the old Roman motto *carpe diem* (roughly translated "take advantage of each day as it comes along"). I observed what a master of timing he is when I promoted the stage appearances of his television show. Not a moment in the show was lost, from start to finish. It moved so quickly and smoothly that few in the audience realized that almost three hours had elapsed when the show was over. I have discovered from my association with Welk over the years that he is a man who is never late for an appointment, has such self-discipline that he never knowingly imposes upon or wastes the time of others, and lives each day as if it were his last on earth. He has often said: "In a sense tomorrow does not exist. It is only today that is a reality for us. If we are to dream of having any success or happiness, we have to do today what makes for such success and happiness."

Power over People

The largest single element of Lawrence Welk's success is his power over people. Everyone I have ever spoken to admits this, and I have observed it myself many times. He harbors absolutely no resentments against others, though he has been the object of much harsh and inconsiderate treatment over the years. He firmly believes that most misunderstandings and animosities are caused by people who project their own frustrations upon others. They are at odds with life themselves, so they project their unhappiness and insecurity upon other people. In other words, he believes that when a person fights others he is really fighting himself; that he first needs to clean his own house from within, uproot destructive thoughts and replace them with thoughts of security, confidence, self-reliance, and peace with God and himself. An example of how he practices this thoroughly Christian attitude came up in a 1970 conversation about the Lennon sisters. "Some people imagine I am angry with the Lennon sisters," he said. "Actually I sincerely wish them every success. They started with me ten years ago and have done probably as well as anyone on my show. Now I believe it is time for them to go elsewhere. Some magazine writers have distorted the whole relationship, but that is only their sensational way of making a big story out of nothing. Nobody could think better of these fine young ladies." He is proud of what he has been able to do for many young people like the Lennons who made their start on his show. Far from being resentful of their leaving him, he is only concerned that they are doing well and have profited by their experience with him.

The scores of people with whom Welk worked in earlier years and who have remained lifelong friends attest to the sincerity of his relations with people. He loves to tell about one of his first business associates, George T. Kelly, who invited Welk to join his group, the Peerless Entertainers (see chapter 2). During their years as partners, Kelly taught Welk some of his first and most valuable lessons on how to deal with people. Evidently this genial, expansive Irishman liked people; he was a born diplomat, a natural showman, and twenty years Welk's senior. Kelly exerted a profound influence upon Welk's character and thinking and to this day Welk likes to recall incidents in his early career in which the strong, magnetic personality of George Kelly dominated his thinking. They lived very closely, often sharing the same room and eating in the same restaurants. No matter how disagreeable the quarters or the food, Kelly always seemed to have a cheerful word of encouragement for everyone. "There isn't anything so bad that there isn't something good you can think or say about it. And that goes for people as well as things," are the words Welk frequently quotes from the mouth of Kelly. "My idea of sharing with others was instilled in me early in my career by George Kelly," Welk recalls. "Basically I am doing with my people today what George did with me as a young man just starting out. It was impressive to see how George would return to his hotel room every week, throw all the receipts on the bed and divide everything equally with me. It made me know right away that this was my business as much as his."[5]

In an age in which piety seems definitely out of place, Lawrence Welk has dared to express himself in the practical wisdom of the Golden Rule, "Whatever you wish that men would do to you, do so to them; for this is the law and the prophets."[6]

Welk's Own Way

When in 1955 Welk signed a broadcast contract with the Dodge Division of the Chrysler Corporation for a weekly, hour-long show on Saturday evenings coast to coast, a real crisis arose. The contract called for only one thirteen-week summer replacement period. All but a few of the executives of the network and the Grant Advertising Agency were pessimistic over the outcome of the show. They wanted Welk to make some improvements in his traditional musical variety format. First they suggested that he add a chorus line to dress up the show; next they wanted a comedian to lend some sparkle to it. Finally they wanted him to invite guest stars as special attractions. They made it clear they were accepting the show only because it had been successful locally in Los Angeles and had the endorsement of the Dodge dealers of southern California. They thought very little of its intrinsic worth. At a time most crucial to Welk's future, he rather stubbornly refused all the suggestions of the television executives and producers. He claimed that the policy he had always followed of using only the people within his organization and playing the kind of music for which he had become known was his way of turning out a successful television program. It might not be Madison Avenue's way or Hollywood's way, but it was Lawrence Welk's way. On the other hand, these professionals of New York and Hollywood thought they had the correct formula for a good television show and, if Welk didn't want to conform to their way, he would simply have to risk the consequences of being cancelled after the summer replacement period was over.

Despite the storms of opposition from highly influential men in the agency and the network, Welk held firmly to his deep-rooted conviction; this was one time he was determined to voice his difference of opinion. The experts insisted that his format would not go over with the American television audience. Though Welk knew his way was not the only way, nor was it necessarily the right way, he did know it was *his* way. Aware that his particular style was not popular with everyone, he knew that it would reach the vast audiences who had followed him throughout his years of show business. He further pointed out that the format he personally

had learned and maintained for more than thirty years—
different as it might be from everyone else's—had already
proven to be a successful musical variety show. And it was
on the strength of this that he finally won out.

Welk has emphasized that his own personal and creative
abilities are meager by comparison with those of many with
whom he has had the privilege of working. Yet he thinks
that, whatever talents a person has, great or small, he should
capitalize on them and make them his trademark. True, he
is probably not a great musician himself, and doubtless his
abilities as an entertainer come nowhere near those of a Bob
Hope or a Danny Thomas. Yet he is in his own way an unsophisticated personality who has appealed to a vast number
of American people by speaking their language and playing
the kind of music to which they can relate.

Shortcomings of Performers

On numerous occasions he has described his own views
on why some of his performers become a problem to both
their own families as well as to his organization. "They receive many compliments which are often undeserved or
insincere. Naturally, praise is very often taken to heart, their
egos are built up, and an exaggerated idea of their own
talents is created. That is when it becomes extremely difficult for anyone to correct the weak points of their performance because they don't see themselves as they actually are."

An honest and realistic appraisal of his own shortcomings
has proved to be one of Welk's greatest assets in dealing with
people. It has disturbed him at times to see performers who
stepped out of character to imitate someone else. "Invariably," he has said, "the results have been disastrous." He believes each person should be satisfied that he is different
from others; that each has his own specific role to play; that
talents, aptitudes, and capacities are singular and distinctive
in everyone. Not everyone can be successful in the same field.
Each has his own inborn talent. Welk himself is an example

of one who has never taken on the role of anyone else. He is always himself. His friends have said: "Lawrence is the same fellow I knew back in North Dakota."

Members of his organization say that he is always quick to congratulate and encourage a person. Many a performer has started with Welk, received experience and further encouragement, given the necessary publicity, and then sent on his way to a successful career of his own. Welk feels that stories of any jealousy toward the Lennon sisters, Al Hirt, Pete Fountain and others have been falsely publicized, and says he is happy for their success, is truly proud of them, and takes great satisfaction in knowing he has given them their start on his show.

Requirements for Success

Unlike so many would-be thinkers, Lawrence Welk is found to be a better observer of his own philosophical maxims than most people realize. You can hardly speak to him very long without hearing him enunciate his three requirements for success in any venture: (1) get a clear vision of exactly what you want to accomplish in life; (2) believe that you can and will succeed; (3) start now to do it and keep at it.

Jack Minor, one of the advertising executives responsible for putting Welk on national television (see chapter 5), cites an example of Welk's goal seeking: "Welk set his mind on a coast-to-coast television show right from the start of his career in Los Angeles. Strangely he never doubted he would succeed, and there was not an idle moment for him during those years on local KTLA." He tirelessly improved his show and made it his business to become personal friends with as many of the local Dodge dealers as possible. It all added up to increased sales and good relationships with his sponsors. Most important of all, it gave Minor supreme confidence that the Welk show could hold its own if it were given a chance on national television. The result of Minor's efforts in behalf of Welk was that on Saturday night, July 2, 1955, the ABC network reluctantly accepted the "Lawrence Welk Show" as a summer replacement. Moreover his contract was renewed again in the fall of 1955. The dream of Lawrence Welk was finally fulfilled. He could now perform on a single Saturday night for more people than he had in the entire thirty years of his career up to that time. He had kept the goal before his eyes; he never doubted he could achieve it; and he never stopped working. Once again his own philosophy was verified.

Less than a year after Welk had begun broadcasting on the ABC network, the Dodge advertising executives arranged for a concert tour to include New York, Philadelphia, and Chicago. The entire TV cast was to fly to New York in March, 1956, and play at Madison Square Garden. When Jack Minor told Welk the details of the trip, the thought of performing before sophisticated Easterners turned him against the whole idea. He insisted that New Yorkers didn't like him and that nobody would come out to see a show such as his. Only after Minor had agreed to take Danny Thomas and Bert Parks along as special attractions did Welk consent to go. When they reached Madison Square Garden on a Monday evening it was raining heavily. To make matters worse it was Monday night in Holy Week. Everything seemed to point to total catastrophe. Bert Parks began the show as master of ceremonies, and he tried his best to cheer up the crowd with a few of his famous stories. Then he introduced Danny Thomas who in his normal, professional way did an equally excellent routine of jokes and stories. When the show had been going on for almost half an hour, Bert Parks finally announced: "Now we present Lawrence Welk and the Champagne Musicmakers." Eighteen thousand people spontaneously rose to their feet with an ovation such as few Garden performers have ever received. This made up for all the opposition Welk had ever received from the network. He had won New York!

When the show was finally over about 11:00 P.M., the

crowd clamored to be allowed backstage. Minor described the scene:

> The crowd was so insistent that they had to have a line of police beside the stage to keep the people from jumping up on the stage before the show was over. As Lawrence Welk, Bert Parks, Danny Thomas and I came off the stage that night we had to walk through this line of policemen to make our way through the crowd so we could get back to the dressing room. As we were sitting in the dressing room, Lawrence remarked to me, "Jack, I shouldn't be in here. I should be out there with my fans signing autographs." I opened the door to the vast hallway which was packed with people and said, "Here he is!" and I shoved him out the door. I turned back to Bert and Danny and asked, "Do you fellows want to go out there with him?" They answered, "Are you out of your mind? We're not going into that crowd."
>
> Instead, the three of us left to go out and have dinner, though it was already past midnight. As we left the restaurant and headed back to the hotel at about 2:30 A.M., Danny Thomas realized he had left his raincoat in the dressing room, so we asked the driver to let us off at the Garden for a minute while he picked up his coat. When we walked in there, we found Lawrence still signing autographs and we waited there for him for almost another hour.[7]

It is a true story, and it is another example of how the Lawrence Welk school of public relations operates. He has a reputation for never having been abrupt with people. He has told me on occasions when I tried to hurry him along to avoid crowds, "They are the ones who are responsible for my success. I owe them a great deal."

Outstanding Associates

Perhaps there has never been a more recurring theme in my personal conversations with Welk over the past fifteen years than his idea of how God has blessed him with truly outstanding people as associates:

There's Jim Hobson, probably one of the best television directors in the business; Myron Floren is not only a top accordionist, but his character and personal abilities make him ideal as my assistant director; George Cates, my music director—I couldn't ask for a better man in his field. There's Curt Ramsey, a hardworking, ingenious music man who has really jacked up our whole music department. Joe Rizzo is tops as an arranger; and how could we get along without Jack Imel on the choreography and dance routines? Bob Ralston is one of the hardest working musicians I have. Then there's Sam Lutz and Don Fedderson, my business executives who keep me in line. They may be hard on me at times, but they're good for me.

At my office I have Ted Lennon, vice-president of Tele-klew, who is simply irreplaceable. Never in my fondest dreams did I ever think I could hire people of the calibre of Norma Zimmer and Henry Cuesta. My private secretary, Lois Lamont, takes care of so many of my personal matters with such care and devotion that I can hardly believe what she accomplishes.[8]

On and on, Lawrence Welk speaks highly about the people who work closely with him—his wife, his children, his friends. Everything he says about them reflects his own interior conviction that he is so fortunate to have their talents and their devotion to him, that he wonders how he could do his work without them. One knows from listening to him that he senses the basic, psychological law that human nature needs to be uplifted, encouraged, and praised, not held down by harsh criticism. No man I have ever known "counts his blessings" so genuinely.

Gratitude to Parents

Going back to his childhood days, he never forgets to express his thanks to God for the parents He gave him:

They may have seemed strict at times in our upbringing, but they instilled in all of us children that deep Christian faith and love for God's commandments. They did a good job of convincing us that, if we go along with God's designs for us, our lives will be happy; and if we go against them, we will only invite disaster. My early training at home is the rock of my life today. I only regret that so many children today are deprived of good, God-fearing parents. No wonder so many lives are wrecked.[9]

Reveals Innermost Thoughts

As I listened to Welk, I realized I had read many of these same ideas before, quoted in hundreds of newspaper and magazine articles about Welk. At the time I had thought they sounded sanctimonious or overly pious. But any doubts I once had about his sincerity were erased when I heard him express his beliefs personally and privately. He is so honest and candid that he disarms people. One reason some are skeptical of his viewpoints is that it is such a rarity to find a person who reveals his true, innermost thoughts. Most people feel that speaking of their inner, spiritual beliefs will be interpreted as wanting to convert or impress others. So they refrain from speaking of God and their inner convictions. But when Welk is asked about his formula for success, his gratitude towards others, his happy home life, or his relationships with people, he is not about to tell it any way but exactly as it is. He doesn't know or care whether he is being poetically profound or trite or guilty of speaking clichés. He's not even concerned very much about his public image and makes little effort to become all things to all men. But when it comes to belief in hard work, deep faith in God, and dedication to the cause of serving his audiences, he doesn't wince at saying exactly what he feels.

One of the most touching conversations I have recently had with Welk took place the night before I left his Country Club Estates in Escondido, California. For three months prior to this I had worked with him at his office in Santa Monica and had just driven him to Escondido to spend a final week at his resort where he operates a large family restaurant, golf course, motel, and provides facilities for hundreds of mobile homes (cf. chapter 9). As I was about to leave I thanked him for generously allowing me the use of his office, his organization's records, for giving me so many personal interviews, etc. But really before I could complete my words he began to thank *me* for all the pleasant times we had spent together over the past few months, emphasizing how much he appreciated my efforts to chronicle the many facts and stories concerning his life and his organization. I said, "Lawrence, you always seem to go out of your way to thank your people for any little thing they do." He responded:

> Let me say that this does not come from any special training of mine as it does from just having a grateful heart. I think if you have real gratitude in your heart, it naturally comes out. I keep thinking of the early days when I played before only four or five couples after I had traveled 200 miles. And when it snowed or rained, sometimes only two couples showed up. Today when three hundred people attend my show at CBS, I realize how well off I am because of the time I didn't have that kind of attendance. You must remember that I worked in show business for 30 years before I came to enjoy this kind of recognition. Let me also say that the largest part of my gratitude comes from my faith. I suspect there are people who get up in the morning who fail to realize that they owe gratitude to God for the beautiful sunshine. They never think that God is responsible for the good things that happen to them. They actually believe that if the world is treating them right, it's all on account of their own doings. My parents' deep faith taught us that ingratitude was one of the worst ways of displeasing God. Even our talents and good qualities are gifts from God, not to be denied.[10]

Welk enjoys reminiscing about the early 1950s when his television show was just getting underway. On May 2, 1951, one of Los Angeles's principal television outlets, KTLA, first broadcast the Welk Orchestra from the Aragon Ballroom at Pacific Ocean Park. When the KTLA switchboard was swamped with calls, station manager Klaus Landsberg offered to sign a contract to keep this remarkable show on his station. However, it was not until August 21, 1951, that Welk's manager, Sam Lutz, was able to cancel all the band's bookings around the country and assure Landsberg that it would be free to appear on KTLA on a regular basis.

Adverse Criticism

Welk's problems, however, were only beginning. He was playing a five-night-a-week engagement at the Aragon and was putting in long hours of rehearsal for the special television pickup. He said thoughtfully:

This showcase being offered us was probably the greatest opportunity ever given to an orchestra like ours. The advantages certainly more than compensated for the added work. Yet there were some who could see only the dark side of the picture—those who found fault with the hours, the boss, the show's producer, the music they were asked to play, and on and on. In a few cases this attitude was so strong that these people could not be salvaged as useful members of our organization.

Welk learned from this experience that one of the worst enemies of progress is a critical approach that harps on petty grievances instead of thinking of the more challenging goals. Much of the extraordinary success of his present organization is traceable to his being able to eradicate negative thinking on the part of its members and emphasize that they all form what he has termed a "musical family." He insists that their common objective—a first-class musical variety show heard in millions of homes throughout the United States and Canada—is bigger than anyone's personal ambitions. He feels the job is essentially teamwork, that each person as an important member of the team contributes his part toward the achievement of a common objective. Thus Welk succeeded in teaching his performers the simple give-and-take of a well-regulated family. Recently when speaking about envies and rivalries, he said:

We don't have too much of that any more, I am happy to say. The reason is that on our show if any individual does well, it reflects upon the whole group. Suppose one performer does a number which makes the show better. The others realize that the success of the whole show may mean more personal success and money for them in the long run. And so they don't feel at all jealous or fearful of the others' work. I believe this is one of the strongest points in our organization. I try to teach our people this whole new kind of social relationship which is based on freedom and encouragement toward personal improvement. This involves, of course, the discipline of work, how to get along with people, how to practice gratitude, and never do anything that hurts others. Now this regimen or discipline has to be taught to people, just as it needs to be taught today in our schools which sadly have tried to eliminate it from their programs of learning. They say it hinders children from growing. Well, it ends up with the teacher losing control over the children. Unions sometimes forget about discipline and self-improvement of the individual in their efforts to get more money for their members. They encourage their people to take more break time than they have coming and seldom insist upon professional excellence in their members. Now all this is just the opposite of what I am trying to do in persuading my people if they do a better job they benefit by it.

Welk's Lighter Side

People who have read about Welk's serious philosophy may conclude that he never enjoys the lighter side of life. But those of us who have spent long hours with him have often been entertained by one humorous story after the other for the entire evening. Remarkably, the butt of each story's joke was none other than Lawrence Welk himself! If you were to question him, however, he would readily admit that he had to really teach himself how *not* to take life so seriously. His German extraction, his frugal upbringing, and his hard struggle and sacrifices to earn his living—all contributed to deeply serious habits of thought and living. "For too many years," he told me, "I had been so intent upon doing such a good job that I was jeopardizing my health. My futile attempt to run a one-man operation with an iron hand threatened me with an ulcer, and I sensed a mood of rebellion in my organization."[11] He claims that most of us make too much of our problems. They are in reality not as monstrous as we think, and we only make them larger in our own minds while we forget the joyous side of life.

Welk wrote an amusing letter to the editor of the *Santa Monica Evening Outlook* (August 18, 1976) in reply to a campaign by Anthony Defina of Santa Barbara, who was promoting Welk for president!

> Dear Editor: Everybody wants to be president this year—except me! In fact, when a fan of ours, Anthony Defina of Santa Barbara, undertook a letter-writing campaign to get me elected, I got on the phone immediately to try and talk him out of it. "I love being leader of the band," I told him, "and father of our Musical Family. But, I have no plans whatever to be father of our country!" Nevertheless, I was understandably flattered by his nomination and I let my mind play around with the possibilities a little. And in all due modesty I have to report that I have some very unique qualifications for the post.
>
> In the first place, I already have my "cabinet" ... (and my cabinet generally operates with a good deal more harmony than most incumbents in Washington). And even though there may not be a Ford in our future ... there will most certainly always be a Dodge in my garage.
>
> And when it comes to accents, I can more than hold my own. Can Henry Kissinger's accent compare to mine? For

that matter, can Jimmy Carter's? In fact, Mr. Carter and I
share a good deal more in common than just an accent. He
is a farmer. So am I. He has a big family. So do I. He has
a big TV smile. Me, too. He raises peanuts for a living and
I— (or so I've been told) —raise corn! So there you are.

And when it comes to Ford and Reagan, I'm still in the
running there. They are fighting right down to the wire
trying to line up delegates from every state in the Union.
And here I am with an orchestra already filled with representatives from practically every state—and a couple from
Canada and Mexico as well. Not only that, but with the
varied races and religions in our group we have a ready-
made diplomatic corps, all set to go to work the minute we
hit Washington!

So maybe I'm better qualified than I thought. And just
think what we could do if I were president! We'd have band
concerts every night . . . and polkas at every party . . . (I could
dance with every lady who voted for me). We could open
every session of Congress with a little Champagne Music
to get the legislators in a good mood—and then maybe
they'd start cutting some of those miles and miles of red
tape, and lopping off some excess bureaus, and lowering
everybody's taxes, and . . . say! Maybe I'll run for president
after all!

Stardom Requires Work

Welk's experience, both with his own performers and with
many all-time "greats" of the entertainment world, has convinced him that stardom and proficiency are *not* something
that people simply stumble onto by receiving some sort of
"break." He believes they must be steadily worked for during many years of study and personal sacrifice. "True, the
break does have to come from some source," he says, "but
if a person is not prepared for it, he will never attain proficiency on any level." He feels that if some musicians and
performers would seriously perfect their own instrument or
skill, they would quickly rise above mediocrity. Instead, they
like everything served to them on platters, even predigested,

so they can benefit with little or no effort on their part. At the age of seventy-seven, Welk is still one of the hardest-working men in the business. Every working day brings him to his office before eight in the morning, and more than one evening a week he works late. He is past the retirement age but doesn't plan on quitting in the foreseeable future. "Too much depends upon my carrying on now. Think of all the people who would be out of a job if I quit!"

Newspapers all over the nation back in 1955 called him "the hottest thing on television," "an overnight success"; they spoke of "the sensational rise of Lawrence Welk to a top spot on a major network." But Welk had actually been working patiently and determinedly for thirty years; and for the last five of those years his fondest goal had been a place on national television. To state that he was an immediate success, as though his accomplishment were due to short-term effort, is erroneous.

His was a lifetime of playing one-night stands, traveling perhaps more miles than any other band in history, all to discover the kind of music and entertainment that would please the rank and file of American people. Television may have arrived for Welk at the crucial moment of his career, but if anyone was prepared for it, he certainly was. Other great "name" bands of the 1930s and 1940s—Guy Lombardo, Duke Ellington, Artie Shaw, Fred Waring, Ted Weems, Wayne King, Sammy Kaye—had made great contributions to the popular music of America. But not one of them achieved a top place on a major network for more than one complete season. There must have been a certain element in Welk's show that the other band leaders knew comparatively little about. It was not simply excellence of musical performance or a characteristic "sound" or a danceable rhythm. Other bands had sounds and rhythm and musical performance and top-calibre musicians to surpass anything Lawrence Welk produced up until 1955.

I have asked scores of people who have been closely asso-

ciated with Welk over the years just what was this extra
something he had that enabled him to successfully meet the
challenge of television. Without exception they agreed: It
is the philosophy of the man himself. He envisioned his goal,
and he never gave up working for it until he achieved it. He
was willing to pay the price in personal sacrifice, effort, and
time to gain the expertise he needed to please his audience
with the kind and manner of musical performance they
wanted. He did not then, nor does he today, play to suit his
own tastes; he plays to suit the audience.

Measuring His Success

One further ingredient Welk has put into his musical
efforts over the years was never to judge a performance by
how much money he made. Though always a careful businessman who paid his musicians their fair share of the
profits, he frankly admitted to me: "I've played many single
engagements in which I either made nothing at all, or else
lost money myself. On my first television appearance, I myself had to pay my musicians the extra money the union demanded for broadcasting. Many a time in my career I didn't
know where my next meal was coming from; that's how bad
things were. I always tried to measure the success of any
performance by how our audience reacted and how much
we pleased them, not by how much money we made." Welk
considers the personal satisfaction in his field of music and
entertainment as paramount. He regards the inner joy of a
job well done as the essential ingredient of his success. Welk
continued:

One of the troubles in this world is too many people are
working more for the money than for the good of the job
they're doing. I want to say something to you about myself.
I have never known how much money I had, and this dates
back to the early days when I didn't know whether I had
one dollar, five dollars, or ten dollars. I believe people today
are overly conscious of money. In my whole lifetime I have

never worked just for money. This may appear strange or unreal, but it probably stems from my habit for many years of concentrating on pleasing my audience. For example, you saw how our young trainee here in our restaurant at Escondido was playing. I was wondering how well he was going over and how the audience liked him. I knew he was playing some songs the folks didn't know, and I was very concerned about it. You see, you have to do a better-than-average job if you are going to succeed in our competitive system. You need competition to stimulate yourself to do a really good job and keep improving. It's not the mediocre worker but the one who does the better job who makes headway. I believe this is what has always been the backbone of our country.

Do you remember that job from Las Vegas which came in the other day when you were in my office? Well, they wanted me to bring my orchestra up there for a week and were willing to give us $175,000. A suite, the use of a car, swimming pool and golf privileges, and all expenses were thrown in for everyone in the band. When I turned it down my manager, Sam Lutz, called and asked, "Would you take $200,000?" I told him it's not the money, but it may not be good for us. In our television audience there are a lot of religious people who don't believe in some of the things Las Vegas represents, and it could hurt the image of our whole organization. So it's not money that really counts, but it's how well we please our audience. We can't let them down.

My reasoning has always been that if you do a good job you don't have to worry about money. That was true when I got my start in Ipswich, South Dakota, and got in trouble with the church for playing beyond midnight. It was the same when I played for barn dances and birthday parties and even here at our restaurant in Escondido. If I can bring some joy and happiness to those people—many of whom have traveled hundreds of miles to visit us—that's what I aim at. It's why I took my accordion with me this evening and played for the people in the restaurant. Personally I would rather have sat with you people who were my guests.

It's not my own personal pleasure that matters most to me; rather I do what I feel will give pleasure to a larger number of people.[12]

One of his favorite prayers is the familiar peace prayer of Saint Francis of Assisi which is hanging on the wall of his office in Santa Monica.

> Lord, make me an instrument of your peace;
> where there is hatred, let me sow love;
> where there is injury, pardon;
> where there is doubt, faith;
> where there is despair, hope;
> where there is darkness, light;
> where there is sadness, joy.
> Grant that I may not so much seek to be
> consoled as to console;
> to be understood as to understand;
> to be loved as to love.
> For it is in giving that we receive;
> it is in dying that we are born to eternal life.

Handling Superior Talent

Something particularly noteworthy about Welk is the manner in which he deals with those who are highly talented. It will be recalled how Bill Karzas, owner of Chicago's Trianon ballroom, tried to dissuade him from hiring Myron Floren on the plea that he would hurt his own image by having a stronger accordionist in his band. Welk thought otherwise. He candidly admits that he has hired many musicians more accomplished than himself. In fact he has always publicly acknowledged superior talent. His familiar expression, "Wonderful, wonderful!" upon hearing an outstanding performance on his show has raised the question, Does he really think so, or is he exaggerating his performers' abilities? His thinking is: Yes, he does see in each performer something he is truthfully able to praise. Though the work may not be perfection in every respect, there is enough good in it to receive a pat on the back from Welk. To fail to give due recognition because of envy only hurts oneself, he believes. His own effort to overcome envy and his sincere desire to see the other person get ahead is one of the intangibles he communicates to the "musical family," the name by which he is proud to label his organization.

His Secret of Longevity on TV

Perhaps the most burning question ever put to Welk is the one that has puzzled broadcasters and entertainment people since he first went on national television in 1955: How does he manage to stay on television year after year? To the average person who watches his show each week, not much change seems to take place. A few of the performers move along each year; some new ones come in. Though the theme of each show is new and different, the performers seem much the same. Yet if you were to look behind the scenes, you would discover significant changes and improvements taking place to keep the music, the singing, the choreography, and the skits fresh and lively. This is precisely the reason the Welk show has made such great strides and why it is still on the air after twenty-eight uninterrupted seasons. Welk himself believes in change. For him to remain static is to go backward. His career has actually been one constant stream of growth. He considered his first television show as only a foot in the door. The real struggle was to maintain that level of excellence that would ensure the yearly renewal of his contract and an increase of audience. This could never be accomplished unless each week's show was just a little bit better than the previous week's. As Welk explains it:

It became obvious that the only way to stay alive in this business was through constant improvement. To stand still in any business is the path to failure. We have tried to upgrade our operation in every conceivable manner. To accomplish this we have enlisted the help of all the members of our organization; we have enlarged our orchestra and our cast of entertainers; we have made a determination that our show will continue to grow in quality as well as in size; and a general meeting before each new television season is devoted to strengthening this determination. Our show has become more and more a group effort. Each week's show is the product of the thinking of many people. We try to keep an open mind to all suggestions, siphon off the best ideas, and strive for gradual improvement through this sort of teamwork.[13]

A Sincerely Grateful Man

In 1965 Welk and his entire television cast appeared in Saint Louis's Kiel Auditorium—their first stage appearance in more than five years. I had the privilege of promoting that show. More than 12,000 people jammed Kiel's Convention Hall, which was sold out three weeks in advance. It was one of the few technical sellouts in the history of that auditorium. Welk was such a hit that he returned to Saint Louis five successive years to full houses. The 1965 show was one of my first experiences dealing with Welk in a business way, and I will never forget how he took me aside before boarding his plane upon leaving. "I want to thank you," he said, "for conducting what I consider one of the most effective promotions I've ever had since I've been in show business. We feared coming back to Saint Louis because of our last experience playing on an election night. Now, thanks to you and your organization, we will never underrate our popularity here." By rights, I should have thanked *him* far more profusely than he thanked me, since he was a benefactor to the religious organization for which I worked in the amount of more than $25,000. I immediately perceived that he is a sincerely grateful man. His gratitude pours out upon everyone with whom he associates. And it is precisely the expression of this gratitude to the people within his own organization that is at the root of much of its teamwork. Each member of his show is made to feel that he has a definite contribution to the success of the whole organization. As a result, each person feels appreciated and finds that, the more successful the entire show, the better his own career looks.

Welk the Teacher

In analyzing the character and philosophy of Lawrence Welk, it becomes surprisingly clear that he is by natural endowment a teacher. Though personally he saw very little of the inside of a classroom, he shows a persistent inner thirst to pass on to young people the same strong convictions he himself has learned to live by. Teachers in our world are doubtless a special breed of people. They are not necessarily of the highest intellectual endowment, nor are they so deeply entrenched in the ways of academe that they miss the practical challenges of life. They are more often persons of modest intellectual attainment who know how to develop and encourage the minds of young people. Thus they are able to speak their students' language, meet them on common ground, and gain their respect and admiration. Lawrence Welk, the teacher, seems always to have an idea, born of experience and vision, that he wants to communicate to someone. For example, I have sat in his dressing room and overheard him explain to a few of his best performers just what he thought was good and what he thought was weak in their work. Without being overbearing, he tactfully encouraged them on points of improvement, and they graciously accepted his advice. I could not help observing that the effectiveness of this man was that of a highly respected teacher who knows the inner workings of the human mind.

I asked Lawrence to outline how "as a teacher" he goes about developing people in his organization. He explained:

> I try to see what potential they have before ever hiring them. Most of the time I've been able to recognize talents and abilities in people. Of course, I have made mistakes, and I'm terribly disappointed when they fail to live up to their potential. But we only take them on a one-year, trial basis. I could use as an example Gail Farrell. She began a few years

ago as a singer. However, it turned out that she plays the piano, she arranges, she dances, she writes music, she has an attractive appearance, and she works well with people. The other day she came in and asked if I had a minute to listen to a new song she wrote. Well, her harmonies were so good that I actually got chills down my back as I listened. I said: "Gail, I've never had anything quite that pretty to go with my orchestra before. It's one of the nicest harmonies I've heard, and I know it's going to be sensational." You can imagine how justly proud she was of her work. When I encouraged her to arrange another song or two like this one, how important she felt as a member of our organization!

I think that what we do for our members is much like what a father does for his children. In most organizations it's curtains if you don't deliver an excellent job immediately. Usually you can't talk to the big boss either. I impress upon these young people what an opportunity they have being on our show, and I try to avoid putting pressure by encouraging them to develop their strong points. When a person slackens off, is tardy for a rehearsal, or doesn't do what is expected, someone in the band is sure to point it out to them. Invariably they'll be chided: "John, why don't you get on the ball?" So when the boss comes along, they've already been warned by their peers. So you can see why ours is called a "family" organization.

Another instance of how people develop in our organization is that of George Cates. He has developed into one of the most beautiful and capable people we have. You see, to develop someone, you have to think of the larger development of the whole organization. In the beginning George was a strong individual who had his own ideas of exactly how to handle people. His mistake was that he wanted things done exactly as he wanted, but he learned the lesson of using those fifty musical minds he works with. Now he encourages our people to talk and make suggestions. He has learned that to be valuable to the whole orchestra he has to get the best out of all the players, rather than scare them into silent submission to his way of directing. He is now one of our most respected and admired people.

Now besides people like Gail Farrell and George Cates—

and I could mention many others who have made even more progress—you also have those who are ill prepared, who try to sing songs not the way they're written but the way they like to sing them. To make things worse, these are just the people who have an exaggerated view of their own abilities and can't see any room for improvement.

Welk's School of Hard Knocks

Welk still subscribes to the principle that the best teacher of all is experience. He believes that all the theory and encouragement in the world given by another will not substitute for what one is able to teach himself through trial and error. He has taught himself golf and swimming to help his physical fitness. His early career demanded that he "double" on other instruments which he taught himself to play. Moreover, he frequently did everything from manage the finances of his band to setting up the bandstand before the shows. With the exception of what his parents and the nuns in grade school taught him in Strasburg, North Dakota, he learned most of what he knows today in the school of experience, or to quote an old cliché, the "school of hard knocks." It is probably because of his wide range of duties and activities that he has a deep compassion for the so-called common man. He can stand up before twenty thousand people at a state fair and tell them stories of his experiences on the farm, or he can talk straightforwardly to a sophisticated group of New Yorkers in Madison Square Garden about world problems. He is especially good at talking to just plain family people about the foibles of domestic life. He has opinions and ideas on almost every political and patriotic subject you could think of, and has had friends and close associates among senators, governors, and presidents.

Superficial Yardsticks for Success

I have read over 1,000 stories in magazines and newspapers describing the success of "The Lawrence Welk Show" and have balanced them with what I have learned from my personal association with Welk over the past fifteen years. The factors emphasized as reasons for success by the writers of the articles are often quite different from Lawrence Welk's own ideas on what constitutes his real success. For the most part the writers only skim the surface of the success story of Welk. They stress merely two things: the duration of his television career for twenty-nine years; and the financial bonanza it has proved to be for Welk personally. He believes that not only are these two yardsticks purely superficial ways of judging success, but they are at the root of much fallacious thinking today. "Parents," he told me, "point with pride to their son who is well known, highly respected, and holds down a well-paying position. Tremendous pressures are put on children early in life to work hard in school just so they can receive a good income later in life. A daughter is pressured into marrying a man of means. Men of moderate means develop an awe and respect for a man who has amassed great wealth. Yet money and earning power by themselves have been responsible for many unhappy lives and have wrecked perfectly good families."[14]

If I am able to interpret the deepest convictions of Lawrence Welk on what constitutes success, I would say that none of these symbols of power or prestige have ever influenced him very much. He thinks he was just as successful in the days before television as he became afterwards. His only view of this medium was the challenge it offered of playing to the whole country simultaneously. He wasn't satisfied until he met it.

I was especially struck by the following quotation from Welk's book, *Guidelines for Successful Living*:

> As far as I know there is only one way of defining and measuring success. It is doing one's best to make the most of oneself. It is not something that can be measured in relationship to others. It is an individual matter and must always be determined by the degree to which a specific person has reached his own highest potentialities. In line with this,

a person of great accomplishments may still be a failure if he is functioning below the best of which he is capable. And one of small accomplishments is an outstanding success if he is performing at the level of his maximum potential stature. . . . To me, success is very nearly synonymous with happiness, and in this respect I have had more than my share. The things that make for contentment are really not material accomplishments, they are a loving and close-knit family, close friends, good health and wonderful associates. All these contribute greatly to what I consider success.[15]

One of the most remarkable stories of Welk's career can now be told. It demonstrates his uncanny achievement of goals. All during the 1964–65 season he had been thinking about how color television was soon to take over. Everyone in the industry was talking about it. So as not to be unprepared, Welk began making plans for his color debut by arranging for a huge color spectacular to be filmed at his Country Club Estates located north of Escondido, California. As was expected, ABC announced in May of 1965 the shows that would start the fall season in color, and Welk was *not* one of them! What was even worse, he discovered he would be sandwiched in between two color shows. This caused him such tremendous concern he could talk about nothing else. Here he had begun the filming at Escondido, had such high hopes for his opening show, and even planned to send out announcements to all his fans before the opening date. It looked as though ABC had really let him down.

In June while he was performing at Harrah's Club at Lake Tahoe, Nevada, he approached his houseguest, Matthew Rosenhaus, president of the J. B. Williams Company, his principal sponsor. Rosenhaus was more than sympathetic over Welk's concern and tried to persuade him not to worry, saying that only 3 percent of the homes had color sets. He assured him that, if he were patient, he would soon be in color. But Welk did his best to persuade Rosenhaus and his advertising executive, Edward Kletter, that starting in color that fall was essential to the future of the show. He was convinced that no show starting the next season in black and white would last out the season. He told Rosenhaus, "If I am not in color this fall, I may decide not to go on the air at all. I predict that by December, 14 to 20 percent of the homes in this country will have color sets." Rosenhaus was so impressed by Welk's prophetic insight that he came backstage that very night at Harrah's Club and assured him that his firm would guarantee the additional cost if ABC would agree to broadcast the show in color.

Welk now went into action. He immediately phoned Don Fedderson and Sam Lutz in Hollywood and asked them to go to New York to negotiate with ABC. And just to make sure ABC would get his message, he phoned the network's president, Thomas W. Moore. He made it perfectly clear to Moore, in his typically friendly way, that he wanted to cancel his show for the coming fall, though he might be willing to do some specials if the network would want them. Moore was just as conciliatory as all the others, promising him that soon he too would be in color. It was not very long, though, before all the executives of the network had the clear message that Welk was ready to gamble his whole television future rather than run the risk of remaining in black and white. He was aware, of course, that the network was salvaging the shows being converted to color and considered Welk's show so well established it didn't need this added attraction. Legitimate as ABC's motive was, he did not agree with this thinking. He insisted on being in color even at the cost of losing his whole show on ABC. Finally, on July 26, he received word from New York that his show would be in color for the 1965–66 season. And so the color spectacular at Escondido was finished. It proved to be such a hit that his sponsor asked him to repeat it the following February. Tourists still drive into his Country Club Estates by the thousands each month to behold with their own eyes what Welk showed them on television. He still jokingly refers to his

color spectacular at Escondido as "the most eff̶
long commercial ever to appear on television." Thi̶
how Welk began his color show is but another exan̶
his philosophy of keeping one goal before his mind unti̶
achieves it. He indeed is a man of many goals, all of the̶
achieved.

His Right-Hand People

One of the unique characteristics of the Lawrence Welk
organization, known today by its corporate title, Teleklew,
Incorporated, is this most enviable record in show business:
most of its key personnel have loyally worked an unprece-
dented number of years under Welk. Sam Lutz, the executive producer, has served for thirty-four years; James Hobson,
producer-director of the show, for twenty-six years; Ted
Lennon, executive vice-president, twenty-three years; George
Cates, musical director, twenty-eight years; Myron Floren,
assistant conductor, twenty-nine years; Curt Ramsey, music
librarian and show coordinator, twenty-nine years; Bert Carter, retired manager of the Country Club Estates, twenty-
eight years; Don Fedderson, syndicator and network adviser,
twenty-five years; Lois Lamont, Welk's private secretary,
thirty-four years; and George Thow, continuity writer,
twenty-three years.

It is obvious that a large measure of the success of Welk's
show is due to the untiring efforts of these talented and
dedicated people. In fact, it is always with great personal
pride that Welk refers to them as "my right-hand people,"
sincerely insisting that he could never do the job by himself.
On his part, Welk has made them all shareholders inasmuch
as they partake in his profit-sharing plan. This plan will be
discussed in greater detail in a later chapter of this book.
However, it is sufficient here to point out that it indicates
an important attitude of Welk toward his associates. He re-
spects them as "human beings with individual rights, each
with a responsibility to guide his own life toward fulfill-

ment." He feels each person has a right to full compensation for his work and deserves honest consideration of his grievances.

It is to be expected that some people who join his organization later wish to drop out. However, the unusually large number who have continued with him for years is a glowing testimonial to Welk's high regard for each individual. Next to Welk's own personality and character, these people are the most important reason why the Lawrence Welk Show has been broadcasting for twenty-eight years.

Horatio Alger Award

Perhaps no one has been more deserving than Welk of the famed Horatio Alger Award, given him on May 25, 1967. It reads: "The Horatio Alger Award of the American Schools and Colleges Association Toward the Enhancing of the American Tradition of Overcoming Obstacles to Achieve Success Through Diligence, Industry and Perseverance." He firmly believes that most of the great accomplishments were achieved by men and women who, according to human standards, had not even a single chance for success. He recalls stories of men like Glen Cunningham, the world-champion runner, and others who overcame severe handicaps to become truly outstanding as athletes, musicians, scientists, humanitarians, statesmen, and businessmen. "They did the impossible? No," Welk insists, "they did what was *thought* to be impossible. It is only what we think is impossible that deters us from doing it."

His Investment in People

Welk has a sixth sense in sizing up people and judging their talents. His investment in people is not only in words. His record of hiring young talent who show promise clearly speaks for itself. Some facets of his faith in these people are not well known. As one of its regular charities, the Lawrence Welk Foundation contributes substantially to college scholarship funds in North Dakota and California to aid deserving students toward a college career in music and the performing arts. The foundation further donates to hundreds of other charities approved by members of its board of trustees. Welk's entire television show has gone on the road dozens of times to play benefits for Shriners' hospitals, crippled children's homes, the Sacred Heart radio and television hour, and hospitals in various parts of the country. In 1968–69, when Welk was chairman of the Cancer Crusade, he traveled across the country at least twelve times making speeches, doing short performances, and lending his efforts toward raising $69 million for the benefit of that organization.

Welk's only frustration in helping young people is that both the American Federation of Musicians and the American Federation of Television and Radio Artists have seemed at times to hinder his efforts. He frankly states: "The unions' rules have proved little interest in young people's development. When unions or government take over management of people's business affairs, they curb human incentive. Young people need encouragement to achieve goals for themselves. Many young musicians would like to start bands of their own, and they need all the help and encouragement they can get. And I believe most business people feel as I do; they want to see young people get ahead."

Welk has expressed his personal convictions on free enterprise as opposed to governmental and union interference in the operation of business in the magazine *Christian Economics,* as follows:

> My proposal to both government and unions is that business people who are willing to share their profits with employees should be allowed to operate on the principles of free enterprise. This would make any business, indeed any job in that business, a rewarding and exciting experience. This is what free enterprise is all about—meeting a need and meeting it a little better than anyone else. The healthy spirit of competition, inherent in this idea, calls upon the

best a man has to offer in the way of services or resources, and builds up his character as nothing else can. I know this works because the people in our musical family, who share in our profits, work with such spirit and enthusiasm. They all realize that to stay in the television world they have to continually try to do a little better job each year; and if they don't try they don't deserve to stay in the business.

It is this free enterprise which sets no limits on what any of us can achieve. It has released so much creative force and energy in this country that we have been able to provide more of the best things in life for the greatest number of people than any nation in the history of the world; yet today we seem to have not only lost pride in this wonderful system, but we have become almost defensive about it.

I feel with all my heart that free enterprise is essential to our way of life. There has never been any form of commerce or business developed that has been more fair or offered more opportunities to everyone, regardless of his origin, and I have only to look to myself to see that one who is born of immigrant parents, formally schooled only through the fourth grade, unable to speak English until I was twenty-one years old, I was still able to achieve so many of my boyhood dreams. Hundreds of thousands of other Americans have been able to do the same thing.[16]

4
Behind the Curtain

What Welk's Closest People Say About Him

The following series of interviews will disclose for the first time the convictions of those closest to Lawrence Welk in the production of his show. From their long experience and association with Welk, they are in a position to evaluate the aims and effectiveness of the program and to point out the various elements that contribute to its longevity and overall success. Both their personal opinions and factual observations are included.

Sam Lutz, Executive Producer and Personal Manager

Sam Lutz became associated with Welk in 1942 when, as sergeant for special services with the United States Sixth Army command in Chicago, he enlisted Welk's free services for the personnel at Gardner General Hospital. During those war years, Welk's band was a regular entertainment event at the hospital. It was there that Lutz observed for the first time the influence of Welk over an audience. "He could pick up his accordion in the midst of a show and turn a crowd of rather indifferent people into a most enthusiastic audience. I recognized this man's power over an audience and was determined that I would one day be his manager."[1]

It was Lutz who, a few years later, was influential in encouraging Welk to make Los Angeles the base for his band's activities. There the two men joined forces and have worked together ever since. Lutz has stood mostly in the background of the television show's production activity, but he has had a major role in its network and syndication development. Moreover, Lutz does all of the bookings for out-of-town appearances of the show, as well as personal appearances by the performers.

In 1951 Lutz opened the way for the Welk Show's appearance on one of the best television stations in Los Angeles, KTLA. It was a happy and planned coincidence that the band had just been booked in the Aragon ballroom at Pacific Ocean Park in Santa Monica. In those early days of television before videotaping, shows and bands around the Los Angeles area were often relayed by mobile truck back to the transmitter because stations were badly in need of live talent. It happened that KTLA-TV had often broadcast shows from the Aragon ballroom in this manner. Klaus Landsberg, manager of KTLA, was against broadcasting the Welk organization, calling it a "polka band," but by sheer persistence and strong persuasion Lutz persuaded him to try the group on a temporary basis. Of course, public response to this event led to Welk's television career. "Prior to that date in 1951," Lutz remarked, "Lawrence could have stood on the corner of Hollywood and Vine, and a thousand people passing him by wouldn't have the slightest idea who he was. But after that date, everyone in the Los Angeles area knew him."

Lutz insists that the success of the Welk Show stems from the personality of the man himself:

> His uncanny sense of knowing exactly what the audience wants at any given moment has sometimes led him to rearrange a whole show at the last minute. His timing and pacing of a show are so masterful that no one can explain it except to say that it is a God-given "sixth sense."

Another factor in Welk's audience projection which endears him to the public is his faulty English. His German dialect has a charm which people enjoy. He has proved the truth of the Horatio Alger story that it is possible for anyone to rise from rages to riches if he just works hard enough. Though nobody I've ever worked for has shown himself more grateful or loyal to me personally, I do find that I have to be on the ball with Welk at all times. There is no letup with him. He works just as hard as anyone else, and he demands a high degree of effort from those under him. I haven't had a vacation in six years simply because we go from one job to another and there is no time for a vacation. When we finish the television season, we go into road concerts. When we're through with the concerts, we go back into the TV season. That's been going on for twenty-eight years. Even when I went to Europe eight years ago I was constantly on the phone answering people's questions. Remarkably, although Lawrence is very demanding, he is also appreciative and loyal. He certainly is to me personally, and I know he worries about everyone in his organization—sometimes, I might say, a bit too much!

The constant theme of Welk's serious observations is that young people need to work if they are to get anywhere in life. He is as determined at the age of seventy-seven as he ever was in this belief. For example, he came back from a golf tournament the other day where he played with the Pittsburgh Steelers in Las Vegas. Well, he won the tournament thirteen down. The first thing he did when he returned was to call me and tell me about what a thrill this experience was to him. He forgot about all the great accomplishments of his life for the moment, though he certainly has had hundreds.

It's the old-school ethic that, if you want to make anything out of yourself, you have to work very hard, and he still works just as hard today as he did twenty years ago. He doesn't neglect one thing which he feels necessary to insure the success of the show. My big problem with him has always been that he never says no to anything. It's certainly not money he's after. He has all he needs, though he lives simply. He just has a determined fixation on the subject of work—for himself and for others: "If you want to be successful, you've got to work." He feels strongly that, if kids are given an opportunity to work, they have a better chance for success and happiness. In fact, he thinks so much of the importance of our free enterprise system that he is trying to convince legislators to change our child labor laws so kids can take a job. In his efforts he forgets that some employers are not as honest as he is and may take advantage of young people if they get a chance to make a dollar on them.

Lutz, who has worked with Welk as closely as anyone for over twenty-eight years, today considers him an "institution," alongside other highly respected showmen and public servants who have come to be looked up to and revered:

Bob Hope, Bing Crosby, Ed Sullivan, and Will Rogers have all been "institutions" in the American sense; and so Lawrence Welk has taken a similar place in the esteem of people. They look up to him, even idolize him. Women flock around him by the thousands whenever he makes personal appearances. All they want to do is shake his hand and thank him for bringing such fine music and wholesome entertainment into their homes. I believe it is all due to the fact that people identify with Welk. They can see in him something of themselves. He plays their kind of music and talks their language. He projects the kind of personality they feel makes him one of them. Wherever he goes, he is an immediate hit with the audience.

As the man who is responsible for making the advertising dollar stretch over the costly broadcasting budget, Lutz says he is a strong proponent of much variety in the Welk show:

Everybody doesn't like everything, but they are bound to like something. Welk's charm is wholesome and warm; his smile is winsome; and he builds up the good in a performer to the point where the audience overlooks little shortcomings and weaknesses. Lawrence has always believed in longevity for the show. It costs less and lasts longer. The agency people write off Welk, saying he has just been lucky to hit the "big time," but they forget that it has been a great deal more than luck. True, he came into the television picture when people were looking for a show like his. But Lawrence has succeeded as he has by dint of hard labor and much dedication to his audience.[2]

Don Fedderson, Network Representative and Syndicator

Fedderson has been closely associated with Welk from his start on coast-to-coast television in 1955. He has played a major role over the past twenty-five years, first in launching the Welk show on ABC network television, and in 1971 in keeping it in the same enviable place on the American scene through syndication. It took courage and vision on his part to back a show that the New York advertising executives with few exceptions predicted would certainly be discontinued after its first thirteen weeks. Don Fedderson, though quiet and outwardly unassertive, was sure Lawrence Welk had something to offer the American public that nobody else had. He takes little personal credit for the transaction, saying:

Lawrence would have succeeded on network television without my help. All I could offer was some experience in dealing with the networks. He had all the desire and drive to put his band on the greatest of our mass media, television. I believe one secret of how he began on national television was timing. He had the kind of music people were looking for at the time. You must realize it was just immediately before the days of rock 'n' roll. "The Lawrence Welk Show" was one of the first real organizations to offer network television a tried and tested performance. Indeed, he is still one of the best organizations in television today. Every performer is hand picked by Welk himself. Each has something definite to contribute in the way of talent or expertise. Everyone pulls together because each believes in Welk, in his methods and his aims.

I asked Fedderson how, as a producer, he would evaluate "The Lawrence Welk Show."

You know this production business in television is a tough, exacting job. It requires people who, week after week, are willing to pull together and not act like prima donnas overwhelmed by their own importance. Just look up there on the stage at those people rehearsing. They've been working together since ten o'clock this morning and surely must feel a certain amount of tension and frustration. But if you could watch them year after year, as I have, you would hardly ever hear an impatient word from any of them. They're simply hardworking, cheerful people who try to get along with one another. They're human and have their little ups and downs, but they have real team spirit given them by Welk himself. He calls them by the rather naïve title "our musical family." Well, strangely they fill that bill rather well inasmuch as they really pull together.

How well would you say these musicians and performers do financially?

You've heard Lawrence criticized, I'm sure, for only paying union scale to his performers and musicians. Well, just count the number of people in his show. There are nearly a hundred all together, counting those behind the scenes. Suppose you paid one musician more than another, or one singer more than another, wouldn't you have a revolt on your hands? Actually Lawrence tries to help his people find side jobs—personal appearances, recordings, tours, and extra jobs which may come up. Invariably he will excuse a person from a television show just so he can make a personal appearance in some distant city.

I asked what he considered was Welk's particular forte.

One of them is his deep insight into people's talent. He can take singers like Joe Feeney or Jim Roberts or Norma Zimmer and give them just the song which makes them look and sound best before the camera. It's somewhat as though Lawrence were a good cook who takes a dash of whatever each performer is able to do best, then mixes it all together in a dish, and the public loves it. Note that it's not so much the individual performer who goes over, but the combination as it is served. This is why he often makes a change in a show at the last minute when he discovers, for example, that two slow-moving numbers have been put back to back. It may all seem so simple, this mixing of songs, and pace, and singers and dancers. But its very simplicity is such a large factor in the total success of the show. You know how many orchestras like Stan Kenton tried to create something totally new in the entertainment world. They were either new types or arrangements, new ways of playing songs, or new styles of singing. In many cases they didn't wear well; they fell by the way. And people either grew tired of them or else they had to cover up their ears after listening for a time.

Lawrence's genius is ultrasimplicity. He will throw aside an overarranged piece. Often he will leave out a complicated interlude. He wants his performers to do the ordinary, simple music extraordinarily well. How often he has remarked, "Throw it out; it just doesn't have the right feel." He senses exactly what the public wants and tries to give it to them.[3]

James Hobson, Producer-Director

Of the twenty-eight years that the Welk show has enjoyed prominence on television, Jim Hobson has been producer-director for twenty-five. He is a former Shakespearean actor who has taken numerous dramatic roles both on television and in motion pictures, and he has directed television specials and series like "The Liberace Show" and "The Tennessee Ernie Ford Show." Welk has often referred to him as "the best director in the business, and an experienced showman himself." He came to the Welk show as a seasoned, capable director; however, he has, like many of Welk's people, grown in sympathy and understanding of young talent just getting their start with Lawrence Welk. People who work with Hobson invariably praise him for his ability to "put the part into the actor's mouth." Since as director he is the creative individual responsible for assembling hundreds of different elements of the television show and turning them into a coordinated, artistic piece of showmanship, Hobson can be considered as the final important link in the long chain of production. In addition, he is also the producer, the person responsible for originating all the different elements of the show. The opinions of this man, it must be remembered, come out of a mind that never stops thinking, planning, or visualizing. He is blunt, straightforward, and strong in his opinions, but he is tireless and positive in carrying out what he thinks best for the show. His critical bent is just as strong toward himself as it is towards others with whom he works.

Hobson summed up his own job in this way:

> My job is to put on a show which represents Lawrence Welk fairly and at the same time offers good entertainment. All of us on the production team must second-guess Lawrence as to exactly what he wants on the show. After all, he is the boss. But we've worked with him for so many years that we feel we can do a fairly good job of it by now. He always maintains the idea that he is trying to train all of us to take over if or when he is out of the picture. But my argument to him has always been: "Lawrence, the production staff is perfectly capable of putting on a good musical variety show, but without you the magic is gone." You know, when you stop to think about it, Lawrence is what holds the whole show together. I've always been the bad guy who insists the show cannot go on after Lawrence leaves, and I still don't believe it can. We of course have an heir apparent in Myron Floren, but you're not going to have the same show. Myron's instinctive input is not the same as Lawrence's. He's second generation like all of us. However, I seem to be the only one who feels this way.

Developing the idea that Lawrence Welk has been in show business for so many years that he instinctively feels what his audience expects, Hobson continued:

You must remember that Lawrence works a great deal through a "sixth sense" of intuitively knowing what is best for the show. There's no real plan in his mind which has been worked out systematically. This is what makes it so difficult at times to work with him. He just thinks this particular problem or that needs immediate attention. For example, he lights upon a current problem he is having with an individual in the show who won't improve himself; or he comes up with some naïve request he heard from a nice old lady he met on the golf course. Many of his ideas come from the mail he receives at the office or from other contacts with audience like the road shows, talking to our studio audiences here in Television City, meeting people in his restaurant at Escondido, or from the various public appearances he makes around the country. Well, the trouble is that, though Lawrence is usually right about such complaints, ideas, or suggestions, they tend to become blown up beyond proportion and often get in the way of our long-range, systematic efforts to keep the shows good and attractive and well produced.

When discussing how he is able to work with such a wide diversity of talent on the show—some beginners, some nonprofessional, others highly professional—Hobson had this to say about the talent on the show:

Ironically, the weakest talent we have on the show seems to have the highest mail rating. Both Lawrence and I agree that we do have some weaker talent, but we're both constantly working to try to improve these individuals. He has lost many of these people over the years through attrition. Some decide they want to go on their own, or others just retire from show business. Unfortunately, because of the way Lawrence builds up our performers, some develop the impression that they're really much better than they are. Also there is a nondiscriminating element in our audience which at times becomes very vocal in support of talent which is really not that outstanding. Frankly, our entertainers for the most part are like the next door neighbor's kids performing. We have some real professionals, but the rest have been brought up from nothing by Lawrence himself. These latter are the ones Lawrence likes the most. The ones to whom he makes himself very vulnerable are those with native talent who easily slacken off and don't work very hard to develop themselves. Invariably these people present big problems. You will have to admit, though, that Lawrence is usually right about the potential of any talent he tries out on the show. When he first brought Anacani on the show, she had some trouble with pitch, and none of us thought much of her ability. Well, Lawrence proved he was right. She has developed into one of our best singers today. The same could be said of several others on the show.

Many producer-directors work under restrictions of one kind or another—financial or budget restrictions, personnel, network demands, sponsor demands, etc. Jim Hobson is given much freedom to produce the show the way he thinks best, largely because he has gained Welk's confidence over the years he has been with the show. However, in discussing the restrictions he feels as producer, he stated:

The restrictions I have in producing this show are in Lawrence himself and his lack of willingness to take a chance on anything. He's the type of person who always bets on a sure thing! For example, he has to actually see what a production number looks and sounds like before he will try it. It took me years to persuade Lawrence to let me march the band through the audience at Lake Tahoe. It took another four to persuade him to let me open up the show with the band on the stage and the entire cast coming through all the doorways and walking through the audience shaking hands with the people. Now ironically he often resorts to exactly these same techniques on his road shows.

I had his daughter-in-law, Tanya, do the hukilau over in Hawaii. Tanya had studied a certain amount of dance technique, and I felt she would be just the person for this skit. You know, the hukilau is an old fisherman's song which is used with almost every tourist group that goes to Hawaii.

They get a group of tourists together and teach them to do the hula-hula using the hukilau. Now if you pick the right people, it's an incredibly funny thing to watch. Well, as you know, Lawrence is a natural for picking people out of an audience to come up and take part in such a fun activity, and he has a knack for picking just the right people. So I said to him: "Lawrence, you don't know what this is, but we're going to do the hukilau with Tanya. What I would like you to do is to go out into the audience there on the grounds of the Sheraton-Waikiki and pick a small group of people so we can teach them to do the hula-hula." This immediately turned him off. "No, no, that's terrible. We just can't do it. It simply won't work." I kept pleading, "Lawrence, why don't you just give it a try?" He kept insisting: "No, it will never work. I know it. Why don't *you* pick them yourself?" So I went out and picked about fifteen people—a fat man and a skinny woman, a tall man and a tall woman—just the kind I thought Lawrence would have picked. I lined them up and we started the music. Tanya said to them: "Now we're going to teach you all to do the hula. You do exactly what I am doing." Lawrence watched it for exactly ten seconds and almost fell over with laughter. Now he was on to it and thought it was great!

The remarkable fact is that Lawrence is completely honest. This incident was not a case of Jim Hobson's thinking of it and therefore it wasn't any good. He's not that way. He just couldn't picture it because he hadn't seen it. But he is so completely honest that he doesn't feel embarrassed if ten seconds later he has to admit he's wrong. My only point is that it's sometimes very difficult to bring him around to that point.

As a person who has for many years dealt with business executives in broadcasting, Jim Hobson had this to say about Welk's attitude toward the broadcast industry:

For having spent twenty-nine years in television, Lawrence not only doesn't know much about the business side of broadcasting, he doesn't want to. He is not familiar, for example, with the National Association of Broadcasters or of the importance of cultivating their friendship or attending their conventions. Further, he is not interested in television awards, though he has received more than his share of humanitarian and service organization awards. The result is that we're really on the fringe area of show business inasmuch as we don't associate with people in other shows. That is, we don't do the things they do. We're strictly a kind of ivory tower in the world of television. Only about three people I know of in our show belong to the Television Academy. Now the way you win awards in the Television Academy is exactly the way you win them in the Motion Picture Academy. When Metro-Goldwin-Mayer wanted to win an Oscar for *Singing in the Rain,* they bought memberships for the three thousand people employed by MGM. In television it's much the same. You have to go out and polish the apple if you want to receive an Emmy. Now Lawrence really doesn't understand much of these mechanics of the business or the political side of television. Of course he does understand how to put on a television show which appeals to his particular audience. This for him is important.

How do you explain the enigma that the Welk show represents in the minds of television executives, advertising people, and show people? Hobson replied:

Our show is more than a puzzle to them, it is an object of hatred. Remember that when Lawrence first went on the air with a network show back in 1955, everybody in the industry predicted that it would last three or four weeks and then fold. Well it lasted sixteen years on the network and eight by syndication to this date. And it's still going strong. At that time it displaced twenty-seven major shows which were thrown against it on Saturday evenings. This was brought out very forcibly to me one time down in Newport Beach. One day the owner of the beach's anchorage was walking along the dock with a friend, who apparently was a television producer. As the producer looked at one of the boats, he remarked: "That's a beautiful boat! Whose is it?"

The friend replied, "That's Jim Hobson's; he's the producer of 'The Lawrence Welk Show.' " Well, the reply he came back with was so full of invective that his exact words can't be supplied here! This producer had put on a show with Peter Falk just opposite ours, and it lasted only two weeks. In fact, the only show to compete with us on Saturday night was "Adam 12," which did eat somewhat into our ratings. This incident proved to me that many people's attitude in the industry is one of more hatred than puzzlement over the Welk show. After all, this man's financial interest in time and money had been wiped out by the success of our show.[4]

George Cates, Musical Director

My interview with George Cates brought out the opinions and observations of a man who has held his position with Welk for twenty-seven years, twenty-four as musical director. Welk himself on numerous occasions has referred to Cates as "a most competent man in his field." Cates is a tall, thin, soft-spoken man with a beard. He was formerly music director for Coral Records of Hollywood. Cates met Lawrence Welk in the early 1950s while the latter was performing at the Aragon ballroom in Santa Monica and making recordings at the studios of Coral Records.

Cates recalled that Welk had come to Los Angeles in the early fifties with the twelve-piece band he had had in the Midwest. Welk had had many minor, one-night stands and recording sessions along with bookings in various parts of the country, and in 1951 was finally able to locate at the Aragon.

It was at this time that Welk used his opportunity to build a larger and better band, because his income from both the weekly television broadcasts on KTLA and his regular contract with the Aragon netted him a considerable sum. Even at his start on national television in 1955, he had a much smaller group than he has now. Welk kept adding wherever and whenever he could—vocalists, instrumentalists, and dancers. It seemed a burning religion with him to build up something really good enough to serve the interests of the public. He has the typical, broad view of what the average American likes. His own taste is a barometer of the taste of the general public. For example, over the years, wherever and whenever he could—vocalists, instrumentalists, or not, Welk would say, "I don't understand it, but I'll let you fellows override me, and we'll assume it's going to go over." Later we would invariably receive complaints from listeners over that very song. Welk has the same "feel" as the audience. Whenever he remarked that a certain show was outstanding, you could be sure the letters would roll in saying the same.

I asked Cates what stood out as most memorable in his long association with Welk.

Most outstanding in my mind from my associations with Welk over these many years is his total dedication to making sure he does what the audience wants. Anything that was 2 percent controversial he would leave out of a show because he didn't want to offend anyone. For example, we would never do a song from a controversial motion picture because of the bias which might be associated with that particular number.

I remarked that Welk managed to maintain a kind of middle style of musical performance while playing many modern types. Cates answered:

Some people think we don't do rock 'n' roll, dixieland, jazz and the more modern types of sounds. Somehow they associate us only with the champagne music for which Lawrence became famous. This is completely untrue. We play all the "pop" tunes of the day; we do tunes of yesterday; and we play tunes that have never been popular but which are great tunes. Since we're in the sound business we naturally don't play those sounds which are rough and without finesse. We perform lots of contemporary music, but we feel sure it's the best and that it is thoroughly polished.

Since we've gone into television, we've increased the number of productions within our musical show. When we started we had only about two or three little productions squeezed in among about twenty-five numbers. Since then, we have used a theme for each show which gives us ample opportunity to bring in more and more little productions for each hour's show. The brain work is done by our whole team of producers: James Hobson, Jack Imel, Curt Ramsey, George Thow and myself. No one person is responsible for the entire show, but Lawrence is the head and has the final say on everything.

When I asked what he thinks is the psychological appeal of the show for the public, Cates answered:

It is often said that one of the secrets of the success of our show is the identification our audience feels with the individuals they see and hear. We make sure our characters are ordinary people and never theatrical types. People see in them their husbands, their daughters, wives, and friends. They're never overly made-up so they will always fit into the family scene, which is the kind of show we try to produce.

We're always touched at the kinds of gifts which are sent by our listeners. For example, to the girls who are going to have babies they send handmade coverlets and crib covers. One person even sent his old violin to Aladdin [Aladdin died in 1970]. This proves that a very personal, intimate relationship certainly exists between our viewers and the people they see regularly on our show.[5]

Les Kaufman, Public Relations Director

Les Kaufman, who originally worked for the Grant Advertising Agency in Detroit, came to Los Angeles in 1952 to do public relations work for the Welk show and to work under Bert Carter, then regional sales manager for the Dodge Dealers' Association of Southern California. He recalls that, in Welk's early days on television, he took such strong hold of the Los Angeles area on Saturday nights from 6:00 to 7:00 P.M. that no sponsor would buy competing television time.

During Welk's first summer on network TV, in 1955, Jack
Minor, vice-president of Grant Advertising Agency of New
York, came out to Los Angeles from Detroit to persuade the
Dodge dealers to back the permanent signing of the Welk
Show. Kaufman recalls:

> They all worked feverishly on a big sales presentation
> to be given at a special breakfast meeting of all the Dodge
> dealers in the Colonial Room of the Ambassador Hotel. The
> program was planned in great detail. Jack Minor was to
> MC the breakfast and manipulate everything to perfection
> so the dealers would be well impressed with the success
> thus far of the summer series on the ABC network. Well, we
> all arrived, and everything was set to begin promptly after
> the breakfast. All the speeches, posters, and diagrams were in
> order. A certain dealer named Lonnie Hull, whom everyone
> respected very highly, raised his hand, stood up, and said,
> "Jack, we don't know what this meeting is going to be
> about, but before we start, there's one thing I have been
> asked to say by all of our dealers—keep Lawrence Welk on
> ABC for Dodge!" So Jack Minor simply announced, "Gentle-
> men, the business is completed; the meeting is adjourned."
> It was the shortest breakfast meeting the Dodge dealers of
> southern California ever had!

Kaufman claims that Welk's relationship with his sponsors
is brought about through a natural affinity he has for people.

> If you are going to buy Welk, he is going to work for
> you. He goes out of his way to give you what you want. This
> is all a reflection of his own innate feelings toward people.
> Actually I have figured it out this way—he is in love with his
> audience. He is grateful to each one of them for giving him
> support. It may all sound naïve or corny, but this is sin-
> cerely what Welk's attitude toward his audience is. He simply
> does not want to do anything that might in the least alienate
> his audience. And after so many years of listening to them
> and catering to their wishes, he believes he knows what to
> do to please them. For example, if his audience says they
> don't like "I Love You Truly" but would rather hear
> "Alexander's Ragtime Band," that's what he is going to

play for them. He just has a "sixth sense" of what people want as a result of his experience playing all those one-night stands throughout America. His staff reads every single letter that comes into his office. They make note of the favorite selections, as well as those the people don't especially like. Now all these results are carefully tabulated, and the results are studied by Welk himself, as well as by his production people. It was basically this desire to please his audience which impelled Lawrence to go into syndication. Although ABC had cancelled him in 1971, millions of protest letters poured in, and he felt that if he didn't continue his show he would let his audience down after they had supported him for so many years.

I asked what Kaufman thought were the advantages of syndication over network broadcasting.

One reason is that the added work and expense of syndication more than evens itself out because the financial returns are somewhat higher. But the biggest single advantage of syndication is that you are not beholden to any one broadcaster, and you are your own boss as to what you put on the air. Network officials often wrongly dictate what a show should be. I've seen a lot of shows in which a network official would tell the producer to change his show's format. They try it, and find they've bombed the whole show.[6]

Curt Ramsey, Assistant Music Director, and Jack Imel, Assistant Producer in Charge of Staging and Choreography

These men discussed their opinions of why the show has been a success, as well as their own personal roles in it. Ramsey, who has been assistant music director since 1950, stated:

The success of "The Lawrence Welk Show" is a combination of many factors and of many people, all of whom contribute their special talents and abilities toward the functioning of a truly airtight organization. The big band era had waned when television started in the United States in the late forties. Today Lawrence Welk remains the only

one which has lasted on a major television network, though
many of the best bands had their try at television.

When asked, "Is it entirely the personality of Lawrence
Welk which accounts for the success of the show?" Ramsey
stated:

> This is a large part of it. He is quite strong in many of
> his ideas about pleasing the public. We've discovered while
> playing one-nighters that his presence on the bandstand is
> almost magnetic. We used to observe on Saturday nights here
> at the Hollywood Palladium how he would leave the band-
> stand for ten or fifteen minutes during the course of the
> evening. Though the band had been playing all the time,
> when he returned it was like a 30 to 40 percent increase in
> audience enthusiasm. He has a few rather basic rules which
> he wants us to follow in putting the shows together. First,
> he tries to do songs which are well known. Next, he keeps
> them short, so that very few are over two minutes in over-
> all length. That way we get more numbers in, and if one
> doesn't please a certain person, the next one will. Some
> dance numbers may take longer, but a straight vocal or in-
> strumental is rarely more than two minutes. Even when
> choosing the new songs, we try to make sure that they are
> well known all over the country before we play them on our
> show. The magazine *Billboard* keeps us well posted from
> week to week as to exactly what recorded songs are doing
> best across the country. Lawrence's next rule is to be care-
> ful in choosing songs with appropriate lyrics. Since our
> show goes into homes, we avoid any lyrics which are sug-
> gestive or vulgar or with double meaning.
> Lawrence insists on another basic rule, that each num-
> ber we play have a "feel." The song must have a beat; its
> structure must be such that it makes sense to the audience.
> This is called "meter" in musical terminology. He likes
> songs with thirty-two–bar choruses, and he rules out songs
> entirely which are "off-beat." In fact, a way of determining
> this himself is whether he is impelled to tap his foot to any

number he hears from a prerecorded tape. He considers this
a minimal test of audience participation for any good song.

Curt Ramsey showed me a large loose-leaf book containing
separate sheets for each performer. On these sheets were
listed the song that each singer or instrumentalist had performed from the beginning of the network television show
in 1955. Opposite each song was inserted the corresponding
number of the show in which that person had performed
the selection. Whenever a song was chosen for any performer,
the producers referred to this book and thus were sure to
pick a selection that had gone over well in the past. They
believe people enjoy hearing a song more than once.

Ramsey showed me another loose-leaf book in which is
recorded every musical arrangement ever used on the show.
The name of the song, the composer, the publisher, and the
arranger are all typed on these sheets and presented to the
stations for the purpose of clearing the music for broadcast.
Most songs are copyrighted; so the stations must pay the
publisher for their use on the air through fees paid to the
two major licensing societies—the American Society of Composers and Publishers (ASCAP) and Broadcast Music Incorporated (BMI).

I asked these producers of the Welk show whether they
felt their production projects were idealized and fanciful
images enabling viewers to identify themselves and their
loved ones with the performers. Curt Ramsey answered:

> We're in a definite category in the public's mind. In fact
> when we hire someone we always ask whether his image will
> be what our show requires. Often Lawrence will try a per-
> son out for a couple of weeks to see whether he fits in. Some-
> times a singer who is very good in person may not come
> across the television screen with an image appropriate to our
> show. Lawrence has been extremely careful in a personal
> way, for example, over the image created by each individual

performer. He has had his secretary, Laurie Rector, tabulate each month in careful detail all the mail coming into the office as "favorable" or "unfavorable" for each performer on the show. This is probably the most thorough study which has ever been made of audience reaction to any show.[7]

Jack Imel, who has been assistant producer in charge of staging and choreography since 1957, further elaborated:

Fan mail arrives in which the writer compares the Aldrich Sisters to the girls next door. One person said Dick Dale looks just like his son. Another said her husband, before he died, looked just like Jimmy Roberts. Our performers are carefully protected from the theatrical look so they can present a proper image to people in their homes. That is, they're never overly made-up. Our wardrobe, too, is never extreme is style. Of course we have to change with the styles. The hemlines went up a lot slower than on other shows. The "mod" look in men's clothes, the bell-bottoms, and all the rest have gradually come into our show in a modified way. Our wardrobe manager, Rose Weiss, is probably the best person in the business here in Hollywood. She does marvels with a very limited budget in fitting these people into costumes each week. She works full time exclusively for "The Lawrence Welk Show" but is called to work on the Academy Awards show each year as a special job. She used to travel each year with Bob Hope to Vietnam to take care of the wardrobe for his show.

Next to Welk himself, perhaps the one man who has the greatest responsibility for the success of the television show is Jim Hobson, the director-producer. The people sitting in their homes watching this show have only what Jim gives them on their television screens, and he has as perfect an understanding of what Lawrence wants as anybody we have working with us. He has been directing the show since its start on the network in 1955, and also has taken over the producer's job since the death of Ed Sobel in 1960.[8]

The one thread woven through this set of interviews points out that the personality of Lawrence Welk is largely responsible for the success of his show. Though manifested in various ways, his personality is especially strong in enabling the audience to identify with him. Don Fedderson stressed that it is the genuineness of his character, his credibility, which enables the audience to relate to him as an ideal father, husband, or friend. George Cates stressed another reason for a more general indentification: the performers are not theatrical looking, but ordinary looking people. For example, he considered the large number of gifts received from the audience as proof of the deep emotional relationship between performers and audience.

Though many elements of success were brought out in these interviews, none is more dominant than the image of Lawrence Welk and his performers bringing about emotional identification with the audience. Therefore it is right to conclude that an idealized fantasy image, as experienced by millions of people week after week, is one of the largest single reasons for the success of "The Lawrence Welk Show."

5
Who Pays the Bills?

Welk and His Sponsors

One of the most authentic approaches to the study of "The Lawrence Welk Show" or any other commercial broadcast is to examine the attitude of the sponsor who pays the costs. Some say it should be no concern of the sponsor in what shows his commercials appear. Indeed, there has been a movement for some years within advertising agencies and networks to sell commercials to sponsors without their knowing where or when they will appear. Networks have long wanted the liberty to place commercials where they feel they would receive the best audience. In practice, however, this procedure has proved to have ingredients of poor salesmanship. As long as networks are in a position of having to peddle their commercial time to the sponsor through the advertising agency, they must be able to show the buyer what he is buying. Demographic descriptions of the specific age group of an audience, its economic status, its educational level, and its ethnic makeup are all available today for any well-established television show. Moreover, sponsors feel that a particular television show creates an image for their product. Advertising research supports this conviction by proving that a favorable image is necessary if any product is to enjoy long-range sales.

Another reason for studying the sponsor relationships of the Welk Show is that, among all television shows of long standing, it has a most enviable record. Over its long twenty-eight years on television, it has had only two principal sponsors: the Dodge Division of the Chrysler Motor Company of Detroit for eight years (1952 to 1955 on Station KTLA-TV, Los Angeles; and 1955 to 1960 on the ABC network); and the J. B. Williams Company of New York for twenty years (1960 to the present). A few other sponsors—for example, Block Drug Company, the Polaroid Camera Company, the Kellogg Company, the National Biscuit Company, and Johnson's Wax—in recent years have had as much as two or three minutes collectively on some individual shows. However, the principal sponsor is considered the J. B. Williams Company of New York, and the public image of the Welk Show definitely associates it with Geritol, Aqua Velva, Rosemilk and Serutan—all products of the J. B. Williams Company.

It might be presumed that the remarks and opinions of a show's sponsor would tend to be favorable. Yet there is no one as quick as the sponsor to sense weakness that might creep into a show. The sponsoring company pays large amounts of money—production costs, air time and agency fees. Though the exact amount is never disclosed, today it can be presumed to be in excess of five dollars per thousand homes reached for each commercial shown.

Role of the Sponsor

The average viewer of television in America often forgets the role of the sponsor. It is actually in a peculiar position of influence over network, producer, and public alike. If it favors a show and is satisfied with the sales results for its product, then to a large extent the show can be considered secure. True, there are other influences that determine the life span of a show. However, the sponsor's favorable attitude is one of the largest single factors in a show's enduring success.

The following analyses of sponsors' attitudes toward the Welk Show begin with an interview with Bert Carter, former regional manager of the Dodge Dealers' Association of Southern California, who sponsored the show on KTLA-TV from 1952 to 1955. Next are statements by Jack Minor, formerly vice-president of the Grant Advertising Agency of New York. Minor was in charge of the Dodge account in 1955 when the Welk Show began on the ABC network. Later Minor was placed in charge of public relations for the Dodge Division of the Chrysler Motor Company, in which capacity he had even closer ties with the Welk Show during the years 1955 to 1961. Later I interviewed Matthew Rosenhaus, president of the J. B. Williams Company of New York, the present sponsor of the Welk Show. And finally I spoke to the regional manager of the Parkson Advertising Agency in Los Angeles, Irving Ross, who handles the J. B. Williams accounts on the West Coast. The opinions of these four men, I believe, will give a clear, factual picture of what the sponsor has to say both for and against the show.

Bert Carter

I asked Bert Carter what the Dodge dealers honestly thought of the Welk Show in its early years, from 1952 to 1955. He replied:

Thanks to Lawrence Welk I had the best selling area for Dodge cars in the United States. Welk sells his product effectively because he believes in it and talks about it during the show in such an adroit way that people associate him with his product. Back in those days, if anybody asked you who Red Skelton's sponsor was, or Danny Thomas's, or any of the top television personalities, you would have had a hard time remembering. But if anyone had asked you what Lawrence Welk sold, you would have known right away. He was the greatest direct salesman Dodge ever had. Now he is doing the same for the J. B. Williams Company.

When I asked Carter just how it happened that he chose Lawrence Welk for the local Dodge account in 1952, he replied:

My wife was a bit experienced in show business. She had heard the Welk band on a few of the remote pickups KTLA made from the Aragon ballroom and remarked that he was "box office." She compared him to Elvis Presley, who at that time was so popular with the youngsters. Nobody knew why Elvis was "box office" either. But he filled every auditorium in the United States with overflow crowds. She said to me: "I want you to look at this Lawrence Welk show from the Aragon." When she turned it on, I said: "You're out of your mind. That guy can't even speak English." "Yes," she replied, "but he is 'box-office'." Her intuitive sense told her that he could sell automobiles. And so we signed Lawrence Welk for the Dodge dealers of southern California in 1952, and that's history by now. Since that first day he went on television for Dodge, he has given his sponsor a bonus of many times 100 cents on a dollar. He works at the idea of selling his product every inch of the way through the program. I know for a fact that he wouldn't take on a product he didn't personally believe in.

I asked Carter to expand more on those early days when he had given Welk his start on television.

When Lawrence was working for the Dodge dealers of southern California, we asked our salesmen to report where their prospects had heard of Dodge. It's on record that 49 percent of the people who bought Dodges from 1952 to 1955 in southern California actually brought up the name of Lawrence Welk without any suggestion from the salesmen. Many individual cases were reported of people who came into showrooms and said they wanted to buy a Dodge because Lawrence Welk told them to buy one!

During those years from 1952 to 1955, we paid Station KTLA only $3,600 a week to sponsor the Welk shows. Of that sum, the station paid Welk $600 for his salaries and expenses. This low-budget type show is the result of Lawrence's inherent German frugality, which led him to avoid any unnecessary expense in turning out his shows even to this day.

Until now, Lawrence has never lost his sense of gratitude to the Dodge dealers who gave him his start on television. This is without a doubt one of his most unusual personal qualities. He never forgets a favor done for him. And the Dodge dealers haven't either; every year they still give him a new car to drive!

After starting Lawrence Welk with his first sponsorship by the Dodge dealers in 1952, Bert Carter was transferred to Detroit as general sales manager for Dodge. In this position, he was instrumental in prevailing upon the Grant Advertising Agency to consider Welk as a summer replacement on the ABC network.

Mr. Grant told me then how they were going to present the whole idea to Welk. They were going to put him in a dress suit, a high hat, and cane. In addition, they would add a chorus line to his show and dress it up Hollywood style! I responded, "Mr. Grant, please. I'm on my knees to you. Don't try to turn the Welk Show into a Hollywood production. It would be a disaster. That just isn't Lawrence Welk." Well, they went along with my suggestion to leave the show as it was and use it as a summer replacement. And it turned out to be the longest-lasting summer replacement show in the history of television.

Carter recalled an incident that took place shortly after the show went on ABC.

The vice-president of Dodge called me into his office in Detroit. His desk was literally covered with fan mail sent to Dodge in favor of the Welk Show. "Look," he said, "we've bought the Welk Show for thirteen weeks, but I don't take favorably to your publicity stunt." I assured him I had

nothing whatever to do with the mail response, and I predicted that this was only the beginning of a deluge of mail
they could expect each week thereafter. My predictions were
more than realized. One of the attractions of the show had a
big appeal to the public—we used a commercial only at the
very beginning and at the very end of the show. That was
all. The public took to the show like a trout takes to bait.
They loved it, and made no hesitation telling the sponsor
exactly how they felt. Soon Welk became known as "Mr.
Dodge." It seemed that anything Welk said about Dodge
cars was accepted as gospel. Dealers all over the country
were so enthusiastic over his being their spokesman that,
whenever he would travel on concert, invariably the Dodge
dealers would meet him at the airport and parade through
the city with the whole show in convertibles.

When I asked Carter why Dodge later gave up the Welk
Show, he replied:

The reason is that the whole operation of Dodge Division
had changed in 1960. They brought in people from other
automobile manufacturers who were going to revolutionize
sales. The new emphasis was on youth; and so they put in a
young but sadly inexperienced advertising manager who
did not understand the value of Welk's image for Dodge.
This was a sorry day for Dodge because they have never had
as close an identity with any television personality since. But
the dealers themselves have never forgotten Welk's close
tie-in with their business and still have a close affection for
him even after all these years. Remember that the Grant
Agency's recommendation that Dodge take the Welk Show
as a summer replacement was purely an experiment they
really thought would never succeed. It turned out to be a
boomerang which started Welk on one of the most successful television careers in history.[1]

Jack Minor

Minor relates:

One of the best selling points I've ever observed of the

worth of "The Lawrence Welk Show" to the sponsor was in 1953, when there was a question of discontinuing the sponsorship by the Dodge dealers here in southern California for lack of funds in the advertising budget. Our forty-five local Dodge dealers voted unanimously to keep the show on the air and reduce their newspaper, radio, and billboard advertisements to pay KTLA for the broadcasts of the Welk band. They further agreed to assess themselves an additional ten dollars per Plymouth and five dollars per truck, in addition to the twenty dollars per Dodge they were already paying. It was one of the strongest proofs of their fondness of the Welk Show and of their conviction that it was doing an effective job of selling Dodges. Welk, of course, made it his business to become personally acquainted with as many of the dealers as he could, and visited them. He always appeared at our sales meetings. All of this, of course, added up to supreme confidence on my part that the Welk Show could hold its own if given a chance on national television.

Early in 1955 I convinced the network to use Welk as a replacement the following summer for Danny Thomas. I approached Robert E. Kintner, then president of the network, and found he was definitely against any idea of using Lawrence Welk even as a summer replacement. He claimed there was far too much opposition from the New York advertising people, who thought Welk was a "North Dakota cornball." I was so determined and confident that Welk could do the same job nationally that he was doing locally here in Los Angeles that I threatened to cancel both "The Danny Thomas Show" and "The Bert Parks Show," over which I had control, unless they would give Lawrence Welk a chance as a summer replacement. It was a desperate move to try to force the hand of the network; and I made no bones about telling them they were prejudiced against Welk and were making a serious mistake in turning him down. The threat of cancelling two shows seemed to do the trick, and so the result was that on Saturday night, July 2, 1955, the ABC network reluctantly accepted "The Lawrence Welk Show" as a summer replacement.

It turned out to be the most long-lived show on their net-

work. In spite of opposition even from the top officials of
Chrysler Corporation, we were able to carry on a large
advertising promotion during those thirteen weeks of the
Welk Show that summer of 1955. People flocked into Dodge
agencies by the thousands just to receive a picture of the
Welk band. This promotion, coupled with some very effective commercials used on the show, made sales soar all over
the country. It began to convince some of the executives in
Detroit that maybe they had something in Welk that would
sell cars. Actually, Chrysler was paying only $12,000 for the
early Welk shows, a figure which even then was ridiculously
low. It was about half of what other shows cost their sponsors. And so it was on this economy basis, plus substantially
increased sales of Dodge and Plymouth cars, that Chrysler
renewed Welk's contract for another thirteen weeks beginning in the fall of 1955.[2]

Matthew Rosenhaus

I asked Matthew Rosenhaus whether he considered his
association with the Welk Show an effective way of allocat-
ing his advertising budget.

Our recent renewal of our twentieth successive year as
principal sponsor of the Welk Show is proof of our belief in
its effectiveness in selling our products. The Welk Show
has developed an unusually loyal audience, especially among
senior citizens. I feel that the sales messages on this show
have been acceptable to that audience, and long-range sales
have resulted. However, there is no scientific data available
to define exactly how acceptable they have been, nor how
many long-range sales have resulted.

Since 85 percent of the advertising budget of the J. B. Williams Company goes into network television commercials,
and only 15 percent of that is allocated to "The Lawrence
Welk Show," it is impossible to separate the effects on sales
of advertising on one network from the influence of all
other advertising and marketing factors.

When I asked if any surveys were ever taken on the relationship of the Welk Show to the products it advertises, Rosenhaus replied:

> Some telephone and mail surveys conducted by our company among Geritol purchasers during the last ten years indicate that 25 percent of our customers were first influenced to purchase Geritol by seeing our commercials on the Welk Show. In a more recent telephone survey it was discovered that one-half of the adults who were questioned did associate Lawrence Welk with Geritol. This is probably due to the long association of the product with the show. We have found that recent demographic surveys of the audience for the Welk Show indicate that, because we wish to reach an audience in the over-fifty age group, the Welk Show is among the least expensive of any show on the air.[3]

Irving Ross

In addition to his regular duties as Parkson Agency manager for the West Coast, Irving Ross today works with Don Fedderson managing the day-to-day syndication of the Welk Show to 225 television stations throughout the country. He perhaps knows more than anyone else about the relationship of the Welk Show with both sponsors and stations. I asked him why, in spite of consistently high ratings on the ABC network, Welk was suddenly dropped from its broadcast schedule in 1971.

> At that time ABC wanted to change their image and appeal more to a younger audience. As you know, Welk's audience is largely made up of people over fifty. But the mail response to ABC was overwhelming. People were angry with the network for canceling Welk. However, you must remember that he didn't lose a single week on the air. Immediately we went into syndication, and to a large extent most of the same stations—actually more than 80 percent— still carried his show. This was very reassuring to the public generally and especially to his ardent fans who were making such a big fuss. Matthew Rosenhaus, the president of the J. B. Williams Company, was so sold on the Welk Show

that he not only promised to back Lawrence if he went on syndication, but he even agreed to pick up any and all commercial time which could not be sold to other sponsors. Of course he didn't have to because there have always been sponsors waiting in line to buy the show. Actually the syndication has succeeded much better than we had even hoped for. It proved to be the largest station lineup for a syndicated show on the air today. Possibly only the World Series can reach our present 225 stations. Our closest competitors are "The Tonight Show" with 212 stations and "The Today Show" with 215.

I asked Ross to explain just why the syndication method has turned out so well.

To begin with, we're on more stations. That's a big reason. When we were on ABC, it was the third network. Naturally the ABC stations grabbed the Welk show in 1971 when it went into syndication. A hundred and ten of our original stations were ABC stations. Now we have about 65 affiliates of each network plus the independent stations. The total is 225. Our preference is to sign up the show for Saturday evening around 6:00 P.M.; however, some good stations like WGN in Chicago broadcast the program on Sunday evenings at 9:00 P.M. This transposing of the show seems to be a common practice of independent stations because the Welk Show brings the highest rating numbers at times when they're competing with the big network shows, and so they can realize more from their local commercials in the Welk Show. At present there is only one of the top fifty markets where we are not broadcasting, and this will only be a temporary condition.

I asked Ross to explain how many commercials he incorporates into the Welk Show and how many are allowed to be sold locally.

Our show is built with four minutes of national advertising. This means eight thirty-second spots. We build it to allow the local stations to sell five minutes within the show, or ten individual thirty-second spots. You see, ours in known as a "barter" show in the syndication business of television. There are basically two ways of selling a show: either straight syndication like ours, or for cash. In the latter case, the station pays for the whole show and all the commercial minutes belong to it. However, a "barter" show has clients like the J. B. Williams Company, the Block Drug Company, American Home Products, the Kellogg Company, the National Biscuit Company, etc. Our income for the production of the show comes from our barter clients. So if I go to WGN with a "barter" show, there are no dollars that change hands. Our show is absolutely free to the station. All they must do is copy our master videotape which we send them each week. We use what is known as a "bicycle" system of distribution. Consolidated Film Industries in Hollywood makes forty-seven copies of our show each week. These are our master copies. We send a master to station A; it in turn makes its own copy for broadcast and sends our master to station B. We work four weeks in advance so that all stations may broadcast the show simultaneously on a given weekend.

My final question to Ross was to ask exactly what are the advantages of syndication.

Actually a tremendous amount of work and expense can be eliminated if you are on a network. However, the fact that we do thirty-two new shows a year with twenty repeats frees Lawrence and his band to do many road shows each year. The road shows are quite lucrative since he invariably plays to full houses wherever he goes. This gives about four and a half months for the band to do such shows as Harrah's Club at Lake Tahoe for three weeks and go on tour around the country. Actually the percentage of advertising income is about the same now as it was in the days when we were on the network, but the fringe benefits to the whole Welk organization from its fifty-two-times-a-year television show are enormous. Many individuals in the show have profited handsomely from personal appearances around the country. And the television exposure is probably the largest single reason why Welk's records sell so well. So, all in all, the syndication idea has worked out very well.

I might add that it was Matthew Rosenhaus, Welk's principal sponsor, who was the first to phone him when he was put off the network. He said he would be squarely behind him if he chose to go into syndication. And I am sure I can speak also for Fred Plant of the Block Drug Company, an even older sponsor, when I say that sponsors are well satisfied with what they're getting in cost per thousand viewers from the Welk Show. Though there are other sponsors waiting in the wings at all times, the present sponsors aren't about to change in the near future. You see, if you keep your cost per thousand just a little below what the networks are asking, you won't outprice yourself, and sponsors will always be eager to buy your show.[4]

An Evaluation of Sponsors' Attitude Toward Welk

Though it is impossible to base reliable conclusions on any one sponsor's opinions, it is possible to draw valid generalizations from the collective opinions of all Welk's sponsors over the entire span of his television broadcasting career.

Bert Carter considers Welk a good salesman who delivers to his sponsor "many times 100 cents on the dollar." By referring to him as "box office," he uses an old movie term to emphasize that Welk brings in the sales. Forty-nine percent of the people who bought Dodges from 1952 to 1955 in southern California spontaneously brought up the name of Lawrence Welk. Questionnaires filled out at the time of each sale are still on record to prove this. Welk's inherent German frugality impelled him to keep down the production costs, and made it possible for some forty-five dealers to pay for his show for three years. Many of these dealers still remember what Welk did for them; and there is a genuine feeling of gratitude on both sides even to this day. They still give him a new car to drive each year.

Jack Minor had supreme confidence that Welk could do nationally what he accomplished locally in Los Angeles. Almost single-handedly he prevailed upon both the Chrysler officials and his own firm, the Grant Advertising Agency, to pay for a trial run of the Welk Show in the summer of 1955. It was due again to the show's low budget and substantially increased sales of Dodge cars during the period that Chrysler renewed Welk's contract.

Matthew Rosenhaus stressed that his firm's renewal of the Welk Show's contract for twenty straight years is proof of its belief in Welk's effectiveness in selling its products. He believes the show has a loyal audience of senior citizens. According to surveys, 25 percent of Geritol's buyers were influenced by the Welk show. More recent surveys indicate that half the adults questioned associate Welk with Geritol. Finally, demographic surveys indicate that the Welk show is among the most economical ways to reach an audience of over fifty years of age.

Irving Ross interpreted the attitude of Welk's sponsors as most favorable. He dispelled any notion that cancellation by the ABC network in 1971 was a reflection upon Welk's audience appeal or the quality of his show. He pointed out that the renewed vigor of the show through syndication has many advantages to Welk's whole organization—if not in direct dollar return from the television show itself, at least through opportunities for road shows and personal appearances.

From these conversations with those who sponsored Lawrence Welk over the twenty-eight years of his television broadcasting, I conclude that he indeed knows how to ingratiate himself with those who are paying for his show. He displays unusual deference to their aims and desires. He becomes so involved with the products he advertises that he personally drives Dodges, takes Geritol, and uses Aqua Velva. He is honest enough to admit that the sponsor is no interloper to be simply tolerated, but rather an integral part of the entire production, run by human beings like himself with likes and dislikes plus the important business objective

of selling their product. Welk has frequently insisted that
the sponsor, as a businessman, must keep down costs as much
as possible, and also prefers to underwrite a television show
that operates the same way.

Probably the largest single reason why Lawrence Welk
has had his sponsors' contracts repeatedly renewed has been
this personal relationship he maintains with the sponsors.
He does not hesitate to write a letter of thanks to his sponsors each year when his contract is renewed. Another major
source of influence for him is his loyal public. Strangely
there always seems to be enough of the great silent majority
to make up the 10 to 15 million homes that tune him in on
weekends. This kind of loyal following is every sponsor's
dream.

6

The Tube Speaks

Feedback from the TV Audience

Throughout this book it has been emphasized that Welk felt his first duty was to his audience. He learned this early in his career and has spent a lifetime studying and playing for the audience's wishes. He admits that some of his most serious mistakes were made when he went against this principle and began including selections that song pluggers wanted him to play. His most painful lesson was learned at the Edgewater Beach Hotel in Chicago when his big opportunity was thwarted and not the success he had anticipated. He had acquired the reputation of an easy mark for song writers and publishers' agents, who prevailed upon him to play their new songs. His good nature made him vulnerable to their pleas. In later years he remarked: "After listening to so many hard luck stories from those song pluggers, I was the one who ended up having the worst hard luck story of all! My contract at the Edgewater Beach was not renewed!" This experience convinced him always to cater to the tastes of his audience, to make a careful study of their reactions to what he played, and to adopt the kind of fare referred to in the music business as "tried and tested, all-time favorites."

Welk's personal manager, Sam Lutz, stated, "Lawrence could pick up his accordion in the midst of a dance and turn a crowd of reserved people into a most enthusiastic audience." Everyone who has worked with Welk knows that, even after twenty-eight successful years of television broadcasting, he is a better performer on stage before a live audience. He senses and responds to their every feeling.

Challenge of the TV Audience

The television audience proved to be a new challenge for Welk. He had broadcast dance music for twenty-five years from some of the great bandstands of America and had a radio broadcasting career that started as far back as 1927 in Yankton, South Dakota. Yet he still found the television audience a thrilling but unique challenge. His radio audience had simply wanted listenable music and knew little about him personally. Now he was told, "When that little red light goes on, you are on television, face to face with twenty million people." It nearly scared him to death. The thought of facing that many unseen people took him back to his first painful ordeal before the microphone at the Edgewater in Chicago, when he was told he would have to say a few words to his new and distinguished big-city audience.

Fortunately Welk knew that it was one achievement to start on television, but quite another to stay on. His problem was how to face an unseen audience and somehow succeed in satisfying their wishes as he had with his ballroom and theater audiences. He tried to convince himself that if he could hold a live stage audience, then he could hold a television audience. But he was aware that the job would not be as easy as when he could look out from the bandstand and see right into the people's faces. Besides, television viewers were probably doing things—eating, washing dishes, knitting, talking, and all the other distracting activities that go on in a home. Moreover, in age, interests, and social environment, they differed from the comparatively sophisticated, dressed-up, young adult group he had come to know in the hotels and ballrooms of America.

Welk finally faced his first television camera. He may have uttered a few inarticulate phrases and placed the wrong emphasis on some of his words. However, both mail response and increased sales of Dodge cars proved that this North Dakota farm boy projected a deep sincerity. People warmed up to him and identified with him immediately. It was precisely this quality of genuineness, the winsome smile and the word of encouragement, that impelled Fedderson, Minor, Lutz, and Carter to do everything possible to place him on national television. It was his power over an audience, in the final analysis, that sold Welk to the American television public.

This chapter outlines one of the most detailed programs of audience participation ever to be carried on by a modern television organization. Students of mass communications might call it feedback, insisting that all valid communication must contain some type of dialog between listener and broadcaster. It is further proposed that the dialog set up by Welk with his listeners is largely responsible for his longstanding place in American television.

Card File of Fans

With the help of his private secretary, Lois Lamont, Welk started building a card file of all his fans dating back to his first year on local TV in Los Angeles. Later, when letters flooded in from all parts of the United States and Canada, he expanded the file considerably to hold as many as 275,000 to 300,000 names. The thoroughness of this system was proven to me personally as I came across the name of a person I knew who had been one of Welk's fans in Los Angeles in 1953. Her letters had been carefully noted on her card, as had Welk's replies to her over the years. As I viewed the card, I casually mentioned to Welk that this elderly fan was presently confined to a Long Beach hospital. Without hesitation he picked up his phone and called to cheer her up. This small incident demonstrated his concern for his loyal fans.

The name and address of each writer are recorded in a file that covers the length of an entire wall. Hundreds of letters are received every day; they are answered by a staff of secretaries who use a special signature writer to trace Welk's authentic signature, making each reply as close as possible to a personal letter. Welk considers this method of handling fan mail essential to keeping in touch with "the most important friends we have, our listeners." By this correspondence with nearly 300,000 active fans, he has made these people feel their letters are welcome and their wishes for musical selections and performers are important. Most significant is the fact that he has succeeded in drawing a larger sustained total of fan mail over the years than any other television program on record. The total is estimated at well over 1½ million letters during the years 1952 to 1980. His fans show interest in almost every detail, from the length of the girls' dresses to what selections the band plays. In most cases they are quite outspoken about their likes and dislikes. This is exactly as Welk would have it. He sincerely wants his television audience to feed back their ideas and suggestions. Thus the Welk Show has become one of the best examples of how a television program can be successful in establishing dialog with its listeners.

People Who Write to Welk

Barbara Curtiss, who for years has been the person in charge of mail response to the many fan letters, stated:

> Anyone who writes to Lawrence Welk receives an answer within a reasonable length of time, especially if questions are asked about the show. Of course there is a small minority of people who write so frequently—almost daily—that we

cannot possibly answer each time they write. However we do stay in touch through an occasional letter.

When asked what particular problems occur—other than their being swamped with mail—she replied:

One problem that does arise involves racial or ethnic slurs made against individuals, or complaints that we are too liberal in our attitude toward minorities. Though we at first tried to answer these people's objections, now it has become impossible to continue defending our practice. Once in a while it happens that Lawrence may be photographed at a concert dancing with a black woman. This has often occasioned some verbal abuse in letters we receive. Adverse comments come in about the two black members of our musical family, and we even receive cracks about our Jewish sponsors by those who are certain that these people are sabotaging our show and have too much control of television in our country. By now we have learned to pretty well sidestep this kind of criticism by simply not answering such letters. Their minds are made up; they're simply prejudiced. Lawrence believes we've made the mistake in the past by being so polite to such people that they've gotten the impression we're on their side. This convinced us that no answer is the better way of dealing with downright prejudice. Other than these types of eccentric letters, it's correct to say that every letter receives an answer in due time.[1]

Each letter received is carefully classified as "favorable" or "unfavorable" in regard to various performers or combinations of performers—duets, trios, or quartets. Remarks about particular shows are also recorded. Even Welk's own dancing on the show is tabulated for listener approval or disapproval. At the end of each month, Welk personally scrutinizes the digest of fan mail that is placed on his desk.

Table 1 tabulates all the mail pertaining to the regular performers over a one-year period, January through December, 1978. No effort was made to record audience reactions

Table 1
Mail Response to "The Lawrence Welk Show"
January through December, 1978

Favorable—Unfavorable

Anacani	380—6
Ava Barber	316—12
Henry Cuesta	111—3
Dick Dale	128—0
Ken Delo	173—24
Arthur Duncan	184—19
Ralna English	116—8
Gail Farrell	119—2
Joe Feeney	370—14
Myron Floren	325—1
Charlotte Harris	141—0
	(7 months)
Neil Levang	38—0
Bob Lido	39—0
Joe Livoti	70—0
Mary Lou Metzger	97—2
Tom Netherton	419—75
Bob Ralston	289—2
Jim Roberts	193—16
Bob Smale	64—0
Kathie Sullivan	205—70
Norma Zimmer	457—25
Bobby Burgess and Cissy King	571—18
Sandy Griffith, Gail Farrell and Mary Lou Metzger	155—4
Sheila and Sherry Aldridge and David and Roger Otwell	578—56
Norma Zimmer and Jim Roberts	154—2
Guy and Ralna Hovis	464—22
Hotsy Totsy Band	20—0

to occasional guest performers. The number of favorable fan letters for each performer is shown by the figure before the dash. The number of unfavorable letters appears after the dash.

Unfavorable letters about any performer on the Welk show usually offer a valuable indication from the outset as to whether his/her performance will achieve the main objective of the show—to please its audience. Such letters are expected immediately after a new performer begins since this has always been the practice of Welk's highly concerned audience. Then a few months after the audience has become accustomed to any new performer, unfavorable letters often taper off. However, if they persist over many months, it is a definite indication to Welk that the person should not remain on the show. This tryout period has been a prerogative that Welk has always insisted upon. The final decision on whether or not to retain a performer is solely his, based on audience reaction. An interesting fact, however, is that comparatively few unfavorable letters are ever received about persons who have been employed by Welk for many years. Another interesting fact is that no one in the Welk organization is ever hired under contract, to allow for flexibility and to obviate unreasonable terms or conditions.

Favorable letters are equally important in establishing a performer on the show. After a reasonable number of favorable fan letters are received on any new talent, the final decision on whether that person will be given a permanent place is based on how many of these letters continue to come in.

Upgrading Talent

The favorable-unfavorable mail response just indicated has the strongest possible influence in upgrading both the talent and the content of the Welk Show. Periodically each person discusses frankly with Welk the type of mail received about himself or herself. Over a period of months and years, these evaluations become much more significant, since they indicate a singer's or instrumentalist's diligence in improving his or her performance skills and also show audience preferences for various themes or types of shows. In general they give a clear idea of whether the entire program is improving or deteriorating. Most significantly, they furnish an accurate barometer on whether the program is losing or maintaining its audience. Judging by an article in *Broadcasting* that points out how Nielsen and American Research Bureau ratings disagree with each other, it would seem that such unsolicited mail response is one of the best criteria for judging the size and faithfulness of an audience.[2]

Even new talent is occasionally discovered through interested listeners who send tapes of singers and instrumentalists. Thus a constant effort is made to improve the show through dialog with listeners.

Volume of Mail Received

Whether complimentary or uncomplimentary, mail reaction demonstrates the listeners' identification with Welk and his performers. Over the five years 1965–69, 90,460 letters were received at the main office in Santa Monica, not counting those addressed to individual performers. Since the show went on syndication (1971) the letters have continued to average about 300 a week. Special times of the year like Christmas, Welk's birthday, or some crisis that may arise when someone leaves the show will bring the mail count to well over 5,000 letters a week. The largest single upsurge in the volume of mail came when ABC dropped the show. Then the volume of mail rose to almost 100,000 pieces from May to September 1971 (not counting the protests sent to ABC). Moreover, it is important to note that the total number of people who have written to Welk over his twenty-eight years on television is more than 1½ million, which according to all statistical experts indicates a listening audience of many millions. The very regularity of this mail pull is further evidence that, as stated earlier, millions of listeners are drawn to the show by deep psychological ties of fantasy identification. To many of them it constitutes a vast storybook of marvelous, idealized characters. The cast may do no more than sing or act or play an instrument; yet their every gesture, mannerism, song, or dance has a message for the viewer of warm friendliness, love, and affection.

Stage Appearances

Further evidence of this psychological identification is the group's reception at stage appearances throughout the United

States and Canada. Its annual tour of twenty or more cities attracts audiences totaling between 400,000 and 500,000 people; and another 9,000 to 10,000 view Welk's forty-two stage shows at Harrah's Club at Lake Tahoe during a three-week engagement each year. *Variety* and *Billboard* report that in almost every community the show is a sellout. Yet these figures are a mere sample of the television viewers who are emotionally drawn to Lawrence Welk.

CBS Studio Audiences

As part of this audience study it is important to note the hundreds of people who queue up in front of the CBS studio at Television City in Hollywood each Tuesday evening to view the show as a live audience. Tickets for the shows requested by mail are sent free of charge, but the waiting period is at least eighteen months. However, it is possible to secure tickets to the dress rehearsals with a slightly shorter waiting period. Both dress rehearsals and live tapings are always filled to capacity with standbys waiting. Over the years audiences at live performances have totaled close to 500,000, a record no other television show has ever come near equaling. Even today the Welk Show is the most popular at CBS, and in the entertainment capital the perennial joke is that the three most popular tourist attractions are Disneyland, Forest Lawn Cemetery, and Lawrence Welk! Hank Grant recently wrote in *The Hollywood Reporter*: "It used to be a six-month wait for tickets to the Lawrence Welk Show. It's now an 18-month wait! Gad, if you're not old enough to be a member of his geriatric fan club, you will be by the time you get your tickets!"[3]

Television Ratings

The A.C. Nielsen Company of Chicago and the American Research Bureau of New York calculate the size of television audiences as well as demographic breakdowns. They classify viewers according to the population of the county in which they live; their household size, family income,

IF YOU THINK YOU HAVE A long WAIT, YOU SHOuld SEE HOW long IT TAKES TO
GET A TICKET TO "THE LAWRENCE WELK SHOW"... 18 MONTHS!!!

and educational level; and the ages of men, women, and nonadult viewers. Such information naturally becomes very valuable to the advertiser who spends hundreds of thousands of dollars to air his commercials. Moreover, television stations and networks find this information helpful in planning their programs and selling commercial time.

Without attempting to go into the vital question of precisely how accurate such information is, it will be pointed out how Nielsen gathers its answers from scientifically chosen sample homes throughout the United States. Laurence Frerk, Nielsen's promotion director, furnished materials explaining how this information is established.

The size of a network television audience is measured

by Nielsen using the Audimeter (Storage Instantaneous Audimeter—SIA), a complex electronic instrument attached to television receivers in a scientifically selected cross-section of 1,200 American homes. Television usage and tuning of all TV receivers in these sample homes is automatically recorded and stored every 30 seconds in the SIA home unit's memory. Each of these SIA home units is connected by special phone line to the central office computer in Dunedin, Florida. This computer center retrieves and inspects the SIA household tuning data at least twice a day. The entire process is automatic and requires no attention on the part of the people in the household.

While the SIA tells whether a household has a set on and what station it is turned to, another method is necessary to determine *who* is watching in the household by age and sex. Sample households in each local market are computer selected from a continually updated list of more than 41 million households. The resulting National Audience Composition Sample totals 3,200 households.

Nielsen also measures the 226 television markets in the United States three to eight times a year, depending on their size. The samples chosen in these markets also vary from 300 to 3,000, again depending on the size of the markets. Each predesignated household is contacted by trained interviewers who make long-distance telephone calls from several centers strategically located throughout the country. The high quality of this investigation, along with the impressiveness of long-distance phone calls, has contributed to the reliability of the information gathered.

After the first interview, a comprehensive, thoroughly tested diary called an "Audilog"® is sent to all selected households. The head of the household uses the "Audilog" to write in which programs were viewed by members of the household during a one-week period, including how long each program was watched and by which family member. At the end of the measurement week the completed "Audilogs" are mailed to the Nielsen computer center in Dunedin, Florida. There the diaries are carefully checked for the inclusion of valid information including data on family size, age, sex, and income. The information is transferred to tabulating cards, using a key verification procedure.

Using IV Phase Direct Data Entry, diary viewing and program name information are entered into a mini-computer where they are subjected to automatic logic editing, verification and correction. The information is then fed into the main computer for further edits and processing. Similarly, "Audilog" data are entered into the computer where they are combined with household tuning information (SIA) and station records.

Thus the Nielsen computer system, staffed by programmers and systems analysts, designs and programs the necessary routines to produce the data that make up the finished Nielsen product. These published Nielsen reports provide information vital to networks, agencies, advertisers, stations, producers and almost anyone else involved in the television industry.[4]

Comparative Ratings: ABC and Syndication

The data in Fig. 1, furnished by Don Fedderson Productions and based upon Nielsen's ratings, tell the story of Lawrence Welk's seven complete seasons in syndication, plus his last (sixteenth) season on ABC-TV.

According to further information released in 1978 by Don Fedderson Productions, a total of 7.1 billion people viewed "The Lawrence Welk Show" in its first six years (1971–77) of syndication on "The Lawrence Welk Television Network"—which, Fedderson claims, comprises the world's largest commercial network with more than 220 television stations.

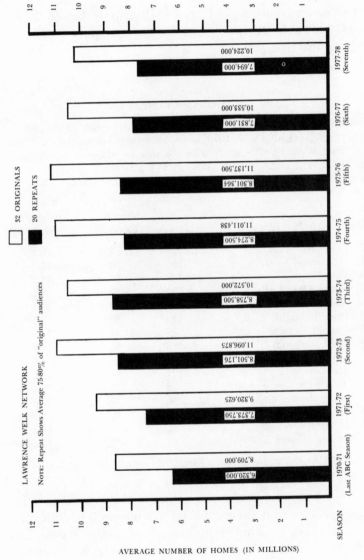

Fig. 1. Homes viewing "The Lawrence Welk Show"

149

First Among Syndicated Shows

A comparative listing of fifteen of the top syndicated shows in 1977 (Table 2), published by *Variety*, puts Lawrence Welk in the first place.

Table 2
The Top Syndicated Shows in 1977

Analyses of the performance of syndicated television programming during last November's Nielsen sweep have been completed, and the "Lawrence Welk Show" clearly wins the title by almost any standard. It is in the most DMA markets, 198, covers the largest percentage of the country, 97%, and has the highest average rating per market, 16.2.

Rank	Program	Markets	Percent Coverage	Rating (Designated market areas)
1	Lawrence Welk	198	97	16.2
2	Hollywood Squares	103	80	15.0
3	Hee Haw	193	95	14.9
4	Name That Tune	104	79	14.2
5	Match Game PM	73	64	14.1
6	Price Is Right	110	82	13.9
7	Candid Camera	88	61	13.8
8	Wild Kingdom	186	95	13.7
9	$25,000 Pyramid	78	64	13.4
10	Muppets	121	84	13.2
11	Truth Or Consequences	28	12	12.7
12	Gong Show	48	50	12.5
13	Jacques Cousteau	31	25	11.8
14	$128,000 Question	70	61	11.5
15	Bobby Vinton	53	53	11.2

Source: "Top 15 Syndie Shows," *Variety*, March 9, 1977, p. 4.

Table 3 shows a random sampling of the February, 1978, Arbitron television sweep of ADI (Arbitron Data Information) markets, showing rating and share audience estimates and day/time of program. These are examples of Lawrence Welk's audiences in various areas of the United States. (A complete Arbitron Television listing of 211 markets is available from Arbitron upon request.)

Table 3
Samples of Welk's Audience Ratings

Market	Station	Day	Time	ADI TV Households Rating	Share
San Francisco	KPIX	Sat.	7-8 PM	15.5	36.5
Boston	WNAC	Sat.	7-8 PM	23.5	45.0
Pittsburgh	WIIC	Sat.	7-8 PM	19.0	32.5
Minneapolis	KMSP	Sat.	6-7 PM	15.5	34.0
Miami	WTVJ	Thurs.	7-8 PM	22.0	35.5
Seattle	KOMO	Sat.	7-8 PM	20.0	38.0
Denver	WBTV	Sat.	6-7 PM	21.0	43.5
Portland, Ore.	KATU	Sat.	7-8 PM	19.5	35.5
Cincinnati	WLWT	Sat.	7-8 PM	15.5	28.0
Columbus, Ohio	WCMH	Sat.	7-8 PM	17.5	31.5
Charlotte	WBTV	Sat.	7-8 PM	24.0	44.5
Kalamazoo	WKZO	Sat.	7-8 PM	20.5	39.5
Orlando	WFTV	Sat.	7-8 PM	24.0	41.5
Wilkes-Barre	WBRE	Sat.	6-7 PM	23.0	40.5
Harrisburg, Pa.	WTPA	Sat.	7-8 PM	16.0	33.0
Salt Lake City	WTVX	Sat.	6-7 PM	17.5	37.0
Birmingham	WBRC	Sat.	6-7 PM	23.5	40.0
Wichita	KTVH	Sat.	6:30 PM	26.5	50.0
Shreveport	KTBS	Sat.	6-7 PM	19.5	37.0
Des Moines	WOI	Sat.	6-7 PM	21.5	39.0
Rochester	WROC	Sat.	7-8 PM	26.0	42.0
Roanoke	WDBJ	Fri.	7-8 PM	28.5	48.5
Omaha	KMTV	Sat.	6-7 PM	25.0	47.0
Cedar Rapids	KCRG	Sat.	6-7 PM	24.0	41.5
Chattanooga	WRCB	Sat.	6-7 PM	16.0	33.5

(Audience estimates copyright, The Arbitron Company, 1978)
(Quoted with permission of the American Research Bureau)

In table 3, "Rating" refers to the number of television households tuned to the Welk show during the average minute, reported in *percent* of American television households. In other words, this figure gives the percentage of all selected samplings actually listening during the average minute, compared with the total number of television households which could possibly be tuned in.

"Share" estimates the audience (during the average minute of the program) in percent of *households actually using television* at the time of the program's telecast. This estimate makes it possible to compare programs even though total usage levels vary according to hour of the day or season of the year.

How Welk Scores

Table 4 is a Nielsen listing of Welk's ratings for the last ten-year period of his ABC contract, 1960–70. It is interesting to note that the Welk show, far from slipping in its rating points since going into syndication, has actually captured one of the finest records of any syndicated show in the country and has improved its ratings substantially since 1971.[6]

Table 4
Welk's Ratings, 1960–70
Saturday Evening—ABC-TV

January	Time	% U.S. TV (Avg. Aud.)	% Share
1960	9:00–10:00 P.M.	22.0	32
1961	9:00–10:00 P.M.	21.4	34
1962	9:00–10:00 P.M.	21.5	33
1963	9:00–10:00 P.M.	19.5	29
1964	8:30– 9:30 P.M.	22.4	34
1965	8:30– 9:30 P.M.	23.1	34
1966	8:30– 9:30 P.M.	22.9	35
1967	8:30– 9:30 P.M.	23.3	37
1968	8:30– 9:30 P.M.	23.7	35
1969	8:30– 9:30 P.M.	20.6	32
1970	8:30– 9:30 P.M.	20.0	30

(Audience estimates copyright, A. C. Nielsen Company)
Quoted with permission of A. C. Nielsen Company

TV Audience Feedback

Critics have long pointed out that far too much emphasis is placed upon television ratings as indicators of "good" television shows. The consensus among broadcasters would seem to be that the public is the sole arbiter of what it shall see and hear; that program schedules are determined by tune-in and tune-out data as furnished by the Nielsen and ARB indexes. One main problem with such a yardstick of program evaluation stems from the obvious fact that ratings are based entirely on the shows that are available. They indicate nothing about what as yet unproduced programs the television audience either needs or would like to see.

This cart-before-the-horse approach to audiences and their wishes has never characterized Welk's thinking. He has never belittled rating points because he recognizes they are the norm of commercial acceptance and make his show salable in the advertising market. Yet he has always insisted that true audience dialog—taking his viewers' wishes into consideration, keeping in touch with his fans, following their advice, seeking their reactions, and thanking them for their support—has been responsible for his success, his longstanding place on television.

7

The Devil's Advocate

Who Doesn't Have Critics?

Despite the fact that the popular press has published thousands of articles on Lawrence Welk, very few by substantial critics can be found. Beyond the stock jokes, the snide remarks about the square "North Dakota cornball," and numerous cartoons about his bubbles, little adverse criticism is available. Music critics seem to pass him over in silence, thus giving the impression that his contribution to the artistic expression of music is negligible. The popular press articles are mainly either feature or news pieces, almost 6,000 of them. They relate human interest stories and highly praise Welk's accomplishments. However, they express a minimum of thoughtful evaluation of his work, his capability, or his contribution to the sociological development of music. Television critics, too, seem reluctant to make any serious comment about Welk. This fact was brought out rather forcibly when I attended a testimonial dinner held at the Hollywood Palladium honoring Welk on the occasion of his receiving the God and Country Award. Ironically that same evening in Hollywood (June 7, 1970) the Emmy

Awards were being conferred on other prominent entertainers in the television world. During his long television career Welk has never received an Emmy Award, though he received a personal nomination in 1954 from the Academy of TV Arts and Sciences.

The success story of Lawrence Welk needs rounding out. For example, if one were to base conclusions about the man simply upon what has been recorded in chapter 3 on his philosophy, one might well ask, Is this man human? One person remarked recently, "Lawrence Welk's philosophy reads like the *Autobiography* of Benjamin Franklin." I reminded him that Franklin was by no means without human failings; and neither is Lawrence Welk. Wise sayings, typical of both men, do not preclude the possibility of human shortcomings.

I had a conversation with Welk when I began my research into his career. He took me into the large living room of his home in Pacific Palisades, which looks out over the city of Santa Monica, and handed me his business card with an embossed image of himself holding a baton. He had written his home phone number on it and assured me he would be eager at any time to discuss whatever I would like to ask about himself. Then he added: "Whatever you wish to uncover about my past life or my musical career, no matter how personal, feel free to publish it. I am not ashamed of anything about myself, as long as it is true." Then he grinned with his characteristic smile and said he hoped that whatever was exposed about himself and his organization would be for the benefit of others who might want to learn about it in the years to come.

An Exaggerated Mystique

Actually there is too great a mystique surrounding the public image of Welk today to gain a clear picture of who the man is, what he has done, and what his contribution has been to the field of broadcasting and the sociological development of music. Two of his closest associates insist that he has become an "American institution." Most people close to him admit that he has become a kind of popular hero in America for adults over fifty. Popular magazines are still publishing articles that praise him so ridiculously that he admits he is embarrassed to read them. People idolize him, make a little god of him, and hang onto his words on every subject from politics to religion. Obviously such is a distorted image of the man, typical of how people tend to build up images of omnipotence around mass media personalities. Precisely one of the main obstacles to an objective study is this very mystique surrounding the man and his work. It militates against a true evaluation.

Historical sketches of statesmen, scholars, and saints have very often fallen into this kind of unrealistic idealism. Consequently they have suffered in the eyes of true scholars. Certainly every worthwhile study of people and human organizations must of necessity tell both sides of the story—the favorable and the unfavorable, the pleasant and the unpleasant.

With this thought in mind, namely that no one-sided appraisal constitutes true scholarship, I shall record statements of Welk's critics, evaluate them, and conclude with an objective, unprejudiced appraisal of his shortcomings as both musician and television personality.

Preliminary Facts

A few preliminary facts must be kept in mind as we approach the subject of Welk's critics. I offer them not as a defense but as obvious facts without which it is impossible to arrive at an honest perspective on what his critics are saying.

1. Welk has been unique in making music that is economically and commercially viable on national television over a period of twenty-eight years. Others have tried and almost all have failed.

2. His show is much the same type of entertainment that it would be if he were not on television. He developed his musical variety style on bandstands long before he went into television.

3. On the other hand, a large measure of his success is precisely due to his exposure on television. It is obvious that television has furthered Welk's success just as surely as Welk has succeeded through the medium of television. If any of the other big bands—Waring, Lombardo, King—had been prepared to meet the challenge of television or had been given the same opportunity, doubtless the American mass audiences would today appreciate them as much as they do Welk.

4. What critics say in an honest and unprejudiced way has a bearing on my whole study of Welk. While they tend to expose the more human side of him and his career, they also expose the American popular taste which really is at the bottom of his success. By their constant refrain of "bubbles, square and cornball," they have reinforced *Look* magazine's cover headline: "Nobody likes him but the public" (June 25, 1957). In fact, the critics, the feature story writers, and the television columnists have unwittingly kept Welk before the minds of the American people by their light-hearted bewilderment over their oft-repeated question: Just what makes this fellow go on television?

5. After twenty-eight seasons on television, Welk has survived almost all of his critics. I began this study in 1969 and uncovered a relatively large body of adverse criticism of him over the years from 1955 to 1965. However, it has become obvious that during the past decade, from 1969 to 1979, his critics have largely become silenced for two reasons: (1) they are no longer critics, and (2) the newer critics in the field of television and music are simply not saying much in an adverse way about Welk. Everyone seems to understand today that

he aims at an audience that seeks simple, basic entertainment rather than sophistication.

The following excerpts will disclose what the critics—Welk's so-called enemies—have had to say about him. The most copious source for the articles quoted in this chapter has been the scrapbooks kept by the office personnel at Teleklew Productions. In other places I have consulted library indexes of *Billboard, Variety,* the *Los Angeles Times,* and the *Chicago Tribune.*

First Classification of Critics

Those who maintain Welk is hopelessly old-fashioned, plays overly simple music, lacks appeal for cultivated music lovers, is "square" and unsophisticated:

Morton Moss, television critic for the *Los Angeles Herald-Examiner,* wrote (1970):

The young bloods and their feminine counterparts consider him a quaintly humorous leftover from the age of the dinosaur. But the "iron-poor bloods" and others on their wavelength find him a beloved shelter from a sliding world whose gyrations elude their comprehension and sympathy.[1]

Terrance O'Flaherty wrote in the *New York World-Telegram* (1959):

Lawrence Welk, America's homespun musical hero, has just returned from a talent tour of Europe which took him (according to ABC) into all the places where music is to be heard. Inasmuch as he was gone only two weeks, the champagne musicmaker must have bubbled around rather fast. "I found they didn't have much to offer in Europe," Welk said.[2]

Larry Wolters wrote in the *Chicago Tribune* (1956):

Lawrence Welk had clobbered TV's top clown [Sid Caesar] with a feather duster: sweet music![3]

Hal Humphrey in the *Los Angeles Times* wrote (1966):

To be a Welk champagner used to require a hide thicker than a rhino's. The Welk music was considered so square and ricky-ticky to the hipsters that anyone playing it had to be broke or tone deaf. That part hasn't really changed, but some "in" groups give points to Welk because they believe he must be putting them on.[4]

Bill Esposito wrote in the *Holyoke* (Mass.) *Transcript-Telegram* (1963):

His years in the medium are a monument to simplicity. All the guy does is lead a band and present very pleasant music. He is neither Leonard Bernstein nor Louis Armstrong, nor does he pretend to be anyone but himself. Of late Lawrence's ratings have slipped, but he still is a strong audience pull. If he lost his TV job tomorrow, however, and in show biz such things happen, he still merits a plaque in the Hall of Fame, TV style. His format is easy. He leads the band through polkas, popular tunes, a smidgen of rock 'n' roll, a touch of jazz, and a bit of the classics and a mazurka or three. Very attractive singers sing very attractive songs. Colorful backgrounds enhance the music. It was and is corn to the corniest degree. But corn is always tasty.[5]

Martin Hogan of the *Cincinnati Enquirer* wrote (1967):

The charm and success of Welk is that he makes no pretense about being chic. The orchestra is rich and full and the musical values are high. It could be that the major objection to Welk's show is that the essentially sound music is couched in terms of absurd settings which, in a cynical age, is something of an anachronism.[6]

Dick Helm wrote in *Variety* (1968):

If the ratings can be taken as a criterion, more people stay home on Saturday night to look and listen to the pride of the Dakotas than for any other admissible reason. And they've been doing it for going on 14 years to keep the big band sound alive and regale the faithful. From the first day Don Fedderson and Sam Lutz sold the show, sponsorship has never wavered. The road ahead looks just as straight and inviting despite Welk's flippancy that "I've got to take things easier or the government will take away my Social Security and Medicare." Welk has been reviewed in these pages for every year of his 14, so there has been very little unsaid about his success. To nail it down, he's folksy and never puts on, as they say up Dakota way. He has flowery compliments for all his entertainers, and never utters an unkind word. And to cap it all, there are millions who say "He'll put on a darn good show every week." His sponsors must think so too.... What producer-director Jim Hobson and Sam Lutz stage every week is a potpourri of earthy entertainment. No comics nor acrobats, just music and songs done by attractive people.... As has been said about Bob Hope, he never gives a bad show; some are just better than others. And this goes for Welk, too; or why would the viewers keep coming back in such numbers to keep in Nielsen's top 20 for nearly all his years? Charisma, perhaps, but showmanship to be sure.[7]

Bob Rose of the Chicago Daily News Service wrote for the *Indianapolis Star* (1968):

What has Welk got? Acording to the music critics, not much. They describe his champagne music as "melodic 7-Up." His manner and grin have gotten him the label "The Liberace of the Accordion" and "Cornbelt Guy Lombardo." But with an annual gross income of two million plus, Welk —like Liberace—cries all the way to the bank.[8]

P. F. Kluge wrote in the *Wall Street Journal* (1970):

While thirteen million American homes are tuned in via ABC-TV to a previously taped episode of Mr. Welk's 15-year-old show, some 4,000 representatives of the Welk Nation—as far in spirit from the Woodstock Nation as it is possible to be—are here at the Hollywood Palladium in person. They have come from every corner of the country where Lawrence Welk's music is *the* music and where Saturday night is his night. The air is heavy with ritual as the

band begins with the theme song, "Bubbles in the Wine."
... Lawrence Welk has not amassed all his wealth by heed-
ing the critics, who have dismissed the Welk brand of music
as hopelessly square, bland ricky-tick rhythms aimed at a
fading generation. This is the kind of music the bandleader
likes himself, and he sees in his success undeniable proof that
others like it too. He doesn't rail against the new sound; it is
just not his thing.[9]

Tony Lioce wrote in the *Providence* (Rhode Island)
Evening Bulletin (1975) :

There was something for absolutely everybody. Lawrence
Welk, when he arrived at the Civic Center yesterday afternoon, brought enough entertainers with him to cover every
conceivable base—forty of them in all. I counted. He had a
lady who sang in Spanish, a "Lovely Italian," even a "happy
Norwegian." He had hoofers and polka dancers. He had a
piano soloist and a guitar soloist and a cello soloist. And
on and on they came, one after another, bang bang bang,
doing songs about mom and dad, and "Amurica" and God
and love—lots of songs about love, the kind of love that just
doesn't go wrong. They even did what old Larry termed
"a pop zong for da younk beople." (Which turned out to be
something from "Camelot," but still the thought was nice.)
Yep, something for absolutely everybody. And the thing is
—and I never thought I'd ever hear myself say this in a million years—it was dynamite. Really. I'm being perfectly
serious. Oh, it was corny, and trite and schmaltzy. Of course.
And the sound system was lousy. But still, there were as many
good vibes in that place as I've ever felt anywhere.[10]

Bill Granger wrote in the *Chicago Sun-Times* (1976) :

Ah, Lawrence Welk, the sheik of the upper Midwest. He
has been doing what he has been doing for so long that his
name is practically synonymous with schmaltzy, waltzy
music. So be it. Welk is also a pro and he has a sense of the
integrity of his kind of show. I watched it all and liked it.
It's all sugar with a German-Polish beat, full of white-haired

ladies and gents who respond to his old melodies and slyly squared arrangements, as though he had played on the strings of their remembrances. He has. If you see tears in the eyes of his audience (at home or in the studio), it is probably because Welk wisely evokes sounds of a world of the past that are still alive in a lot of memories.[11]

Conclusions

These critics are correct in pointing out that Lawrence Welk lacks sophistication and presents simple music. However, it is illogical to conclude that he has no appeal for people with cultivated musical tastes, or that his music is old-fashioned and square. He admits that he deliberately aims to play simple music that the majority of people can understand. Yet he does it with the greatest finesse, and it is performed by some of the finest musicians on the West Coast. Though most people with cultivated musical taste are broad in their appreciation of all types, they do not dislike simple, melodic music, ballads, and quiet dance music. They know that in every type of music can be found the good and the bad. For example, there can be good jazz and bad Gregorian chant. Either form is good or bad depending upon performance or composition. It has always been characteristic of great showmen to understand the secret of performing both simple music and simple drama extraordinarily well.

Second Classification of Critics

Those who point out that Lawrence Welk's personality is both an asset and a liability:

Hal Humphrey in the *Detroit Free Press* wrote (1955):

I don't know that all the critics and the TV academy are all against Lawrence Welk. It is true that Lawrence failed to get an Emmy nomination last week, but some of his critics approach his TV programs much the same way they would Walt Disney's Mickey Mouse Club. . . . Maybe the critics and the other performers are tired of eulogizing those per-

formers who attain their success by dint of only hard work
or just being themselves. Welk has diligently applied himself since the days he helped around the farm at Strasburg,
N.D. I doubt that even his most fervent fans would credit
him with being the Heifetz of the Accordion, however. . . .
His personality holds a sort of shy, clodhopper charm and
heaven knows he is sincere. But perhaps in entertainment
and critical circles there is a growing feeling that more aes-
thetic qualities should be required to qualify for genuine
stardom. Arthur Godfrey, Ed Sullivan and Tennessee Ernie
Ford were blanked out by the Academy this time, too. Maybe
for the same reason. Is it possible we are returning to an
age in show business when the performers will be referred
to as artists?[12]

An unidentified writer in *The Charlotte* (North Carolina)
News wrote (1963) :

Lawrence Welk sent 10,000 happy people home from the
Coliseum Monday night after a Cancer Crusade benefit performance. For them, almost all of them his fans, he had
played his champagne music for two and a half hours, and
they had loved it. Welk is good in his own way. Whatever it
is about him that is unique is 100 percent Midwest American,
red, white and blue, though lacking in musical taste. But
his is a successful formula, and in this country who questions
taste or quality in a performance if success is already apparent? The Welk audience is not a critical one and neither a
flat nor an off-key note lessens their enthusiasm. They came
to have a good time, and with Welk they had it. . . . Welk is
indeed popular in every way. If he did anything that was
disappointing, it was that he failed to ask ladies from the
audience to dance with him.[13]

Jack Wasserman of the *Vancouver* (British Columbia)
Sun, wrote (1967) :

Despite all the moaning and groaning about a sudden
shortage of money for entertainment, some 5,800 people

found $20,000 that enabled them to fill the Forum for Lawrence Welk Wednesday night. The turnout was in the face of a football game and a major league opera, both of which had plenty of empty seats. The answer which will probably disturb the dickens out of the "with it" generation is that Welk, the biggest "square" this side of Eaton's parking lot, is an honest-to-goodness, genuine star. I've never been one of the people who stayed home Saturday nights just to watch Welk's syrupy TV show. But I've got to say that his hold on his people is little short of stupendous. And the feeling is mutual; Welk likes them.[14]

Conclusions

Welk's appeal is to the millions of Americans. His personality and devotion to hard work are only a part of this appeal. He also definitely attracts people by the type of music he plays, by how he plays it, by the psychological identification of the audience with the members of his show, and by the general atmosphere of naïve friendliness that his show projects. True, he does have segments that seem excessively emotional, even syrupy, in their sentimental appeal. But this is part of any popular show in America today. Grand opera is full of excessive emotionalism. Most television drama is also guilty of this fault. Critics who say Welk needs to improve the artistic taste of his show are correct. However, it is rare to find any show about which this cannot be said. He is no Arturo Toscanini and doesn't pretend to be. If he were, I doubt if he would have ever achieved his wide level of acceptance in the mass media.

To properly evaluate the above criticism, which emphasizes the personality and television success of Lawrence Welk as opposed to real artistic skill and impeccable taste, one must bear in mind that popular taste in America, even among those rather well educated, is not remarkably high. Welk makes his appeal to the masses of the American public through the hit tunes he finds from reading *Variety* and *Billboard*. He plays every type of music, even the hits made popular by the Beatles, a fact overlooked by many.

Yes, Welk could raise his artistic tastes, but so could the audiences to which he plays. Critics, though, are remarkably silent regarding Welk's middle style, a kind of Addison-and-Steele, middle-of-the-road image that is at the core of his popular appeal. If there is any validity of the old Addison-Irving-Pickwick literary sequence, and if Charles Dickens could learn to write by following Irving's portrayal of an updated Roger deCoverly, then there is middle-style precedent in the taste of the middle-aged and the elderly. In Welk's performances, the middle style is there with its homeyness and nostalgia; he even brings the oldsters in on the dancing. Dancing oldsters—indeed very mediocre dancers long past their prime—are a source of embarrassment to the sophisticated Anglo-American critic.

Third Classification of Critics

Those who point out that Lawrence Welk is not recognized as a true musician, but is rather a shrewd, top-flight business man:

Gary Stevens, music critic for *Variety*, wrote (1966):

Lawrence Welk is an unexplained phenomenon. His simplicity is cashable at any bank. For years, he was strictly a territory band, strictly midwest. His sojourns into New York went from failure into mild success. His dates at the Edison and Roosevelt Hotels were just fair and few people broke down the box office rushing to hear him at the Capitol Theatre. Yet, golden bantam corn won out. He became television's biggest music attraction. I can cry through my laughter because I was one of the doubters.[15]

Edgar Penton wrote in *Showtime* (1965):

The Lawrence Welk Show is perhaps the prime example of a show for which viewers have a voice heeded in production and planning. . . . Growing is something the Welk troupe has been doing. In 1955 the Music Makers numbered 16. Today there are 43. There may be more before another year rolls around. Welk is an easy target for somebody with talent. Back in 1961 when Barbara Boylan and Bobby Burgess won a Welk dance contest at the Palladium, he put them on his television show. Audience response kept them there. Welk admits he gets much pleasure from discovering a young, gifted performer for his show. And there is evidence his audience is growing younger, probably because of the hit record "Calcutta," a million-copy seller. The older folks don't buy a million copies of a nonvocal disc such as Calcutta. Though no one has kept count of how many punch lines have been created at Welk's expense, you may be sure he has supplied many a comedian with a laugh line. Far from being upset about it, Welk enjoys these jokes. When Johnny Carson said Welk's music was "way in," the Maestro laughed hardest of all. It's an old joke, but true in Welk's case that he laughs all the way to the bank. If it's more than music people like in Welk, it may be they are attracted by the man and his classic American success story—one that has a lot of determination and hard work in it.[16]

Jack O'Brien, a New York columnist, wrote in 1965:

Lawrence Welk does not coincide with our taste in popular music, but that schism has never left us disgruntled. We have been enormously "gruntled" in fact that Welk's lively square sounds have found their own large and devoted millions, and far from suspecting or suggesting that these Welk partisans are wrong, we only maintain they are different. It is our personal concept (in some cases, personal knowledge) that LW fans range widely in many income brackets. If they have a common denominator, we'd say it's an attraction to folks who never have bothered to pay steady exploratory attention to modern popular music sounds and trends or to musically progressive values. There's nothing wrong with folks who dig Welk. They're not imbeciles; they're not always even squares, even if the Saturday Welkin ringing strikes us as somewhat four-cornered or eight. A lot of Welk admirers would consider us in many spheres of their influence or confluence to be squares indeed. We know a few scientists who consider Welk to be what we insist Duke Ellington, Neal Hefti, the Elgarts, Modern Jazz Quartet, etc., are. In fact, some Welkphiles are far more feverish Champagne Music fans than anyone might suspect is possible. Joseph P. Kennedy, father of a President and of three U.S. Senators, a man of many sprightly enthusiasms, was one of Lawrence Welk's earliest TV fans. Back when the Welk show was considered a not-too-permanent summer fill-in, Ambassador Kennedy was singing its praises to us.

We were resistant, if not insistently, to Joseph P.'s stubborn loyalty to Welk's programs. They did give us a small opportunity to see what made as rich a man as Joseph P. Kennedy take time to admire, and in a spectacularly small way, to help.

Welk hadn't been on the TV air nearly so securely in those days. Our only peripheral complaint about the Ambassador's expanding admiration was that it delayed the start of the Saturday evening movie; because Joseph P. would insist upon seeing the Welk show before the start of the movie, we had to wait. It became a good-natured weekly argument we knew we would inevitably have to lose. Welk was growing bigger than our aural resistance to his ricky-ticky, mickey-mouse rhythms and sounds. Joseph P. Kennedy did much more than donate his attention each Saturday evening. One day he took pen in hand, signed several checks, then dictated a letter to the President of the Chrysler Corporation. In it, he explained he never had bought nor even driven a Dodge station wagon in his considerable lifetime. But he was buying this little motorized wagon train for the Kennedy compound at Hyannis Port, Mass., solely because he had received much pleasure from the Lawrence Welk Show.

There is no telling how much this meant to the Welk show at option time. We would guess a lot.[17]

Janet Kern in the *Chicago American* said (1960):

Sullivan and Welk resembled the old advertisement line "They laughed when I sat down to the piano," but both are having the last laugh. Their anniversary shows prove that in TV as in everything else, he who laughs last laughs best. . . . and longest.[18]

A Shrewd Observation

Here Welk's critics have put their finger right on one of the most central points. It is their shrewdest observation of this man and his work. Their remarks might be even better summed up this way: For a musician, he is probably one of the sharpest businessmen in America. Musicians are not known for their astute abilities in handling money or business matters. Welk is a definite exception to this rule. Though he is not a great artist himself, he is a good average musician who has an inherent knowledge of the tastes of the American public gained from years of experience. Further, he has put that knowledge to work and has built up one of the largest musical business organizations in the country. In no small way, his business abilities have kept him on major television all these years (cf. chapters 5 and 9).

Fourth Classification of Critics

Those who pan Lawrence Welk for being a country bumpkin, an amateur performer, and for encouraging photographic smiles from his performers:

Thomas E. Murphy, television critic for the *Hartford* (Connecticut) *Courant* wrote (1964):

Riveted to a soft chair the other night by sheer inertia, which is another term for laziness, I found myself staring vacantly into the putty-like face of Lawrence Welk. Despite the approval of a million little old ladies in tennis shoes, Lawrence is not my dish. Indeed I pair him with the ineffable Liberace, for they do have something in common as I shall soon demonstrate.

As Mr. Welk was dragging his North Dakota patois behind him like a collection of verbal tin cans, I noted that behind stood an aggregation of individuals who were all grinning furiously. To be sure those who were playing wind instruments had their pans pretty well hidden. But I am sure that behind the flute, sax and trumpet there were grins. Certainly the accordionist, the violinists, the pianist and others all had wide Cheshire-cat smiles on their faces. The girl piano player particularly was grinning with such furious intensity that I am surprised it did not blow every TV tube in the land. I understand that it is standard practice for the Welkites to grin. Grin or get lost, something like that.

Perhaps it was this great collection of crockery that set me to musing on the fact that in all other species, when the teeth are bared, it is a preliminary to a bite. When a cat, dog, lion, leopard, even a monkey bares his teeth he means business. I felt I had come upon a great fundamental truth that only man grins as a mask of good fellowship. I use the word mask advisedly, because most displays of crockery are a real prelude to "putting on the bite" in the modern sense of that term: a preliminary to asking for something.

Leaving idiots out of it, if you will think hard you will recollect that most of the people who show their teeth are trying to curry your favor: ham actors, used-car salesmen, politicians, people waiting to borrow money, door-to-door magazine peddlers—are all members of the charm-by-the-teeth school. And the wider the smile, the more crockery on display, the more predatory are the designs. For we are akin to the primitives in that when we show our teeth, while legend has it we are exuding good fellowship, in actuality we have designs on the smilee.

In both Welk and Liberace the design is to make little old ladies like them. And both succeed beyond the fondest dreams of man. It is one of the more fascinating sights of our swell culture today to see the ladies line up to dance a few steps with Lawrence Welk. There must be some solution to the enigma, for he too, like Liberace, is not what anyone would say conforms to the standards of masculine beauty. Both share the fixed grin, the display of crockery, an immense quantity of cornball music, and fantastic success. The little old women fall all over themselves to dance just a couple of steps with Mr. Welk. Personally I act on the theory that anybody so lacking in taste that they would want to dance with an old gaffer like myself, has such poor judgment I wouldn't want to dance with them.

This theory means that you don't dance with those who are most desirable to dance with because they won't dance with you, nor with the old dames with whom you do not want to dance. In short, no dancing. But Lawrence Welk apparently thrives on his dance marathons. I am not sure whether I enjoyed this phase of the program better than the music, Whispering Hope being the norm for the program.

There used to be a popular song "There are smiles that make you happy. There are smiles that make you blue. There are smiles that steal away the teardrops, as the sunshine steals away the dew." I think that should be the theme song for the Welk show. For one thing, it catches both the poetic level of performance, and it also describes the great categories of smiles that are displayed by the entourage. As one final note let me quote from Bill Shakespeare who said: "A man can smile and smile and still a villain be." (I don't mean that as a reference to Lawrence, obviously a nice guy, but merely as a warning to beware of strangers who show their teeth.) They may be reverting to type.

Indeed the smile may be as deceiving as the old folk belief that an honest man will look you in the eye while a crook will not. In fact the opposite is most likely to be true. He will look you in the eye, and darn it, he will smile furiously while doing it. That's the way to spot a con man. (Reprinted with permission.) [19]

The following February (1965), Murphy's column in the same newspaper was headlined "Hello Larry":

I could tell by the envelope that it was important. There was a large embroidered W on the face of it, and when I turned it over there was the name Lawrence Welk. Why should the great man be writing to me? With trembling fingers I opened the letter. At the top of the letterhead it read, "The Champagne Music of Lawrence Welk" and in the right corner an embossed likeness of the man himself, wielding his familiar baton. I read, and now I share it with you:

I recently had the somewhat dubious pleasure of reading your column headed "The Teeth." Having always been extremely fond of the Irish people, seeing the name Murphy at the top of the story shook me up quite a bit. I had the pleasure of playing in the Bob Hope Desert Classic with a gentleman named Tom Murphy, a happy, congenial, smiling fellow—characteristics I have always associated with the Irish.

I can't go along with your philosophy belittling our so-called senior citizens. God willing, most of us will reach that status eventually. I have long felt that the elderly were a badly neglected segment of our population, especially in the area of entertainment. Therefore, I see nothing wrong with slanting our show at an audience that includes little old ladies. Even if we deliberately play up to them, it doesn't seem to hurt our programs.

As for dancing with them, I really enjoy it and apparently quite a few of them do also. We are proud of the fact that so many mothers and grandmothers invite us into their homes each week. According to the latest surveys it would appear we manage to attract a fair share of the men and young people in the household too.

Regarding the smiles that seem to offend you, we have found through long, personal experience that most people don't object to watching performers working with a smile. Since we thoroughly enjoy doing our show, smiling is quite natural. In fact, it's rather difficult to enjoy something without smiling. Just try it sometime and if you get the habit, I might even put you on my show the next time you come to Hollywood.

I hope in time we can win you over to our theory of entertainment. Meanwhile, we'll keep trying, and keep smiling. I trust you will do the same." Signed, Lawrence Welk.[20]

"J.B.," writing in *Television-Radio Age,* said (1967):

If ever a show looked like a local Chicago show, this is it. Lawrence Welk has the personality of a road-show Ed Sullivan. He has an accent that won't go away and a clumsy, embarrassed way of reading lines. If ever there was a rube, Larry baby is it. He even starts the band with "a one and a two" stuff that went out with the A&P gypsies. The band is one hundred percent eligible for medicare. They pop up and down like Los Chavales de Espana, only they look awkward and posed. They play square when they are presumably doing a Herb Alpert, New Vaudeville Band, or Beatle number. They remind one of a talented amateur Rotary Club band in Indiana. They might win the state contest but they'll never make the big time.[21]

John Hartl wrote in the *Seattle Times* (1967):

The man has become such an institution that his deficiencies have almost become assets. His attempts at humorous introductions (here's a long-haired musician in the old sense of the word), his "uh-von-und-uh-two" downbeat and his never ending smile are an established part of the American scene. Despite his many years of public exposure, Welk still has the ability to suggest that he doesn't quite know how to go about things—as last night when he seemed to have trouble crowning the new Seafair Queen at intermission. And that is what his fans seem to enjoy most about him.[22]

Alfred G. Aronowitz wrote in the *New York Post* (1971):

He's a nice old man, Lawrence Welk, who likes to keep things plain and simple just like he was taught down on the farm in Strasburg, N. D. He didn't really learn how to speak English until he packed up and left for the big city, Aberdeen, S.D. where he got a job playing the accordion with the Jazzy Junior Five, a group of 10- to 11-year-olds under the direction of a lady named Mrs. O'Brien. You've heard the jokes about why people like Lawrence have hunched shoulders and flat heads. Because when you ask them a question they shrug and when you tell them the answer they slap their hands on their brows.

Poor, plain and simple Lawrence. He still talks like he just stepped off the boat. . . . All he ever learned was how to make money. When his ABC show was cancelled after 16 years, he syndicated the package and immediately sold it to 188 stations, only one less than the number he had with the network.

They call him the "Corn Belt Guy Lombardo" and the "Liberace of the accordion." Whatever else they call him he's such a nice old man that it's hard to dislike him even if he was the one to force the Sid Caesar Show off the air. Lawrence knows about ratings. He used to carry an applause meter on tour with him but now his ear has gotten so finely attuned that he doesn't need any mechanical help in telling whether he's going over or not. He may talk funny but Lawrence can count. Did you ever hear him starting off his orchestra? "A-one and a-two and a-three. . ." . . . .

He'll be 69 next March 11 and he's still touring. He was in Roanoke, Va. the other day when he called me up to hustle his appearance in Madison Square Garden tomorrow night. They've only sold 14,000 tickets out of a possible 20,000![23]

Helps People Relate to Welk

This type of criticism, far from hurting Welk, only helps his popularity. It actually makes it easier for the average person to relate to him. It is much like the newspaper and magazine cartoons that caricature the appearances and actions of prominent people—including Welk. Most of the cartoons do no harm but rather bring out humorous aspects of their subjects' personalities. It is indeed a matter of record that the men who were most influential in selling Welk's show to the ABC network and for the Dodge account in 1955 did so on the strength of his personality as it came across on the television screen. Average people may smile or even laugh a bit at Welk but still relate to him because they see in him something of themselves.

It is the deep sincerity of this man that comes through, despite his few handicaps and mixed-up expressions. There is a certain type of sophisticated person who delights in ridiculing Welk just because of his success. The almost endless cartoons that appeared in the 1950s through the 1970s about corn and bubbles and Geritol were all of this category. They did a great service for Welk by crystalizing his popularity and bringing his name before the public. Actually no one enjoyed their humor more than Welk himself.

Fifth Classification of Critics

Those who attribute Welk's success to his "playing up" to his audience and choosing music to suit the uncultivated taste, primarily of people over fifty:

Larry Wolters of the *Chicago Tribune* wrote (1960):

They said it couldn't be done—the jazz addicts and the rock 'n' rollers—but Lawrence Welk has done it. On Saturday the Welk-in rings for the fifth solid year, on the same network, under the same sponsorship, and with undiminished interest by his following of upwards of twenty million persons.[24]

Hank Grant of the *Miami Herald* stated (1962):

Welk probably has the most loyal fan following of any personality on television. The demand for tickets to his show is so great that rarely can requests be filled less than six months in advance. That the younger ones are coming around is evidenced by the increased numbers of teenagers who appear at his recordbreaking performances around the country. And that teenagers are buying his records is evidenced by the fact that his recording of "Calcutta" is still selling with a current total of 1,850,000 sales.[25]

Rex Polier, music critic for the *Philadelphia Inquirer*, wrote (1965):

Lawrence Welk and his Champagne Music Makers never looked as good as they do now in television's current kick of exalting teenage beat music and the weirdos who play it. ... It is about the only place on TV you can hear music pleasantly played, sung to, and danced to by a group of equally pleasant people on a consistent basis. How consistently is pointed up by the fact that on Saturday, 8:30 p.m., Channel 6, Welk and his group mark their 500th program. They've been at it steadily since July, 1955, when they first went on as a summer replacement. Everyone knows how they made entertainment history.... Competing networks long ago gave up trying to find a competitive-type program. From his kingly perch, the maestro is entirely unconcerned about any new attempts that might be made. His program is the result of more than 40 years spent playing to audiences from coast to coast. He learned in the rocky school of one-night stands how to please an audience, and that remains the guiding principle of the present show.[26]

Lorne Parton in the *Vancouver* (British Columbia) *Sun* wrote (1967):

While a hipster might wonder what was with it, under the nice exterior of Lawrence Welk beats the heart of a shrewd showman, and under the one-and-a-two pulse of the band boasts the rhythm of a very talented group of musicians.[27]

Bob Hull, television editor for the *Los Angeles Herald-Examiner*, wrote (1963):

If the establishment is serious about establishing an arts and culture committee to further the finer things, it should welcome Lawrence Welk, a gentleman who knows all about popular tastes and the appetite for aesthetics. The band leader with Champagne Music enters his 11th year of TV broadcasting with a single network, this month. He has done more for entertainment than Pablo Casals or any other so-called fine artist, including the "intellectuals" who have discovered folk music. When Welk started on Channel 5 in the summer of 1955, as a replacement for re-runs, critics told him what to do. Get back to the cornfields of Dakota, they said. The advertising people also told him what to do. Get some dancing girls, comedians and guest stars, they advised. ... Welk's notions were sound. Thanks to the knocks of the critics, his show gained notoriety. People watched it, liked it, and said so. Then, as now, the mail averaged 5,000 letters per week. Welk had to go out and really "join em" to catch the kids. Cautiously, he has incorporated what he calls "non-hysterical" rock-and-roll music, mainly because his own children are fans and he wanted to give them something like it. Oddly, the reaction to rock-and-roll tunes has come from the opposite age. Oldsters love it—the way the maestro plays it, that is.[28]

P. F. Kluge in the *Wall Street Journal* wrote (1970):

As a matter of fact, it [the younger generation] doesn't like him. But at 67 Lawrence Welk is beyond catering to the whims of youth. "Our strongest audience," he declares, "is the mothers of the American home." That audience has made his side of the generation gap a lucrative one indeed. ... Mr. Welk sees no reason to apologize for his own definition of patriotism or for his one-man rule over the program. "The other bandleaders (the ones who are gone today) thought they were artists," he reflects. "They said, 'Play for yourself.' I play for the audience. If you let musicians play for themselves, they might play something nobody understands." Lawrence Welk's audience is still listening, still understanding—and still aging. An ad man familiar with the show characterizes the Welk Nation as "over fifty, more rural than urban, more lower class than upper class, more uneducated than educated."[29]

Bruce Blackadar of the *Toronto Sun* wrote an article headlined "The Sounds of Cocker and Welk: A Report from Different Worlds" (1974):

One of the most mindblowing events this summer at least for me had to be the Lawrence Welk Show at the Ex. What was truly astounding about the whole epic was the absolutely irreversible gap between his audience—and it is one of the most devoted I've seen anywhere, what with old ladies crying and hundreds rushing the stage to get autographs—and the one that reads this column. Being in the grandstand with

Welk LIVE, so to speak, is much different from his television show for some strange reason, and the feeling for any younger people there—and there must have been at least four of us—could only be described as a stupefyingly bizarre peyote trip....

Nothing could have prepared one for the fantasy world of cleanliness, order and simple farmboy virtues that Welk's ethos represents....

Welk's musical range stretches from bland to bland, of course, so it's pointless to talk about the content of the evening. And yet, after it was over, I found it hard to put it all down, because the simple truth is that Welk speaks musically to millions and obviously gives them tremendous pleasure, and these are good people, solid types, lovely old ladies and pleasant gentlemen who are crazy about polkas and nice "classics" like an excruciatingly bad version of Rhapsody in Blue that Welk inflicted on us that night. But what a gulf there is in music now! Joe Cocker and Lawrence Welk together on stage? Now that would really be something else.[30]

John V. R. Bull, entertainment writer for the *Philadelphia Inquirer*, stated (1975):

If sugar could kill, I'd be dead by now for listening to Lawrence and his Musical Family. Saturday night was a saccharine venture into a world that no longer exists. Welk brought his so-called Champagne Music into the Spectrum for a concert that nearly filled the huge hall with members of the over-40 generation. Welk and his musicmakers spun a cotton candy–like confection of sweetness and light in three-quarter time as his musical upside-down cake evoked memories of a simpler, less complicated era. For Welk's music is of the 50's, that decade that now seems almost naively innocent when compared with later years. Welk's music seems fittingly artificial: his arrangements turn almost every tune into a waltz. There's great emphasis on religion, the home, mom and pop and romance. Welk insinuates that life really is free and easy and we can merely dance our troubles away. This may be dated, but there sure are a lot of people who like to pretend that's the way things still are. A Welk concert is like a wedding, with the maestro giving away the bride and dancing in the aisles with all the mothers and grandmothers in the audience. And if the words "wonderful," "beautiful," "great" and "lovely" were banned from the English language, Welk would be a mute. Some might call this corny, but it's part of Welk's schtick and we're stuck with it now. . . .

There's jitterbugging and tap dancing (now, when's the last time you saw tap dancers?) and some of the soloists, obviously selected for their physical beauty rather than their vocal prowess, are often backed by a chorus that has a confused identity problem with the Mormon Tabernacle Choir. Everyone is excruciatingly cute, the girls literally giggle and squeak their way through inane greetings, and Welk presides over all, his baton moving about in controlled spasm.[31]

A followup article by Bull was headlined "Never pick on Lawrence Welk!" (1975):

Philadelphia area senior citizens, sometimes using obscenities and scatological references, have lashed back at what they regard as an unfair newspaper review of a Lawrence Welk concert at the Spectrum last weekend. . . . The review provoked two dozen letters, an uncommonly large response to a musical review, and several phone calls from persons outraged by what they regarded as an attack upon Welk. . . . Among other things, I've learned not to pick on Lawrence Welk![32]

Lawrence Maddry writing in the (Norfolk) *Virginian Pilot* said (1971):

The marquee outside the Hampton Roads Coliseum carried the message "Lawrence Welk and His Allstars" but you could tell just by looking at the paying customers that the Mr. Wunnerful of bubble music was in town. It was a very hip crowd. Not hippies mind you. But about one of the old folks in five who took a final swig from the Geritol bottle and crawled out of the jalopy immediately planted a cupped hand smartly at the hip—just to ease the pain, you know. Generally speaking, it was the kind of halt and lame crowd that shows up at the orthopedic wing on Monday mornings. Only now they were wheezing across the treacherous wilds of the Coliseum parking lot in support hose for an appointment with the musical doctor of broken dreams. The prescription is always nostalgia. Perky doses of the stuff dispensed over ABC-TV on Saturday nights—lilting oldies and the new ones like "I never promised you a rose garden" only very soft with the thorns off, all dispensed by pretty girls in pinafores and nice young men who keep their pompadours in place with Command hair spray and flash Dentyne smiles. Inside the Coliseum now. Lord how they talked. "I'll tell you, Myrtle, I'd give a week of bus tokens just to stand in Mr. Welk's shadow. He's sooo handsome! I always eat fried food on Saturday nights because his music is so soothing on stomach gas, you know"....

Welk was big business Thursday night at the Coliseum. All the old gals had doused themselves with sachet before coming, and the auditorium smelled like a linen closet. And when Mr. Wunnerful walked on stage, he picked up the cue by waving a baton longer than a veterinary needle over "Everything's Coming up Roses"....

And soon Mr. Welk was putting all those nice show people through their paces with snappy dialog like "That was very nice, Larry, and now we'll hear from Norma." Later, Welk, who is 68 but resembles a middle-aged Pat Boone, was right down front dancing with the ladies in the audience. He wore a blue blazer and white ducks like the hero of an ice cream parlor musical. The bubbler flowed like an overloaded Bendix.[33]

Like Bull, Maddry wrote a followup (1971):

Tuesday morning I walked into the office and found a noose dangling from the ceiling over my typewriter. You could tell it was from the Lawrence Welk mafia because it was twisted from a pair of support hose. I immediately drew up my will and made a hurried payment on my life insurance.

The copy boys say my chances of survival are slimmer than Tiny Tim trying to run back a kickoff on the Baltimore Colts. All we did was write a little column saying that the crowd which turned up at the Lawrence Welk concert in Hampton Roads Coliseum last Friday night was a hip audience. . . .

Since then I have suffered much abuse from the bran-flakes set. It's as though I'd rapped out a solo on the ceremonial drum in the Welk orchestra. . . .

A lot of the callers said that the column showed I was prejudiced against elderly people. That is a lie. I wouldn't want my daughter to marry one, but I sit next to them on the bus all the time. They also have—presumably from listening to champagne music—a kind of natural rhythm.

The people I am opposed to are the nappy-headed, 80-year-old ladies with naughty mouths who do not know good writing from the squiggles in their varicose veins. The ones who phone threatening either to hang me with their girdles, to strangle me with their hearing aid cords, or to spike my effigy with crochet needles.[34]

Not only that, but Maddry addressed Welk himself (1971):

Mr. Lawrence Welk, Hollywood, Cal., Dear Mr. Welk: A couple of days ago my brain cut out on me like a Honda with bad sparks and I had the extremely poor judgment to bad-mouth you and your followers in my column. To put it mildly, I have lived to regret this in the way Hitler came to regret jumping on Poland or Custer regretted giving lip to the Indians. The only journalist I know who has suffered like this was the California movie reviewer who had the bad judgment to say something terrible about a Walt Disney movie. He implied that Snow White was not pure. . . .

By now you are probably wondering about the purpose of this letter, Mr. Welk, so I will get straight to the point. What I want you to do is simple. Lord knows it is simple. Please send me a card saying that all is forgiven before I come apart faster than a Hong Kong afghan. I can't tell you how many letters I've received from old and young people threatening to wring my neck faster than your Myron Floren plays his accordion. A lot of the phone calls are worse, suggesting that the reason I don't appreciate elderly people is that I never had a father. Never did I dream that a column could upset your viewers like that. I hereby take back everything I wrote, especially that part about your followers being a "halt and lame crowd." It was a lie. In truth, your followers are as active as they are enterprising. Last night a little old lady in leotards breezed by our house in an MG with dual carbs and hurled something flaming through the living room window. Who would have thought that you could make a Molotov cocktail with no more than lighter fluid and a Geritol bottle?

If you could hurry with that card, Mr. Welk, it would be appreciated, for I hereby apologize and am more repentant than a bawdy house madam on Judgment Day. Signed, Lawrence Maddry.[35]

Welk's Own Audience

There is little doubt that Welk caters to an older audience, makes no apologies about it, and considers it one of the secrets of his television success. Some say it is part of his shrewd business sense, and no one could contradict that statement. Since he has grown up with that audience, he maintains it belongs to him, and he is nobody to let a good thing get out of his hands. He feels their tastes are good enough to appreciate the old nostalgic tunes of two and three decades back. It is these people who have kept him on the air.

Sixth Classification of Critics

Those who have predicted the worst for the Lawrence Welk Show—lowering of ratings, loss of popularity, eventual dropping of the television show entirely:

Clarke Williamson of the (Phoenix) *Arizona Republic* said (1968):

Top View voters (a private poll of the paper) again place "Family Affair" and "Walt Disney" as the best performers of the season. Lawrence Welk falls from favor of middle-age voters and suffers most from the disdain of youth. Star

Trek gains most; Family Affair, CBS, 85.5 rating—an all-age favorite; Walt Disney, NBC, 83.1 rating—an all-age favorite; Mission Impossible, CBS, 77.7, recommended for young and middle-aged; Lawrence Welk, ABC, 66.6 rating, acceptable; Star Trek, NBC, 61.1 rating, acceptable.[36]

Lawrence Laurent, of the *Washington Post,* wrote in the *Chicago Sun-Times* (1970):

> Give Lawrence Welk just one more year on network television. And put Ed Sullivan down for the same sentence. This is part of the annual forecast by Herb Jacobs, the television industry's most honored prophet. Jacobs has been batting well over .900 in the annual "new season" forecasts he began seven years ago. Welk and Sullivan will have to go after the 1970–71 season, he says, because of television's new emphasis on programs that appeal to persons under 50. This is the emphasis that led CBS-TV to cancel both the Jackie Gleason Show and the Red Skelton Hour. The reason Jacobs thinks Welk is heading out of television is that "enough of his audience have gone to their Maker, and it's safe to bet, after next season, he'll be back in North Dakota giving polka lessons."[37]

P. F. Kluge of the *Wall Street Journal* stated (1970):

> Despite their devotion to their minstrel, the show's ratings have slipped a bit lately; this past season it hovered around the bottom of the top 20, sometimes in, sometimes out. Although one ABC official maintains the show has "a very good survival rating," the slight decline in audience has caused the trade press to speculate that Mr. Welk's star may wane as his followers dwindle during the Seventies.[38]

Erroneous Predictions

Welk's ratings did drop slightly in the late 1960s and in 1970. However, when he left the ABC network and began distributing his show by syndication, he not only gained stations but through this impetus brought his ratings to a higher level than on the network. His ratings in the 1979–80

season will likely go up again, since he aims to increase his
audience by 2 million people. Almost all the advertising experts agree that, though Welk's ratings may go down for a
while, they always have had good survival power and can be
counted on to deliver a consistently high 15–20 million
homes each week. At seventy-seven, Welk is still a man of
unbelievable drive and enthusiasm who is capable of inspiring his co-workers as few others in the entertainment world
(cf. chapter 6).

Seventh Classification of Critics

Those who harp upon the number of performers who have
left Welk and accuse him of being harsh, overbearing, and
penny-pinching in his dealings with his employees:

Paul Jones of the *Atlanta Constitution* wrote (1962):

> Lawrence Welk has a bubbly personality but he doesn't
> seem to be able to get along with people—at least not the
> people who work for him on his Champagne Music program.
> During the last three years at least six of the show's most
> popular personalities have left the show in a huff after a
> run-in with the maestro.[39]

P. F. Kluge wrote in the *Wall Street Journal* (1970):

> Accounts of employees past and present, however, suggest
> that no one steps on Lawrence Welk and that he runs his
> organization with Prussian discipline. One of his former
> employees said: "He is Germanic, he is stubborn, he has the
> answer before you ask. My definition of a stubborn Dutch-
> man is Welk!"

> Most complaints about the Welk organization have con-
> cerned money—particularly the bandleader's practice of sel-
> dom paying his musicians a penny more than union scale.
> This, they complain, often results in a wage of less than
> $300 a week. Mr. Welk replies that the musicians enjoy regu-
> lar employment and don't have to worry about where their
> next job is coming from; that their exposure on the Welk
> show allows them to get lucrative outside engagements, and

that a Teleklew profit-sharing plan enables an employee faithful over the decades to amass comfortable savings.[40]

Bob Rose, of the Chicago Daily News Service in Hollywood, wrote in the *Indianapolis Star* (1968):

Welk has had rules, mostly unspoken, about such things as how his performers dress and act. But he hasn't had to say much about them in recent years.... The last time Welk had a major ruckus with one of his performers was nearly ten years ago when Alice Lon, his champagne lady of six years' standing, left the show. She complained he was too ironfisted and unyielding about her songs and dress. Welk admitted that he felt she had tried to be "too sexy—and I will not stand for such things." He also said she kept nagging him to let her sing numbers that were not in harmony with his folksy format. Even so, Welk called Alice "a peach of a girl" and said that someone was just advising her badly. Looking back on the affair, Welk says some of the columnists were "trying to make a rough man out of me—which I basically am not. The thing was she wanted to sing a song which I did not think was good for the show. We try and use good standards." The hipsters, of course, consider such music so square that anyone playing it must be broke or born dumb. But some of the avant garde musicians watching the Welk orchestra get juicy TV salaries year after year, sort of wish they had learned to read music and write home to mother.[41]

In the nationally syndicated *TV Mailbag* of Feb. 22, 1976, the following question was put by a reader:

Lawrence Welk's show always looks like one big happy family. Do they all love Welk the way they seem to?—P. K., Merrit Island.

No. Welk is a tough taskmaster, and to at least three current members of his group he often appears both "stubborn and self-righteous," a viewpoint shared by many who are no longer with the bandleader. "It seems to me," Natalie Nevins said some time ago, "that anyone who keeps telling people they should emulate the life of Christ as closely as possible ought to be much more forgiving and understanding than he is."[42]

An evaluation of the above classification of newspaper critics will be found below under the subheading "Those Who Leave Welk."

Eighth Classification of Critics

Those who were once critics of Welk but who now find themselves unable to say much in an adverse way about him:

John Wendeborn, music critic for the (Portland) *Oregonian,* wrote (1974):

> I suppose many music writers privately consider the music of Lawrence Welk blandly commercial and insipid. I must admit that my opinion of it hasn't been altogether in the rave category. But after spending about an hour with Welk the afternoon of his June 5 Coliseum concert date and then 2½ hours listening to the band at the show, I have changed my scoffing posture to one of relative admiration. From a professional standpoint, the music was played outstandingly, and there was a lot more punch to the band than I remember hearing on TV. I can't say, though, that it will turn my head around from other styles; it's just that I have respect for the entertainment values Welk espouses.[43]

Charles Hanna of the *Detroit Free Press* wrote (1971):

> I used to sneer at Lawrence Welk. Now on Saturday nights I sit around sipping Geritol and yelling "Go, Lar, Go!" I think the change in my attitude started two years ago when I was among a clutch of West Coast reporters. We met Welk at the airport when he came into town to bubble all over everybody with a concert of his Champagne music. . . . I expected to see him come off the plane dressed in his precise television best, carrying that long baton lightly in his right hand, the point placed daintily across the upheld palm of his left. It wasn't that way. A stream of musicians shuffled off the plane. Toward the rear, there was this guy in a blazer

and a tired face. He was carrying a fat garment bag over his shoulder. His hair looked like it was taking those few precious hours away from the bright lights to rest up from being meticulously parted and groomed. It was he: Lawrence of Dakota. Praised and heralded by millions for his weekly TV hour, derided and scorned by million more for precisely the same reason. . . . King Cornball! Few if any of the newsmen there would have admitted they watched Welk regularly on the tube or were in any way or at any time entranced by his music. Least of all I. . . . We walked with him up the long concourse to a lounge where we would talk. The garment bag looked so heavy and he so tired, several reporters asked if he'd like help. "No," he smiled wearily, "I've lost it too many times that way." In the lounge he answered our questions earnestly, with an attitude that might best be described as shyly brave anxiety. . . . It charmed us all. Here was a man who had started out in 1927 with a six-man band in Yankton, S.D. With a fourth grade education, he managed to build a big band and a following through years of one-night stands and bone-tiring bus tours. Then in 1955 when the big bands were nose-diving into obscurity, Welk won a weekly spot on ABC-TV with his score of musicians and performers. There he stayed, a weekly reminder to the older generation that people who survive a Great Depression and win a Big War, are also people who take time out for cute, snappy songs sung by clean, orderly people who smile ever so coyly and ever so much. I agree.[44]

Victor P. Hass wrote in the *Omaha World-Herald* (1975) :

Lawrence Welk had a program the other Saturday evening that he called "Nostalgia." It was filled with lovely, long-ago tunes sung by beautiful young women and handsome young men, well-scrubbed, their hair neat and tidy. They made a pleasing appearance, they seemed to take pleasure in their work, and the results of their efforts were entirely agreeable. It was an hour of melody that must have carried many a listener back to a time when life seemed simpler, more relaxed, more livable. I thought as I listened that

Welk, for all his corny comments, is an uncommonly astute program planner because he echoed the ache in many hearts and minds these days, the longing, half-expressed, half-felt for something better than the bash and smash, the predatoriness, the scruffiness of so much of life today. I thought, too, of Peter Citron's remark in a review that "Welk sounds better all the time" after the ear-shattering experience of a rock concert that left him, literally, deafened by the assault on his ear drums.[45]

An Evaluation of Welk's Critics

In evaluating what the critics say about Welk, there are some deeper facts to bear in mind. First, from the outset of his musical career Welk looked ahead to something entirely different from that which most musicians call success. His goal was definitely not to give an accordion recital in Carnegie Hall! Instead, success for him was conceived of primarily as business success. He worked for independence, the freedom to run his own little orchestra and to support his family. It would be accomplished through the medium of his first real skill—accordion playing. In the beginning, that skill was the only commodity he had to sell. Later there were the services of other musicians and performers he had hired. Music and musicians have always been for Welk what some would term a business enterprise. They were a means by which he could step up the ladder of success. In his particular case, his business was to entertain people, to bring them pleasure and relaxation and offer them a beautiful setting for song and dance. The entertainment of people meant jobs. It further meant money, personal satisfaction, and success.

Like business people who must earn their living by the use of somewhat unpleasant means, Welk found that he was sometimes dealing with unpleasant, temperamental musicians. At times he had to make excuses for them when they were detained or failed to fulfill their family responsibilities because of drunkenness or carousing.

At one time early in his career his whole band walked out on him because of an accusation that he was "just a farm boy who could never make his way in the big city." When he finally succeeded in hiring musicians who could be trusted to remain on the job and perform satisfactorily, he felt he was making great progress. Musicians who think that being on the road offers an excuse for "living it up" have always been a source of dismay and frustration to him. To this day, the basic dichotomy of trying to run a successful band and having to make allowances for this type of musician causes him deep concern. Yet up until recently this has been the frustrating story of Lawrence Welk's many years in the entertainment business.

This account of earlier dealings with musicians furnishes necessary background when considering what critics have said of him in more recent years. Earlier he learned that he could not pay salaries during sick leave because soon his whole band became sick! He is even accused by some critics of being a penny pincher. Doubtless in one sense he is. He learned frugality early in life and will not forget it, no matter how many millions he may have invested. He staunchly adheres to his conviction that he helps no one by giving him or her unearned money. As for being harsh and overbearing, he is firm rather than harsh. His inflexibility is probably the result of both his strong inner convictions and his Germanic temperament. If he is convinced he is doing the right thing, nobody can change his mind. His deep sense of justice demands that he adopt the only objective norm for paying each person equitably—union scale. He considers it necessary to use this rule to keep peace in his musical family. He has observed that dissatisfaction grows when one performer is paid more than another. One thing is clear to everyone in the Welk organization—each person *earns* his salary.

Welk's whole attitude toward musicians as commodities to be used in his business was reflected in an interview I had with Vincent DiBari, secretary of the Los Angeles local of the American Federation of Musicians. DiBari summed up the relations of the union with Lawrence Welk in this way:

> We have had no open disagreements with Lawrence Welk nor with his manager, Sam Lutz. Of all the people we do business with, they are perhaps the most cooperative and pleasant. They also have done more for musicians than most employers in Los Angeles. Yes, Lawrence Welk is a bit defensive when it comes to musicians. He has had to be reminded of union rules, just as anyone else; but he is most gracious in complying with them. I think that like many employers, he is a bit frightened of unions, not understanding exactly what we are trying to do. Not being a musician himself in the sense of understanding the artistic temperament of our people, I believe he has built up a kind of defense against musicians. Some of our people have given up on him because they say he simply does not understand music, cannot appreciate good music, and is basically jealous of what an artist the musician is.[46]

Lawrence Welk is totally absorbed in talent scouting. He lights up instantly when he tells how fortunate he is to be able to hire such people as Norma Zimmer, Myron Floren, or Bobby Burgess. He speaks warmly, though regretfully, of players like Al Hirt, Pete Fountain, Dick Cathcart, or Anita Bryant—all of whom once performed for him. He would hire them back if he could have them. His attitude toward talented performers is like that of an agent who makes his living by booking talent. The only difference is that he himself is both agent and employer. Some might think he would become envious when his talent upstaged him. But talent for Welk is a business commodity with which he makes capital, and there is no one more interested in the talent business.

Those Who Leave Welk

There is need to bring up the subject of why some people leave Welk's organization after a number of years of very successful work. Perhaps better than any newspaper or music critic, such people are in a position to criticize Welk honestly and objectively. Welk naturally has faults in both his professional and private life. Just as he has countless friends and admirers, so he has enemies who are critical and quick to condemn him. To fail to give a hearing to this group, though it is small, would be both unfair and inaccurate for a study such as this. The following accusations have been made by former musicians and singers:

> Lawrence is a tightfisted penny pincher who doesn't believe in sharing his own personal good fortune with people in his band. Though he has made a fortune, he seems surprisingly frugal. He is far from generous with his staff and pays his performers a lot less than they could get on other shows.

> Another quality which some have difficulty in understanding is his vindictiveness towards certain people who have gotten on his blacklist. If a person does something he doesn't like, that person is out of his good graces permanently. He never forgets a wrong done him, whether it is intentional or not.

> Lawrence expects people who are in his organization to devote their lives to his cause. For example, his unbending rule about traveling on tour is very difficult for some to obey. The dedication he demands of people for the salaries he gives is simply unfair.

> He is forever making rules for people to follow, and if you don't measure up to his rules, you're out in the cold. This is not the life for people of artistic temperament.

> For a person who is always telling others to follow the teachings of Jesus Christ, you would think that he could bring himself around to practice the forgiveness that he preaches.

Once Welk has put his mind to anything, you can't change him. He's stubbornly Germanic and is unwilling to listen to other people's viewpoints.[47]

Such criticisms seem to be those most frequently leveled at the character of Lawrence Welk. As examples of his so-called mistakes in handling people, the disaffected refer to the parting of Alice Lon, the Lennon Sisters, Cissy King, Jo Ann Castle, or Clay Hart. It is not that each and every one of these people was fired by Welk. Actually, what happened in most instances was that, because of disagreement over something like his policy of paying only union scale, the person simply decided to leave. In other cases some glaring fault a performer himself did nothing about occasioned the person's being fired. Sometimes, a musician's performance sank so low that audience response became negative, and Welk simply advised the person not to stay. But in the majority of instances, people have left Welk because they wanted to pursue their careers in an unhampered, individual manner. His alleged interference with style or manner of performing has brought about most of the departures.

The question is: Do these faults in the character of Welk really exist? Or do they exist only in the minds of those who have become bitter and disgruntled over their own lack of success in his organization? In light of the thousands of positive statements made by his friends and closest associates and recorded in this book, I would propose the thought that yes, there may be a shred of truth behind what each of his detractors has said. No person is perfect, and Lawrence Welk is the first to admit this truth about himself. It is quite unlikely, however, that his success could have resulted from a character seriously besmirched by any or all of these faults. With the exception of the few mentioned earlier, almost all those who have left Welk have passed into oblivion. Some have worked the nightclub circuits around the country, but relatively few are well-known entertainers.

I have personally listened to Welk discuss for hours the subject of his critics. He may not group them as I have done for this study, but I would say he is more aware of what his critics write than one would think. Because he is in some ways introverted, adverse criticism preys upon his mind. He has difficulty in setting it aside or forgetting it. He brought me an article that appeared in the *Los Angeles Herald-Examiner* in June, 1970, and asked me if I would analyze what this critic was saying about him. Of course, much of what is said by critics is humorous, and Welk is always the first to enjoy it. However, some statements contain biting, underlying insinuations, which he is also quick to catch. Some writers have remarked that he is not bothered by all the barbed criticism thrown his way. However, because of a sincere desire to please and be accepted by people, sharp criticism does hurt him deeply.

Welk Is His Own Worst Critic

I have thought long and hard over all these categories of critics and have concluded that, if one listens carefully, one will hear Welk say exactly what these critics are saying. Ironically, he speaks most critically about himself. The constant tenor of his conversations with me has revealed that, in his quiet moments, he is deeply aware of his own deficiencies— his lack of education, his farm background, his inability to express himself, his lack of musical genius, and his past need to work twelve to fifteen hours a day to make something of himself. He constantly speaks of having learned deep lessons in life based on bitter experience, want, bad breaks, and mistakes. Today he insists they are lessons he could never afford to forget. They made such a deep impression upon him that they have colored his subsequent life. Surprisingly, this very personal side of Welk has been revealed to very few people.

In conclusion, I would say that the classifications of critics

I have quoted above are fairly accurate in their estimate of Lawrence Welk. However, what they give for the most part are surface impressions that do not go deeply enough into the background of his life. They might well take into account the five preliminary facts in the beginning of this chapter.

8
Can TV Learn
from Welk?

And What Happened to That Big Band Sound?

Television is among the most amazing phenomena of our age. Technically it is but a broadening of radio's use of the electromagnetic wave spectrum to broadcast picture and sound simultaneously on several successive frequencies called channels. However, like so many technical developments, its many practical uses and sociological ramifications had to be worked out of necessity after the invention itself became a reality. Social scientists and students of broadcasting find themselves in much the same position as Thoreau was when considering the telegraph. He questioned the wisdom of erecting telegraph lines to Texas before it was decided what to say to Texans! Similarly we find today that we possess this instantaneous means of communication with millions within the privacy of their homes, yet we really don't have a perfectly clear idea of what we want to say to them. That is, we don't fully understand the sociological, political, economic, moral, and personal implications of television. Indeed, what is worse, problems of this nature have already arisen that defy solution. Television has developed so quickly out of our fast-moving technological and electronic revolution, and we have become so thrilled by its miracle of instantaneous communication with people and events around the globe, that we are like children who are playing with a new and fascinating toy. We simply have not had the opportunity to sit down and reflectively define its purpose and set its goals.

Critics of TV

Writers generally have hailed television as the great platform of free expression of opinion in a democratic society. However, some critics like Harry Skornia and Robert Lewis Shayon have felt that it has fallen into the hands of relatively few big business interests who have used it for anything but freedom of expression and have exploited it for financial profit.[1]

Other critics have hailed television as the great recorder of events in a revolutionary age, a major tool to bring people into contact with the reality of the social environment in which they live. However, Gary A. Steiner's research indicates clear evidence that, for many millions of viewers, it has become a major means of escape from reality: a way of cushioning life's shocks through television's world of fantasy, and a means of relaxing for hours on end in a dream world of beer and late movies.[2] More recent articles in the popular press would support this contention.

There is little doubt that, as a platform of political expression, television is unrivaled. By its emphasis on the close-up, it can convey the charisma of a John F. Kennedy or the unpolished soldier in a Dwight D. Eisenhower. There is nothing it misses, from the nervous gesture of a Menachem Begin to the heartwarming concern for peace of an Anwar Sadat as he stands before the Israeli parliament. Yet television, ironically, shows nothing of a political nature that is not controlled by the cameraman, the director, and ultimately by the television executive. Thus the answer to the question put to students twenty-five years ago by Kurt and Gladys Lang—"How much truth is there in the television picture?"—is determined "by the man who directs the camera in the parade welcoming General MacArthur."[3]

TV Idols and Heroes

With so much control centered in the hands of the relatively few gatekeepers, one might expect television, much like motion pictures, to produce a large number of idols and heroes. Yet it is in fact the most culturally iconoclastic of all the mass media. With the exception of the few great stars inherited from stage and screen, television on its own has produced very few really lasting heroes. Even its most popular shows are apt to be dropped after only a few seasons. Almost any one of the other media—newspapers, radio, comic books, motion pictures—is more enduring in its popular appeal. The taste of the television audience seems fickle and unsure of what it wants. Indeed the whole of the television industry would appear to operate on the premise that no show should last very long; that yesterday's successes may be tomorrow's failures; that the public wants something new, not necessarily good; and respect for the past is a fool's illusion.

Extent of TV

In the past thirty years, television has built a hall that holds almost 70 million families. There are now over 970 stations on the air in the United States. The National Association of Broadcasters expects the spectrum to soon close out with 1,000 stations: about 720 commercial and 280 public. The average family listens 5½ to 6½ hours per day; and grade schoolers listen an average of 20 hours a week. Over $3 billion represents the investment of Americans in television receivers, as compared with more than $1 billion in transmitters and equipment owned by the industry. The average hour-long dramatic show costs about $350,000 to produce, about $450,000 for air time; and a fifteen-minute news report on any of the three networks costs more than $75,000. The gross income of network television is about $3 billion to $4 billion a year, while the total volume of advertising sales on all television stations is in excess of $7 billion a year, with that amount increasing yearly by almost $1 billion. In not too many years, it is expected that television's advertising sales will surpass even those of newspapers, which now hold first place.[4]

A. William Bluem of the Newhouse Communications Center of Syracuse University has said:

> Television has become the great "either-or phenomenon" of modern society. It is either saint or sinner. It is either thought of as the direct path upward toward fulfillment of the individual within our free society, or it is thought of as the primrose path downward to the subtle social hall of "mass man" in a consumer *society*.[5]

In other words, people tend to think of television in extremes as either the all-good public servant or as manipulated by business interests for their own ends and to the detriment of society. Actually the realistic and honest view of television in the United States is that it is either a business or else it does not exist at all. If business does not support the huge cost of operating television, then there is no logic in even discussing such a question as, Are business and public service compatible?

Business interests have made possible both television and radio as we know them in the United States. Both came on the scene at the psychological moment to participate in and stimulate the growing American revolution in consumption. Hence it was quite natural that business would move in to take over both radio and television as effective tools of advertising. However, unlike newspapers, magazines, billboards, and other printed media, the use of television and radio for advertising constitutes the taking over of both the public domain and private property in order to reach the public. That is, the broadcast salesman does not hawk his wares as other vendors, but must use public airwaves, and receiving sets that are the private property of individuals.

Impact of TV

It must be remembered further that the very means that broadcasters use to reach their audiences—music, drama, narration, and news events—frequently take on the impact of rhetoric. They bring about an emotional impact upon their audiences far in excess of what is sometimes innocently referred to as mere entertainment. Commercials can be dramatic experiences involving audiences in an emotional identification with actors, stories, and products. By the power of suggestion, imitation, and other techniques of rhetorical persuasion, such commercials and the dramas of life that accompany them have a cumulative cultural impact that is enormous. This total cultural content of television and its social effect as a communications medium lend to it an importance that trenscends its economic usefulness. That is, broadcasting may not be the biggest business in terms of the advertising dollar, but it is definitely the most influential business in molding the minds of people. All thinkers today agree that it is one of the greatest single teachers of values, convictions, and attitudes.

Social Problems and TV

Thus television, as it operates in America today, has inherent in it some of the thorniest social problems. Because TV seems to be answerable only to the interests of big business, business frequently resorts to anything and everything that makes TV a more effective tool of commerce and looks upon the results as lily white and acceptable to society. The industry's plea sounds so plausible—"We're giving them what they want"—as attested to by the rating points and audience share published every two weeks by Nielsen. "What they want" may reek of violence and filth, but that seems of little concern. Since by law the content of television may not be precensored (just so it falls slightly short of explicit pornography or killings in cold blood), who is there to even mention the word *obscene* or *objectionable?*

To sum up what some consider the central problem of broadcasting in America today, I quote David M. Potter:

> The most important effects of this powerful institution [advertising] are not upon the economics of our distributive system; they are upon the values of our society. If the economic effect is to make the purchaser like what he buys, the social effect is, in a parallel but broader sense, to make the individual like what he gets—to enforce already existing attitudes, to diminish the range and variety of choices, and in terms of abundance, to exalt the materialistic virtues of consumption.[6]

Inadequate Feedback

Critics like Nicholas Johnson, formerly of the Federal Communications Commission, have pointed out that a particular social problem exists in America because the mass media speak in only one direction—that is, towards the audience in a kind of monolog.[7] This is true to the extent that the audience is unable to respond at the precise moment of an actual broadcast. However, it is false to conclude that the American people have no dialog whatever with broadcasters. I propose that one of the most revealing ways to consider television is precisely as a medium of communication wherein both the broadcaster speaks to the public, and the public in turn speaks back to the broadcaster. In this connection Norbert Wiener, when speaking about communication systems, states: "Feedback is the control of a system by reinserting into the system the result of its performance."[8]

Most critics agree that television today sorely needs the involvement of people who take time to think about what is happening each day in politics, social affairs and other vital areas.

What Type of Feedback?

It might be asked, How precisely does the general public feed back to the broadcaster? Though people do not respond effectively as isolated individuals or private citizens, they can respond collectively as voters who favor or oppose a given political issue, the pros and cons of which have been presented over the broadcast media. Further, as members of sociological groups representing business, government, education, religion, and the arts, the public is able to, and actually does, shape the messages of television, film, and radio. However, it must be noted that, of all the different ways that television audiences are able to feed back and shape the messages they receive, none is more effective than what is called commercial feedback—what products people buy at the store.

It is an easy criticism to assert that American television and radio are overly commercialized. Such a statement overlooks the fact that the commercial thrust is precisely what has made the broadcast media the strong influence in American life that they are. In 1967, Thomas W. Moore, president of the American Broadcasting Company (Television), expressed himself pointedly at a dinner in New York on this subject. We were discussing "The Lawrence Welk Show," and he said:

> Lawrence Welk just sent me a profuse letter of thanks because we renewed his contract. I appreciate the good relations this letter engenders in our office staff because he is the only one of our performers who does this. However, as much as we think of Lawrence personally, once Geritol and a few other products we advertise on his show decline in sales, that will be the end of "The Lawrence Welk Show."

Here was a brutally frank admission from a prominent

television executive of how slavishly dependent his entire network's operation is on the advertiser's dollar—and in turn on the sales dollar. One's first reaction might be to rebel against such a situation, saying it should not exist; but it would be unrealistic to say that it does not and will not exist as long as our mass media operate the way they do. And so, you might ask, Does the commercial public talk back to "The Lawrence Welk Show"—or any other television show? Most emphatically, yes—by what they buy in their stores.

Thus, both critics and research scholars are in agreement that improved social effects will be realized in proportion to the actual feedback that television achieves from its audience. It is precisely in this area of serving its audience and listening to feedback that the Welk Show stands as an outstanding example to the television industry today. *More specifically, this means that Welk has unwittingly set up guidelines for the industry, which logically grow out of this study.* I shall attempt in the following pages to specify eight of these guidelines for a successful television operation.

Guideline 1: Present a Solidly Salable Business Package

Welk has always stood for the principle that there is more than one way to put on a successful show. Hollywood's way would not necessarily be his way, nor would his way necessarily be the best. But it would definitely be *his* way. He knew from fifty years' experience in show business that he had a workable formula that pleased a sizable segment of the American public. Nobody could tell him differently.

Note what Don Fedderson said in chapter 4: "His was one of the first organizations to offer a tried and tested show to American network television." Welk started in a small way by applying for bookings at the Aragon ballroom in Santa Monica, California, where a local television station originated live, late-evening shows. He surrounded himself with influential men who were as convinced as he was of the show's worth. At first he had only himself and Sam Lutz. After his first shows succeeded on local television, the number of backers began to grow. It included Bert Carter, Jack Minor, and Don Fedderson. Now he had a sales team that had its foot in the door of an agency, a likely sponsor, and a new network. His production costs were so small that hardly any sponsor could turn him down. His first shows cost Dodge the ridiculously low figure of $12,000. Furthermore his record of selling Dodges in southern California had been so phenomenal over a three-year period that the local dealers solidly supported the idea of a national sponsorship. Despite opposition from the network, the agency, and the Chrysler officials in Detroit, the show was given a summer replacement period solely on the basis of Welk's ability to sell Dodges. ABC was a new network that needed shows, and Welk was able to offer it a well-established production that had done well on local television. His timing was just right, his salesmanship excellent, the cost unbelievably low; and so the network took the show. This is known as a *solidly salable business package.* To this day his sponsors (note chapter 5) consider his show one of the best buys on television.

Guideline 2: Remember That One's First Obligation to the Sponsor Is to Please the Audience

On network TV, Welk was as totally engrossed in his responsibility of selling Dodges as he had been on KTLA. He clearly understood his obligations to his sponsor. He took his show to almost every major city under the sponsorship of the local Dodge dealers. The early commercials on his show began to identify the program with Dodge cars. People went into Dodge dealers everywhere just to receive a free picture of the Welk band.

He began intensifying his personal contacts with his vastly expanded audience. His card file, which he had begun a few years earlier, was now holding upwards of 300,000 names of loyal fans. Each writer to the show received an answer. Personal appearances around the country only strengthened the loyalty of his audience. He began encouraging listeners to write and express their preferences for songs, singers, types of shows, and band selections (cf. chapter 6). Mail kept coming in at the rate of 1,000 or more letters a week. Gradually the production of the show became more attuned to the tastes of the audience.

All during these early days of network broadcasting (1955–58), Welk took pains to improve every possible facet of his program—the musicians, the singers, the dancers, and the production technique. Yet he was careful not to allow costs to mount to the point where his show would become too expensive for the sponsor.

Guideline 3: Adopt a Simple Format; Keep Improving It Within Its Own Confines; and Never Play Your Performers Beyond Their Capabilities

Early in his career Welk adopted a musical-variety style and a format within which he could bring out the best his performers were able to produce. Note in chapter 3 how he was unwilling to conform to Hollywood ideas of using a chorus line and guest stars. However, within his own format, he always improved his show. He was careful not to branch out into too elaborate or too difficult a production, so that no individuals were compelled to perform above their own capabilities. That is, they were given only the special types of songs and dancing they could do best. Note what Don Fedderson said in chapter 5: "It's not so much the individual performer who goes over, but the combination as it is served. . . . Its very simplicity is such a large factor in the total success of the show."

Welk has always known how to bring out only the best in his performers, showing the camera only their best styles, their best singing combinations. His choice of talent is worthy of note. He tries to pick only those performers with whom average Americans in their homes can relate, not theatrical-looking people. He often hires performers who have only one talent to offer, though he has certainly never discouraged people who may be able to develop a combination of abilities (cf. chapter 4).

Further, Welk's choice of musical selections centers around those that people know and love—the time-tested, all-around popular songs, whether old or contemporary, that have proved themselves to be top favorites. He never rejects any one type of music but works on the principle that the good and the bad exist within each type. He plays all types of music, even rock 'n' roll, but with unusual finesse and simplicity. He never plays long selections but limits them to about two minutes, so that if a viewer should find any particular number distasteful, within a short time the next selection would please him (cf. interview with George Cates, chapter 4).

Guideline 4: Instill Confidence in Your Performers, Sponsor, and Network by Establishing a Smoothly Functioning Business Operation

A smoothly functioning business operation has been at the bottom of the entire Welk Show for the past twenty-eight years. It has instilled confidence in his employees and has resulted in a nucleus of thirty-five or more people who have worked for him for more than twenty-five years (cf. chapter 3). Through his profit-sharing plan, he has given each person strong incentive to build up a cash reserve for retirement. The same pay scale is given to all of his musicians and performers—AFM and AFTRA union scale—so that no one feels either slighted or privileged. Fringe benefits for everyone are made available. These include the opportunities of outside appearances, recordings, and a three-week vacation for the entire family while band members perform at Harrah's Club in Lake Tahoe.

Welk's own careful business management has had a powerful influence upon his sponsors. They are convinced that he delivers more for their advertising dollar than most television shows (cf. chapter 5).

Guideline 5: Do Not Neglect Day-to-Day Personal Dedication to Running the Organization

The personality of Lawrence Welk himself, more than any other single influence, is responsible for the organizational functioning of his more than 150 employees, his scores of associates, and his millions of listeners. It is all done by Welk on a person-to-person basis right from his office, from his home, or his Country Club Estates where everyone has access to him. He keeps in touch with his vast audience through letters, stage appearances, personal conversations, and especially through his weekly television program. The interviews cited in chapters 3, 4, and 5 point to his power over people. He fondly refers to his band and performers, as well as all who work for him, as his "musical family." He has worked incessantly for over fifty years to build personal loyalty to himself, for he believes deeply and honestly that he depends upon these people and cannot do his job by himself. Naturally some degree of failure is found, as in every human organization. Yet the overwhelming evidence, as presented in this study, proves that under Welk's personal guidance and inspiration hundreds of people work together as a closely knit, smoothly operating organization to produce a highly successful television show.

Guideline 6: Set Up a Systematic Dialog with As Many Different Segments of Audience as Possible

Welk's aim of always playing to the wishes of his audience has been repeatedly emphasized in this book. However, he does much more. One of the most remarkable programs of audience participation ever carried on by a broadcasting organization has established a true dialog with his millions of listeners (cf. chapter 6 for details). Basically it consists of a careful tabulation of every letter received at his office for favorable or unfavorable comments on performers, particular shows, or songs. If letters unfavorable to any performer persist, they indicate that he or she should not continue on the show. Favorable letters, on the other hand, have established almost all of Welk's performers as permanent members of the show. Welk always holds to the principle of trying a performer temporarily in order to receive sufficient audience reaction before he or she receives a permanent place on the show. Such audience response has done much to upgrade the show by stimulating performers to study their instrument or skill. Further, the strong tie-in with the audience has not only made the viewers the judges of whether he will retain a performer; in many cases he has considered new talent at the suggestion of listeners.

There are other segments of audience with which Welk keeps in close contact. He meets and personally speaks with his studio audience before each dress rehearsal and final taping on Tuesday evenings at CBS Television City. Also, he meets an average of seventy-five or more live audiences each year in auditoriums around the United States and Canada, playing to almost 500,000 people. He has frequently stated that his principal reason for traveling with his show is to determine by personal contact what the preferences of these people are.

While Welk has always been concerned over his Nielsen and ARB ratings, he has been able to do comparatively little to influence them directly. However, he has succeeded in indirectly influencing them by carefully improving the show and promoting those direct contacts with his audience that were discussed in chapter 6.

Guideline 7: Become So Identified with the Product You Sell That You Really Believe in It Yourself

Chapter 5 has pointed out how Welk identifies himself with the products he sells. Everyone who watches the program can tell you immediately who its sponsors are. Perhaps no one in the television world has taken such personal pains to know and use the products advertised on his or her show. Welk is most concerned over who his sponsors are, whether their products do what they are purported to do, and whether they create a suitable image for his show. The time allotted to commercials in his show is about average—nine minutes of total commercial time for the hour. While Welk has little direct control over the actual content of the commercials, he has appeared in some of them himself and has arranged for other members of his cast to actively participate in the commercials. Furthermore he has strong suasive influence if he thinks any are in poor taste or misrepresent the product. One of Welk's strongest appeals to his sponsors over the years has been the way he personally "plugs" a product immediately after the commercial with a few words of recommendation. In this way he so identifies himself with the product advertised that he lays his own credibility right on the line in behalf of the sponsor and the product. Thus when he tells his audience to try Triscuits or Sominex or Geritol or whatever product it happens to be, it means that he endorses it personally and believes that it is a quality item.

Guideline 8: Choose the Kind of Talent the Audience Can Relate to Through Fantasy Identification and Nostalgic Images

Erik Barnouw proposed a theory of how mass media audiences identify with the personalities they see on television and thus establish a true communication cycle. This theory is verified in the case of "The Lawrence Welk Show" and is largely at the root of its success in establishing its long-standing, faithful audience. Anyone who watches the show will agree that a quality of dreamlike perfection pervades the entire production. The women are pretty, pleasant, ladylike, and apparently ageless! The men are all attractive and gentlemanly. The lighting is bright and clean, and there are no depressing colors. The costuming follows the same light, bright, feminine, flowing look for the girls; and a clean-cut, well-fitted look for the men. Yet the most obvious emotion generated by the show is that an almost perfect family is gathered here, one in which each member performs to the encouragement and applause of the others, without the slightest undercurrent of jealousy or ill will. Welk himself is, of course, the central figure of the group. He creates the biggest fantasy image of all. He is many things to many viewers—a father image to some, a big brother to others, a loving friend to many; but most of all he is a strong, supportive figure, one with whom listeners can identify and a man they can respect and admire (cf. Don Fedderson's interview, chapter 4).

A preliminary of psychological identification is that people recognize something of themselves in a character they see in the mass media, as though they were gazing into a mirror. This is particularly true of those qualities they most secretly admire in themselves—their struggles and ambitions, their loves and conquests. When an audience—individually—is able to identify with a performer, imagination soars into endless fanciful images of how manly, how lovable, how full of joy and happiness this person's character is regardless of how unrealistic these images may become. We are told by psychologists that children especially need to indulge in fanciful release to compensate for their repressions. However, adults are also said to be in need of this kind of emotional release.

Welk's winsome smile, his handsome appearance, and his quality of humanness—which seem to go out in a kind of embrace of his audience—are the best inducements any audience could have to identify. They see him as they would like to see themselves—as a boy from the farm who could not speak English until he was twenty-one years old; or as one who had little formal training or education, yet made a success of himself in at least three or four areas. They become comfortably at ease with him because they see him as part of themselves, at least in their fanciful imagination. Further, Welk represents for many Americans a kind of folk-hero image in an age when heroes are scarce. He personifies the good qualities most people would wish to have themselves— moral steadfastness, honesty, truthfulness, patriotism, respect for God and religion, dedication to loved ones, hard work, help for others who are struggling, and a deep human sense of compassion and lightheartedness. These qualities are ideals that represent the loftiest goals in people's minds. Remarkably, they can find them verified in Lawrence Welk, at least enough so that their imaginations can supply through fantasy all that their emotional needs require.

Fan Magazines

The aura of fantasy that surrounds the Welk television show carries over into still another field, that of the fan magazine. Here he is one of the leading personalities. Doubtless this area of popular journalism is not given much serious attention by scholars because it so often deals with pure sensationalism. Yet, quite contrary to their own wishes, Lawrence Welk and his performers have been deluged by requests from fan magazines to include their pictures and stories in these publications.

This form of journalism is admittedly unreliable because it capitalizes upon the lowest forms of salacious gossip and insinuation; yet it has a surprising impact upon our culture and is a barometer of how ridiculously fantasy identification can seize the minds of people. Its readers live in an unrealistic, fantasy world fed by gossip. Yet they become an imaginary part of the lives of the stars about whom they read.

Stage Appearances

A further example of this fantasy identification is evident when the band makes stage appearances around the country. Auditoriums are invariably packed to overflowing with ardent fans. I have personally observed this when traveling with the band, but particularly in Welk's restaurant at the Country Club Estates in Escondido, California. People flock around him for autographs and pictures. They compliment him lavishly, and they hold his hand and thank him for bringing his show into their homes each week. I have observed how gracious he is, but also how perceptive of the dreams and hopes he is able to fulfill by saying a few friendly words. He has confided to me that he is grateful for this praise and admiration because he experienced none of it during the first half of his musical career. No one more than Welk could realize how hypocritical it would be for him to think he deserves it. Yet because he himself lived with long dreams for many years, he instinctively recognizes the power of the fantasy images of entertainers that people dream up in their minds.

Another aspect of the Welk Show's fantasy image is that it recalls a time that in retrospect seems gentler and sweeter than today. It is proverbial in show business that nostalgia plays a major role in psychological identification. Welk is today almost the lone survivor of the great bands of the 1930s and 1940s. In the medium of television he is in fact alone. People who danced to his music and heard his faltering English during the big-band era find themselves swept by memories whenever they hear him, and they recall with nostalgia those years at the Edgewater Beach Hotel, the Aragon and Trianon ballrooms in Chicago, the William Penn Hotel in Pittsburgh, and the Roosevelt in New Orleans. They were loyal followers in Saint Paul, Denver, Dallas, Saint Louis, Milwaukee, and a hundred other smaller cities in the heartland of America. Invariably someone will stand up before the show at the CBS studios in Hollywood and tell Welk they remember him from a particular city back in the Midwest. No doubt the nostalgic urge of days gone by creates a fantasy identification with Lawrence Welk in the minds of millions today (cf. chapter 4, interviews with Don Fedderson, George Cates, and Curt Ramsey) .

Other Reasons for Welk's TV Success

Welk Perpetuates the Big-Band Sound

The climax of what TV has learned from Welk can be stated briefly: He has perpetuated the big-band sound for millions of Americans today. His critics agree that he does not have the characteristic sound of some of his great contemporaries—Ellington, Dorsey, Lombardo, or King. He never really developed his own unique style or characteristic sound, though he has successfully imitated every one of them. Still he has probably enjoyed more popularity with American audiences than any of the so-called greats of the big-band era. Speaking recently on the demise of the big bands, Welk said:

> The sad fact is that the big-name bands have almost all fallen apart. I knew many of these bandleaders back in the thirties and forties, and I used to ask them, "How was your attendance last week?" They would brag about how many people came to hear them; then I would ask, "How was your band received?" Invariably they would say: "Mr. Welk, those people were eating out of the palm of our hand. They loved us." Well, I repeated these questions to so many of the big bandleaders that it was almost like a game with me. Remarkably, none of them ever told me they couldn't figure out why people *didn't* like them nor why they weren't invited back to the same place. Now one of the big reasons these big name bands aren't around any more is that all too often they went on the assumption that the people loved what they played, but they seldom ever made a study of their faults—for example, why everyone started leaving the place at ten o'clock. In other words, they just weren't critical enough of their own shortcomings.
>
> There used to be such intense rivalry among those great bands of the thirties. Each band strove to outdo the other in originality, excellence of musicianship, outstanding soloists, precision, rhythm, and enthusiasm. They worked tirelessly

to perfect their performances, would usually rehearse on their own time often without pay. Of course union rules then were not as stringent as they are today. Now these bands all had one thing in common—the urge to excel, to be the best in their field. The idea of monetary reward was frequently only incidental to their high motivation. In fact I can remember some great musicians who were willing to take a salary cut just to play with a band they considered musically superior.

Among those early name bands the most famous were: Paul Whiteman who gained fame as "King of Jazz" and "Dean of Modern American Music." There was the West Coast band of Art Hickman; Isham Jones and his orchestra were renowned for a wonderful ensemble sound; Ted Weems was noted for his fine arrangements; Hal Kemp was famed for the machinelike precision of the brass section; Wayne King, who gained notoriety as "Waltz King"; Duke Ellington, whose compositions and arrangements have made him a jazz legend; and let's not forget the family band that crossed Lake Erie from Canada to Cleveland in 1927 and became one of the most famous and successful musical organizations of all time, Guy Lombardo and his Royal Canadians. When I first heard Lombardo I really did think it was the "sweetest music this side of heaven." Yes, I might as well confess that I have borrowed something from almost every one of these great bands.

When asked to pinpoint some additional factors that contributed to the fall of the big bands, Welk replied:

Somewhere along the way something happened to this vast and wonderful business in America. The exact date is hard to say, but it appears to have been some time in the fifties. It is attributable to several factors: television, the change in our living habits, new musical tastes especially on the part of the young, and of course the resulting generation gap in musical appreciation. However, I believe there are probably some deeper causes like the growing tendency of bands to "do your own thing." They became more inter-

ested in playing for themselves than for their audiences. But
of all the elements that have hurt our business and caused
the decline of the big bands, there was a change in attitude
on the part of musicians themselves brought about by re-
strictive measures imposed by unions.

Sadly because of increased emphasis upon wages, en-
forced payments for less and less work (in some cases, for *no*
work at all), unions have practically eliminated that wonderful quality of initiative, that striving for excellence, and the
spirit of rivalry which was so dominant in the big-band
era. Even rehearsals are discouraged by the prohibitive
hourly wages imposed by the unions. It is impossible to instill in an organization that enthusiasm so necessary for a
great band when the main consideration has become "what's
in it for me?"[9]

Welk's Unique Contribution to Music

Ironically, though, Welk stands exactly 180 degrees opposite the great bandleaders of the past in the unique contribution he has made through the medium of television to
the musical entertainment of America. His business acumen
and personality have enabled him to use this challenging
medium, as no other bandleader, for the economic advantage
of everyone involved. Sociologists agree that music, with all
of its economic potential, does in fact generate large amounts
of money. The problem has been that a comparatively small
percentage of the money is ever channeled back for the
benefit of composers and musicians. Today popular music
shows and festivals, light operas and symphonies seldom
function without outside support from patrons. As a result,
the music profession is probably at its lowest economic level
in a hundred years.

Out of this economic wasteland of music and musicians
emerged a figure who made a unique contribution to his
field. He turned music making, musicians, singers, dancers,
records, and even music publishing into one of the most

successful television operations in America today. Of all the big bandleaders, Welk has been almost alone, not only in making a successful financial organization for himself, but in probably doing more directly for music and musicians than any other employer in Los Angeles (cf. chapter 7). He bought fifty-eight smaller music publishing firms and amalgamated them as the T. B. Harms Company. He developed them into such lucrative enterprises that he is considered among the top few music publishers in point of volume of royalties received and paid to composers. Though Welk employs scarely more than 150 people within his organization, his far-reaching influence extends to the whole of the entertainment and television industries. Tens of millions of dollars in business are stimulated each year just by the advertising carried by his show. Sellouts of the personal appearances of his band in cities throughout the United States and Canada over the past twenty-five years have astonished show business critics, as evidenced by the articles that appear regularly in *Billboard* and *Variety*. Decca-Coral record releases from 1949 to 1959 amounted to $25 million in sales; and the Dot-Ranwood releases up to the present more than tripled that figure (cf. chapter 9). Welk's California real estate investments have been in excess of $30 million. The Hollywood Chamber of Commerce has repeatedly published the fact that the greatest personal attraction for tourists to the entertainment capital is Lawrence Welk.

Welk operates his business affairs and his entire organization with a personal regard for his employees but has a firm hand against anyone who tries to dictate to him what he should do. He believes in free enterprise; but unlike so many who profess to believe in it, he also practices it with a sense of responsibility toward those whose services he uses. Though he is unable to say exactly what his holdings are or how much he is worth, one thing is certain—almost every dollar he controls is at work in some way to benefit thousands of people besides himself.

Summary

And now a final look into the question of why Lawrence Welk—above all the big-name bands of a bygone day—has succeeded through the medium of television. As a shrewd merchant, he deals with music and musicians as his stock-in-trade. Though always sensitive to their human dignity, he understands that the business success of his organization depends upon the cooperative efforts of many artistic and talented performers. He readily accords them due praise and encouragement. He does not hesitate to hire an Al Hirt, a Myron Floren, or a Pete Fountain, any one of whom is a more talented musician than himself. He has always recognized that highly talented people help the business interests of his organization. Indeed, discovering new talent is precisely his forte. He prides himself whenever he discovers promising talent because he knows it is an important commodity for his business. He even uses his own personality as a business commodity. For example, he recognizes how people relate to his Horatio Alger story of an American who struggled against difficult odds to achieve ultimate success. He stresses these personal characteristics because they have commercial value for his business. His principal aim is to please his customer, the audience.

It is precisely Welk's business approach to television that constitutes his unique contribution to that medium. Many another entrepreneur has made millions by capitalizing on the talents of composers, musicians, and performers. But in most cases, the stronger the power of the entrepreneur, the worse the plight of the rank and file of musicians and entertainers. There are relatively few like Welk—and none like him on television—who have been dedicated for so many years to combining both personality and business ability in an organization to benefit, not only himself, but every member within the organization and even thousands outside of it. In the years to come, television may well offer a competitive bandstand for other musical variety shows, but it may be hoped that the industry will have learned something from the guidelines established by Welk over the years 1955 to the present.

9
Welk's Wealth

Where It's Going

When furnishing material for this chapter on Welk's financial and business interests, Ted R. Lennon, executive vice-president of Teleklew Productions, Inc., opened our meeting with a startling comment:

There is a fact that few people are aware of or would believe. Lawrence, you know, has never worked for money, nor does he have much concern today over how much he is making. This has been a fact of his life. Of course, like many people, there was a time he had to be concerned about making ends meet. For years he divided everything equally with everybody, and he always took the lion's share of heavy jobs like carrying the instruments for the band and setting up the music. He even carried the cost of running his bus during those early years with the orchestra. In more recent times I remember so often how he became concerned when we went too deeply into investments; for instance, the recent Escondido expansion project we just started. He went down there the other day and saw all that grading going on for the new mobile units and other buildings. It even frightened me, because I never dreamed while processing all of this that it would be so gigantic an operation. Lawrence only reflected my own concern and asked me whether we were going in too deeply. I assured him I had gone over the cash flow carefully, that we could stand it comfortably, and that we were acting superconservatively. "We'll have no debt for the corporation," I assured him. "Yes, I know, but I guess this appears to be more than we can stand," he said. I didn't blame him for his concern over not going into debt, since his policy has always been to pay cash for everything, and he has a right to insist upon it. You see, it is very difficult for him to comprehend the extent of his assets, as well as their solidarity, and even their liquidity! It's my job to try and keep the corporation afloat and still maintain the policies which Lawrence has always insisted upon.[1]

Background and Present Holdings

The corporate title of the organization that controls all of Welk's financial and business interests in Teleklew Productions, Incorporated. *Tele* is short for television, and *klew* is Welk spelled backwards.

The organization was formed and incorporated in 1956, the year after Welk began to broadcast on national television and the year he began a second network show on ABC entitled "Top Tunes and New Talent." It was a turning point in the financial career of Lawrence Welk. Edward Spaulding became the first executive vice-president in charge of all his business interests including the television show, but stage appearances remained under the care of his personal manager, Sam J. Lutz.

In 1957 Welk acquired his first major publishing firm, that of the noted composer Harry Von Tilzer. With this purchase he became the owner of many copyrights of hit tunes, which were a source of income for the new corporation. Previously he owned only one small publishing company, Champagne Music Corporation, which he founded himself and built up with the help of several associates who contributed new compositions and arrangements of old songs.

In 1958 Welk acquired the property upon which he later built a six-story office building. It is an eighty-foot frontage on Wilshire Boulevard and is located on the southeast corner of Chelsea Avenue and Wilshire Boulevard in Santa Monica. The building, named the Lawrence Welk–Union Bank Building, was originally planned as a much smaller structure to simply house his own offices. However, through a friend, Bert W. Martin, Welk was able to contract for the tenancy of the first two floors by the Union Bank of Los Angeles. Though the actual transaction was delayed for over a year, ground was finally broken in September, 1960, and the structure was completed late in 1961.

During these same negotiations in 1958 and 1959 with the Union Bank, Welk purchased as an additional real estate investment the southeast corner of Wilshire and Ocean Boulevards in Santa Monica, overlooking the Pacific Ocean. On this property were located a service station and an apartment building. Today it is the site of a new, twenty-one–story office building and a sixteen-story luxury apartment, which are known jointly as the Lawrence Welk Plaza.

Music Publishing

In 1963 Welk purchased another major music publishing company, Vogue Music, Incorporated. This enabled him to control many of the hit tunes that were licensed through Broadcast Music, Incorporated. By now he has gathered together a total of fifty-eight smaller publishing firms. He discovered as a user of music that the music publishing business was a beneficial adjunct to his investment portfolio. Each time he broadcasts one of his own songs, he receives royalties from either the American Society of Composers, Authors, and Publishers (ASCAP) or Broadcast Music, Incorporated (BMI), the two principal licensing societies in the United States, averaging $300 to $400 per broadcast. This money is derived from the high license fees paid to ASCAP and BMI each year by both networks and individual stations. In addition, of course, to his own use of the many songs owned by his companies, he receives royalties from other shows using these songs. Some of the companies have increased their value as much as 200 percent as a result of income generated from hit songs. Finally in 1970 Teleklew bought one of the larger music publishing companies in the United States, the T. B. Harms Company, for $3.2 million. This purchase made Teleklew Productions the largest controller of music publishing firms outside of New York. Much contemporary music as well as hundreds of all-time popular songs from years back are now owned by Teleklew. In the T. B. Harms collection there are 4,600 songs ranging from "Look for the Silver Lining" to "Going Out of My Head" and all the other Jerome Kern and Rodgers and Hammerstein compositions that are still under copyright.

While about half the income of these companies comes from performance royalties, no small amount is derived from the mechanical reproduction of these thousands of songs on records and tapes. For each individual recording, $2\frac{3}{4}$¢ is paid to the copyright holder. This sum can mount so high that, when the company has a hit tune like "Blue Velvet," its royalties alone will pay for the original cost of the whole company.

All the copyrights owned by Teleklew Productions have now been amalgamated under one name: T. B. Harms Company (DBA The Welk Music Group). This company is a wholly owned subsidiary of Teleklew Productions.

Real Estate Holdings in Escondido, California

An additional large real estate holding of Lawrence Welk is in Escondido, California, about thirty miles northeast of San Diego. On this 877-acre tract is situated the Lawrence Welk Country Club Estates. There are 204 mobile home spaces, all occupied; an eighteen-hole golf course; a 670-seat restaurant with banquet facilities, and a forty-four–unit motel. This is where the first color films of "The Lawrence

Welk Show" were shot in 1965 to inaugurate his new series of color programs that fall on ABC. The property has largely served as a retreat for Welk and his friends who wish to get away from the city for a while.

Welk planned his Country Club Estates as an enjoyable and luxurious environment for his fans who wanted to retire there; for many years profit was not his primary motivation. However, he always considered it a good public relations investment, and the retired people who make their homes there are a source of moral support for him. He has built a beautiful coach house for himself where he spends a few days each month. But Welk does envision the Country Club Estates as an ideal location to videotape outdoor segments for his television show.

Present expansion plans at Escondido call for the construction of an additional 253 mobile home spaces, forty-eight more motel units, a new recreation building, and about twenty thousand square feet of commercial space, which will include a theater-museum in which visitors will be shown a film depicting highlights of Welk's career in the music and broadcasting business. A shopping mall will adjoin the theater-museum to provide for the needs of both residents and visitors. A further Phase II of this development will be a full-size golf course and 300 condominiums. At this writing zoning approval for this latter phase is being sought, and it will not be under construction for a year or more.

Paul Ryan, manager of Welk's Country Club Estates restaurant, commented upon the phenomenal success of this business venture, which attracts an average of 1,500 people a day.

It's a combination of factors that accounts for its success. Lawrence is very well known throughout the country through his weekly television show. His name is our biggest drawing card. Secondly, good food is a big attraction. In addition, our people try to attend to the needs of the people who come here. You see, people who come here really feel

like Lawrence is a personal friend, like their brother or
father. They have seen him on television every week for so
many years that they feel they are a part of him. The first
question they ask is: "Where is Lawrence? We've come to see
him." Everyone feels they know him well even if they've
actually never seen him in person. Of course it is impossible
for him to be here to speak to all of these thirty-five or forty
thousand people we serve in a month's time, but we try to
please them in such a way as to represent Lawrence as well
as we can with his fans. It's a reflection on him if they're not
taken care of, so we try to go out of our way to do everything
possible to make them feel at home. One of the remarkable
facts we experience all the time is how people from out of
town who haven't been to San Diego for years say this is the
first place they come. We find that about 60 percent of our
business is repeat customers who have been here before, have
liked the place, and perhaps bring relatives or friends to
eat with us.

Our whole operation here is just like Lawrence's show, a
family operation. He has done very well by all of us, and as
a result we want to make the place go well for his sake. If it
takes sixteen or eighteen hours a day to do it, we are here,
because we're dedicated to the task of making it a success.

Even though we're forty miles from San Diego, very few
places like ours can enjoy the national publicity we've
received over the years. Lawrence originated some of his
early color shows right here, and he has had a training
program which began here with people like Anacani, Tom
Netherton, the Otwell twins, and the Aldridge Sisters. People
hear about Lawrence Welk's Country Club Estates when they
listen to the show because he frequently mentions it when
referring to these young performers who got their start enter-
taining right here in our dining room.[2]

Financial Statement

The following figure for the year beginning July 1, 1977,
and ending June 30, 1978, gives about as clear a picture of

Teleklew Productions' financial status as is possible in these pages.

Consolidated gross revenue generated
through fiscal 1978 .... $15,000,000

Financial Return from Recordings

The retail sales volume of records made by Teleklew Productions for Decca-Coral Records from 1949 to 1959, for 35 album releases, amounted to $25 million; and the retail sales volume for the period 1960 to 1970, under the Dot-Ranwood label, amounted to $50 million, with 127 album releases. The Ranwood label from 1970 to 1980 will net in the area of $35 million. Only a fraction of these figures (total not available) would accrue to Teleklew Productions.

Profit Sharing Plan

In order to provide more stability for the members of his organization, Welk has established an Employees' Profit Sharing and Retirement Plan. All employees who qualify become eligible for participation in the plan after one year. The company agrees to contribute to this trust fund for its employees not less than 5 percent of its net earnings and such additional amounts as its board of directors may determine, but not to exceed 15 percent of compensation paid to all participants. Contributions under the plan are made in cash to the trustees and then invested to bring a fair return for participants.

A portion of such contributions made on behalf of each participant will be invested in ordinary life insurance policies to provide life insurance protection prior to retirement. These policies can be converted to annuity contracts just prior to retirement. The fund is to be used only in the event of the termination, retirement, death, or total disability of a participant. Each participant receives a share of the company's contribution based on the proportion his compensation bears to the total compensation of all participants for that year. The normal retirement age is sixty-five, or twenty years' service, whichever occurs first. However, if the company desires to continue a participant in active service, and the participant consents, he will continue to take part in the plan until actual retirement. When a participant reaches retirement age and retires, he will be paid 100 percent of the value of his account in the trust fund in accordance with the plan and trust agreement and under one of the following options, as determined by the Committee: (1) a lump sum payment; or (2) purchase of a paid-up annuity contract, providing for fixed installment payments for the joint lifetime of himself and his spouse; or (3) equal annual installment payments for five years. In the event of death, his beneficiary is entitled to be paid the amount of his account as it appears in the trust fund within thirty days of his death. Or if he becomes totally disabled he will receive 100 percent of the value of his account, payable under any one of the three options above. If he should terminate or be dismissed, he shall receive a 10 percent interest on his account balance for each year of participation up to 100 percent of his vested interest —i.e., ten years, 100 percent. Each participant receives an annual statement, showing his share of the trust in detail, as of the thirtieth day of June each year.

This profit-sharing plan for employees of Teleklew Productions has been in operation since 1957, and the average performer who has been in Lawrence Welk's orchestra for ten to twenty years would have an account balance of $50,000 to $100,000, which continues to earn a substantial annual income for him.

The Lawrence Welk Foundation

The Lawrence Welk Foundation was established in 1958. The corporation has voted the maximum allowable contribution to the foundation in cash each year. This amounts to

5 percent of the net income before taxes, or about $150,000 annually. The actual annual contributions made by the foundation to various charities amount to about $170,000. Many more requests for charitable contributions are received than can possibly be covered by this figure. However, at the annual meeting of the directors of the foundation, those charities are chosen that are most closely in line with Lawrence Welk's work and interests. He has been especially generous to local charities in the Los Angeles area, with special emphasis upon cancer-related research. For example, Welk's chairmanship of the National Cancer Crusade for two successive years, plus his participation in the local Arthritis Telethon in Los Angeles for twenty-five successive years, are indications of his eagerness to personally raise money for these charitable causes. Reliable statements from both these organizations insist that Welk's wholehearted donation of time and effort has netted them unusually large amounts of money. Also, the Welk foundation gives to various music scholarship funds at universities and colleges, including North Dakota State University at Bismarck, North Dakota. Local boys' clubs and hospitals in the Los Angeles area have all been helped by the Welk foundation.

10
What Does
Tomorrow Hold?

Opinions of Welk's Top People

Nothing could be more dominant in the minds of everyone in the Welk organization—including Lawrence Welk himself —than, What does tomorrow hold? Welk expressed it this way:

> To some extent I am trying to stay in the background these days, hoping my people will learn the business and be able to carry on for another twenty years or so without me. Not everyone agrees with me in this matter, but in the past few months since I have worked with the orchestra from a distance I think it has gotten better. One reason is when the boss is around all the time they don't feel comfortable putting in their own ideas. Keep an eye on the next three shows before our season ends, and I really think we'll end up with a higher rating and a stronger, more loyal audience then we've ever had before. You see, people develop better when you give them more responsibility. If I am there to tell them what to do, they'll do it, but they don't learn as much as when they do it themselves.

The above remarks by Welk, it must be noted, did *not* refer to his being totally absent from the show, but only to his allowing the band to rehearse without him and plan each segment of the show on its own.

Welk's Remarks on the Future

A more pointed question I put to him recently was: "Lawrence, I'm sure you've given a lot of thought to this, but I suspect you haven't committed yourself as straightforwardly as I am going to ask you now. What do you honestly feel would happen to your band *today* if you were out of the picture?" Welk replied:

At the present time my band would fall apart. The good Lord willing, if I am allowed to live for a few years longer, that may be changed. By comparison with a year ago, my people are doing a 20 percent better job without my actually being there for rehearsals.[1]

Lutz's Opinion

Sam Lutz, Welk's personal manager, stated:

It's quite true that the Welk show is a one-man operation. It all starts with Lawrence, and he's the key to the whole show. Besides his being the motivation for all the performers, the audience too prefers to see Welk in evidence. True, it could go on without Lawrence, as other big bands have for a time. Myron Floren could conduct, and we could continue to bill it as the Lawrence Welk orchestra, which is in fact what it would be. But it wouldn't have the main attraction if Lawrence were out of the picture.

In all likelihood, there would be reruns of the Welk show. We own all the tapes which are in storage and I think they could be sold as an afternoon show if the regular TV production ceases.[2]

Hobson's Predictions

James Hobson, producer-director of the show, doesn't agree with Welk's thinking on preparing his people to take

over. On one occasion when speaking to Welk, Hobson insisted: "Lawrence, the production staff is perfectly capable
of putting on a good musical variety show, but without you
the magic is gone. You're what holds the thing together. Anyone can put on a good musical variety show, and there have
been many that have started since television began, but
they've gone off after a short time."

Hobson allows that he may be playing the bad guy, but
he holds to his opinion. "We may have an heir apparent in
Myron Floren," he continued, "but you're not going to have
the same show. Myron's instinctive input is not the same as
Lawrence's. He's second generation like all of us" (cf. chapter 4) .

Carter's Assurance for the Future

Perhaps the most thoughtful answer to our question on
what tomorrow holds was given by the one who was responsible for originally putting Welk on television, Bert Carter.

> As long as Welk is at the helm, I can see no reason why
> the show will ever fail to have the following it has today.
> Lawrence will tell you straightfaced that he has turned the
> whole show over to his production people, that he loves to
> get out and let the boys juggle it themselves. Well, that's a
> bit misleading. Actually he's on top of everything. The fu-
> ture of the show depends upon him. If anything happens to
> him, I fear what would happen to the show. He is presently
> in the pink of condition and is able to supervise everything
> that goes on—every song, every act. If he believes anything is
> a lttle off-key, he will immediately throw it out. As an ex-
> ample, consider George Cates who has been a pivot man in
> his highly responsible position of doing the musical arrange-
> ments. If you'll notice, Welk is gradually easing Cates out.
> There is less of Cates and I believe this is good for the show
> because the public relates more to Welk. Another example
> occurred a few years ago when the band played at the Holly-
> wood Palladium on Saturday nights. When eleven o'clock

came, Welk would disappear and go home. Myron Floren or whoever happened to be in charge would take over. The show immediately took a nose dive in audience interest. As long as Welk can keep up the pace he's now holding, the show will continue with the same excellence as always.[3]

One fact that becomes apparent from the above statements is that many of the people closest to Welk consider him so important in the operation of the show that, if he were not in an active role as its head, the television operation would soon come to a screeching halt. Welk only partially agrees. "At present my band would fall apart," he admitted. Strangely, he is determined to change that situation. When Welk is determined enough to do anything, he often accomplishes a miracle. It has been the story of his life to do what anyone else with half the odds against him would have given up on. This is but one more goal he has set for himself— at age seventy-seven. Few TV executives ever thought his "polka band" could ever make its way on television, even locally. Welk not only created a sensation with his local broadcasts on KTLA in Los Angeles but entered the national scene and became what his friends facetiously term "the longest-lasting summer replacement show ever to go on a national network." When the network dropped him after sixteen years, he still didn't give up. He established his own network, improved his ratings, and became the most widely distributed and most successful syndicated show on the air. Now at seventy-seven he would appear to be reaching out for immortality. Yet all evidence points toward one incontrovertible conclusion—while Welk is at the helm, the show will go on. That is *all* that can be said with any degree of certainty.

Does this mean that in the event of disabling sickness or death his whole life's career will be lost? Not in the least. Much can be said of his system—almost unique in show business—of hiring promising young people long before they reach maturity as performers, working with them, believing in them, encouraging and praising them until they become truly professional. He points out:

> I'm sure you're aware that instead of these people I could hire the most professional performers in Hollywood. I'd certainly have an excellent show, but it wouldn't be the same. You've seen those fine young people like Mary Lou Metzger who did the Wee Bonnie Baker number recently. There is no way I could find a professional to do such a number with the same naturalness, enthusiasm, and feeling. It's that kind of work and dedication that makes the difference in our show. Many made their first start here and the relationship is somewhat like a father with his children.[4]

Welk's System

Welk's system of building the careers of his own people, dealing with them as a father with his children and taking the time to help them on a person-to-person basis is so different from the impersonal way big business handles employees today that it makes him almost unique. In dollars and cents, Welk's system extends even to sharing his financial income with everyone in his organization. Of course, a profit-sharing system is not unique in business today; what is unusual is the extent to which Welk goes to let each employee understand that his or her work will be rewarded financially in proportion to effort—because the whole organization will profit. Welk states:

> It is the sharing with employees as persons that makes the working relationship familylike. While there is always a natural tendency to become stars or outshine someone else, it happens less in an atmosphere like ours. I've tried to teach our people this special kind of relationship based upon encouragement and freedom toward personal improvement. It requires self-discipline, mutual help, and concern. It definitely must be *taught* to people.

Encouraging Professional Excellence

Welk went on to explain:

> Some of our schools have tried to eliminate discipline from
> their programs of study, claiming it hinders children from
> growing. Ironically it ends up with the children becoming
> so out of control that the teachers can in no way communi-
> cate with them. While some unions are trying to get pay
> increases for their members, they neglect to emphasize the pro-
> fessional betterment and improved qualifications necessary
> to warrant a higher pay scale. They seem to encourage undue
> benefits and leisure, but seldom insist upon professional ex-
> cellence in their members. What I am trying to do is just
> the opposite. I try to persuade our people to do a better job
> and thus benefit by it. Also our flexible system allows them
> to share in all the profits. We encourage our people to
> moonlight through personal appearances around the country,
> which sometimes enables them to reap substantial benefits
> financially. Myron Floren is an example. I commented to
> him recently: "You're doing well with all your personal ap-
> pearances. You must be getting close to a quarter-million
> this year." He replied, "Oh no, Lawrence, it would be
> closer to half a million." This demonstrates my point that
> each person who freely improves himself has an almost un-
> limited chance to earn outside income.[5]

With all of this input from Welk, it brings us again to our
question, What does tomorrow hold? No doubt people will
be hearing the music of Lawrence Welk for many years to
come. His records and television replays will continue long
after the regular show has disappeared from the TV schedules. Obviously, though, what will be remembered will be
the character of the man who for more than three decades
made his imprint upon the hearts of Americans through his
weekly musical visit into millions of homes. People may
recall the "Musical Family" or the organization that made it

all possible. But they will remember much more vividly that it all stemmed from the genius of one man, a farm boy from North Dakota, who dared to accomplish what no other big band of his day could even attempt: to capture the greatest of all showcases—television—and in so doing, to capture the hearts of the American people.

Appendix

Awards, Trophies, Certificates, Medals
Presented to Lawrence Welk

1952/53   State of North Dakota
           Certificate of Pride
1952   City of Minneapolis
           Honorary Citizen
1952   California Federation of Music Clubs
           Outstanding Musical Achievement
1952   Sister Elizabeth Kenny Foundation
           Award for Distinguished Service
1952   Knights of Columbus
           Meritorious Service to Boys' Town of the West
1952   Kiwanis Club of Altadena, California
           Contribution to the Community
1952   Houston National Auto Show
           Award for Public Service
1952   Aquatennial Association, Minneapolis
           Honorary Skipper
1952   Chamber of Commerce, Ocean Park, California
           Award for Shows Originating at Ocean Park

1952	Knights of Columbus, Northern California
	Consistently High Standards in
	Wholesome Family Entertainment
1952	LeBlanc Corporation
	Award for Outstanding Contribution to
	Instrumental Music and Personal
	Example to Young Musicians
1952	National TB Association
	Distinguished Service Award
1952	Long Beach *Independent*
	Award for Most Popular TV Show
1952	Epsilon Sigma Alpha (South Dakota)
	Cerificate of Merit
1952	Hospitalized Veterans
	Plaque for Outstanding Service
1952/53	City of Santa Monica, California
	Most Popular TV Show
1952	Independent Dancers and Terpsichorean Club
	Plaque for Distinguished Service
1952	Optimist Club of Pacific Palisades, California
	Honorary Member
1952	*TeleViews* magazine
	6th Annual Award Poll for:
	1. Favorite Orchestra
	2. Favorite TV Personality
1952	Fireman's Benefit Association, Los Angeles County
	Honorary Battalion Chief
1952	American Cancer Society
	Ester Award for Special Benefit
	Dance at Hollywood Palladium
1953	Long Beach *Independent*
	Terry Vernon Award for Most Popular TV Show
1953	Polish National Alliance
	Award for Merit
1953	Electronic Employers' Association
	Award for Best Orchestra on TV
1953	Student Body, Santa Monica High School
	Most Popular TV Show
1953/54	*Down Beat* magazine's Annual Poll of National

Ballroom Operators' Association
Best Band and Show

1953–58 U.S. Department of the Army
Distinguished Civilian Service

1954 Long Beach *Independent*
First Place in TV Popularity Poll

1954 Academy of TV Arts and Sciences
Nomination for "Best Entertainment
Show" on TV

1954 *TV Guide* magazine, Readers' Poll
Favorite Local TV Program Personality
in Los Angeles

1954 Academy of TV Arts and Sciences
Nomination for Most Outstanding Male
TV Personality

1954 Sheriff E. W. Biscailuz Award
Award for Splendid Contribution
to Home Entertainment

1954 American Legion Auxiliary,
Beverly Hills, California
Unselfish Service, Cooperative Assistance

1954 Dodge "400" Club
Superior Salesman Award for Dodge

1954/55 California Congress of PTA
Recognition for Service to Children
of the Community

1955 Bexar County, Texas
Honorary Deputy Sheriff

1955 Lions Club, Huntington Beach, California
Award of Appreciation

1955 U.S. Department of the Army
Medal of Appreciation

1955 Knights of Columbus
Testimonial Certificate

1955 Torrant County, Texas
Honorary Deputy Sheriff

1955 American Society of Composers,
Authors, and Publishers
Outstanding Contributions to Music

1955   *Independent Press-Telegram,*
        Long Beach, California
        Best Local TV Show
1955   Chamber of Commerce, Fargo, North Dakota
        Recognition for Contribution to Music
1955/56 *Radio-TV Mirror* magazine
1956/57
1957/58
        Medal and Certificate for Favorite
        TV Musical Program
1955/56 Terpsichoreans of Aragon Ballroom,
        Ocean Park, California
        Award for 100 Weeks of America's
        Finest Dance Music
1955–58 *Down Beat* Magazine's Poll, National
        Ballroom Operators Association
        Best Dance Band Award
1956   National Father's Day Committee
        Music Father of the Year
1956   *Radio-Television Daily*
        Musical Show of the Year
1956   City of Chattanooga, Tennessee
        Honorary Deputy Sheriff
1956   Automatic Music Industry of America
        Wall Plaque
1956   Easter Seal Association
        Appreciation as National Orchestra Chairman
1956   Social Service Association
        Special Award
1956   Music Merchants Association,
        Milwaukee, Wisconsin
        Recognition of Finest Musical
        Program on Television
1956   American Accordionists Association
        For Inspiring Musical Education
        Among Youth of America
1956   Chamber of Commerce, Milwaukee, Wisconsin
        TV Entertainment Award

1956	City Council, Santa Monica, California
	Plaque Commemorating Lawrence Welk Day
1956	*Radio-TV Daily*
	"Musical Show of the Year"
1956	American Red Cross
	Award for Outstanding Service in
	1956 Fund Campaign
1956	University of Portland (Oregon)
	Doctor of Music, *honoris causa*
1956	Press Club, Spokane, Washington
	Certificate of Merit
1956	Kiwanis International
	Certificate of Recognition
1956	*Radio-TV Daily*
	For Aid to Worthwhile Charitable Organizations
1956	Unified School District, Santa Monica, California
	For Outstanding Contribution to
	Music and Entertainment
1956	City of Boston
	Honorary Police Chief
1956	City of Redondo Beach, California
	Honorary Police Chief
1956	St. Monica's High School, Santa Monica, California
	Recognition for Fine Personal Life
	and Fidelity to God
1956	Mutual of Omaha
	Distinguished Service Award
1957	Strasburg, North Dakota, High School
	Honorary Diploma
1957	State of Michigan
	Certificate for Meritorious Service
1957	City of New Orleans
	Mayor's Certificate of Merit for
	Opportunity Given to Pete Fountain
1957	Coral Records
	Selling One Million Albums
1957	Tau Kappa Epsilon Fraternity
	Remarkable Achievement in Exemplifying
	Traditions of Tau Kappa Epsilon

1957	State of Texas
	Honorary Citizen
1957	United Cerebral Palsy Association
	Star Performance in the 1957 Campaign
1957	Knights of Columbus, Ohio State Council
	An Outstanding Family TV Show
1957	Chamber of Commerce, Venice, California
	Honorary Membership for Outstanding
	Service in Music
1957	Federal Bureau of Investigation
	In Recognition of Contribution to the FBI
1957	American Legion Auxiliary
1957	American Heart Association
	National Chairman
1958	Golden Mike Award for Highest
	Standards in Entertainment
1958	Minneapolis Chamber of Commerce
	Medal for "Town Topper Award"
1958	North Dakota Legislature
	North Dakota Hall of Fame
1958	Newspaper of America
	Highest Standards for Youth
1958	United Airlines
	"100,000 Mile Club" in Appreciation for
	Contribution to Air Transportation
1958	Catholic War Veterans
	Honor et Veritas Award
1958	KABC-TV, Los Angeles
	In Appreciation from Friends at the Station
1958	State of Minnesota
	Order of the North Star
1958	City of Yankton, South Dakota
	Certificate of Merit
1958	Shrine Club, Santa Monica Bay
	For Distinguished Service
1958	Alumni Association, University of North Dakota
	Honorary Membership for Distinguished Service
	in Music and Entertainment

1958   Secretaries Association, Santa Monica, California
        Certificate of Honorary Membership
1958   Old Grand Dad Club
        Honorary Membership
1958   Children's Village, Fargo, North Dakota
        Honorary Director
1958   Knights of Columbus of Minnesota
        For Highest Moral Standards in Entertainment
1958   State Highway Department, South Carolina
        For Outstanding Contribution to Safety
        on Our Nation's Highways
1958   North Tonawanda, New York
        Honorary Mayor
1958   City of Yankton, South Dakota
        Honorary Mayor
1958   Los Angeles County, Board of Supervisors
        Citation
1958   Knights of Columbus, Norwalk, California
        For Outstanding Family Entertainment
1958   Freedom's Foundation, Valley Forge,
            Pennsylvania
        Award for Outstanding TV Show
1959   Accordion Teachers' Guild
        Commemorative Award
1959   City of Hollywood, California
        Honorary Mayor
1959   San Francisco *Examiner,* Reader Survey
        Favorite TV Program
1959   Catholic Big Brothers
        Award for Outstanding Contributions to the
            Big Brother Organization
1959   City of Detroit
        Proclamation of Lawrence Welk Day
1959   Federation of Women's Clubs, Los Angeles Chapter
        For Good Taste in Providing Family Entertainment
1959   Los Angeles County
        Citation for Contribution to Entertainment
1959   City of Santa Monica, California

	Proclamation of Lawrence Welk Day
1959	Veterans of Foreign Wars
	For Highest Standards of Entertainment
1959	City of Santa Monica, California
	Key to the City
1959	City of Wilmington, Delaware
	Key to the City
1959/60	Knights of Columbus, California State Council
	Public Relations Award
1959	Fraternal Order of Police, State
	Lodge of Michigan
	For Promotion of Highway Traffic Safety
1959	Optimists International
	"Friend of the Boy" Award
1960	Sheltered Workshops, Inc.
	For Making Possible the Training and Gainful Employment of Disabled and Aged People During the 1960 Campaign
1960	Dodge Key Club
	Certificate of Membership
1960	State of Oklahoma
	Honorary Colonel
1960	City of Lynwood, California
	Parade of Bands Award
1960	Accordion Makers of Italy
	For Service in Bringing Musical Pleasure to the People of America Through his Accordion and Orchestra
1960	State of Arkansas
	Ambassador of Good Will
1960	City of Fort Worth, Texas
	Honorary Citizen
1960	City of Fort Worth, Texas
	For Clean, Wholesome TV Programs
1960	City of New Orleans
	Honorary Citizen
1960	American Heart Association
	Heart and Torch Award
1960	Arthritis and Rheumatism Foundation
	Distinguished Service Award

1960	Recreational Dancing Institute
	For Contribution to Dancing
1960/61	Limelight Award
	Best Musical Show on TV
1960	Fraternal Order of Eagles
	Civic Service Award
1960	Great Lakes Naval Training Center,
	Great Lakes, Illinois
	For Entertaining Officers and Men
1960	Kentucky State Police
	Colonel, Aide de Camp
1960	National Ballroom Operators Association
	Recognition of Outstanding Contribution to the
	Ballroom Industry
1960	City of San Diego
	Honorary Fire Chief
1961	Community Chest
	Leadership Award
1961	Little League Baseball
	For Recognition of Participation in
	Organized Baseball
1961	World Crusade for God
	Award for Highest Principles in Business Dealings
	and for Using Talent for Betterment of Humanity
1961	Legislature, State of California
	Recognition for Contribution to Entertainment
1961	City of Santa Monica, California
	Certificate of Appreciation
1961	State of Michigan
	Certificate of Appreciation
1961	Dot Records
	Gold Record for "Calcutta"
1961	*Cash Box* magazine, Readers' Poll
	Most Programmed Band on Records
1961	Legislature, State of California
	Resolution and Commendation
1961	Franciscan Award, Order of Friars Minor
	For Outstanding Contribution to
	Family Entertainment

1961	National Academy of Recording Arts and Sciences Recognition of Best Performance by an Orchestra for Dancing: "Calcutta"
1961	Volunteers of America Recognition of Wholesome, Family Entertainment
1961	Franciscan Retreat Award, Order of Friars Minor In Recognition of Highest Standards in Music
1961	Chamber of Commerce, Hollywood, California Certificate of Welcome to New "Home" at the Hollywood Palladium
1961	Historical Development Association, Mandan, North Dakota Honorary Membership
1961	State of North Dakota Certificate in Leather Commissioning Lawrence Welk Honorary Colonel in the Teddy Roosevelt Rough Riders
1961/62	San Francisco *Examiner,* Readers' Poll Favorite Program on TV
1962	Hollywood, Florida Key to the City
1962	Goodwill Industries Award for Outstanding "Good Will" Toward the Handicapped
1962	Veterans of World War I, Department of Massachusetts Recognition for Valuable Services
1962	Alumni Association, University of Portland (Oregon) Honorary Lifetime Membership
1962	Chamber of Commerce, Hollywood, California Tourist and Convention Bureau Award
1962	*Cash Box* magazine, Readers' Poll Most Programmed Orchestra on Records
1962	Chamber of Commerce, Santa Monica, California City Beautiful Award for the Lawrence Welk-Union Bank Building
1962	City of San Antonio, Texas Lawrence Welk Day Proclamation and Honorary Mayor

1962 State of Nebraska
   Certificate Awarding One Square Foot of Land
    Adjacent to the Homestead National Park,
    Beatrice, Nebraska
1962 City of Portland, Oregon
   Key to the City
1962 March of Dimes
   Appreciation for First Annual March of Dimes
    Dance at Hollywood Palladium
1962 State of Tennessee
   Honorary Colonel
1962 Press Club, Greater Los Angeles
   In Appreciation for Services on Behalf of
    Eight Ball Welfare Foundation
1962 Knights of Columbus, Fort Wayne, Indiana
   Appreciation for Inspiring Example and
    Courageous Leadership in Field of
    Wholesome Entertainment
1962 American Society of Composers,
    Authors, and Publishers
   Statue in Recognition of Welk's Work as
    "Pied Piper to Millions"
1962 Fraternal Order of Police,
    Tennessee State Troopers
   Associate Membership
1963 State of North Dakota
   Illustrious Son Award
1963 State of North Dakota
   Theodore Roosevelt Award for
    Outstanding Achievement
1963 City of South Gate, California
   Recognition for Interest in the American Family
1963 City of Chicago
   Medal as Honorary Citizen
1963 City of Little Rock, Arkansas
   Key to the City
1963 City of Baltimore
   Key to the City
1963 City of Nashville, Tennessee
   Honorary Mayor

1963	State of Tennessee
	Colonel, Aide de Camp, Governor's
	Staff-Commission
1963	Red Carpet Club of Nashville
	Certificate of Membership
1963	Boy Scouts of America, Crescent Bay
	Area Council
	Statue to Lawrence Welk, "A Good Scout"
1963	Independence Hall of Chicago
	Gratitude for Concern About Welfare and
	Destiny of Our Nation
1964	WFTV, Orlando, Florida
	Award to Highest Rated TV Show in
	Central Florida
1964	The J. B. Williams Company
	Award presented on Lawrence Welk's
	10th Anniversary on Network TV
1964	Institute of High Fidelity
	For Contribution to Musical Arts in
	Radio and Television
1964	Peter DeRose Memorial (given by
	Mrs. Peter DeRose)
	Award for Loyalty and Support in Perpetuating
	Music and Compositions of Peter DeRose
1964	Harrah's Club—South Shore Room, Lake
	Tahoe, Nevada
	Wall Plaque in Remembrance of 1964 Engagement
1964	Sarah Coventry Jewelers
	Americana Award For Distinguished Performance
	in the Entertainment World
1964	Accordion Association of Southern California
	Award of Merit for Outstanding Achievement
1964	Junior Members of the American Legion
	Auxiliary of California
	Certificate of Appreciation
1964	City of New Orleans
	Proclamation of Lawrence Welk Day
1964	City of Louisville
	Ambassador of Good Will Award

1964	Marquette University Parents' Association For Recognition of Family Entertainment
1964	State of North Dakota Diamond Jim Award for Meritorious Service to Native State
1964	Commonwealth of Kentucky Commissioned as Kentucky Colonel
1964	State of South Dakota Order of the White Buffalo
1964	City of New Orleans Honorary Major, Police Department
1964	City of Charleston, West Virginia Key to the City
1964	City of Louisville, Kentucky Key to the City
1965	National Federation of Music Clubs Award of Merit
1965	North Dakota Chamber of Commerce Honorary Life Member
1965	City of St. Petersburg, Florida Honorary Citizen
1965	North Dakota State University Doctor of Music, *honoris causa*
1965	American Society of Composers, Authors and Publishers Honorary Membership in Recognition of Contribution to Music
1965	Sioux Tribe of North Dakota Honorary Tribal Membership Presented to HO-WA-STE (Goodvoice)
1965	City of Escondido, California Honorary Citizen Award
1965	Chamber of Commerce, Escondido, California Plaque for Distinguished Contribution
1965	KOCO-TV, Oklahoma City Good Luck Wall Plaque
1965	Women's Bowling Association, San Fernando Valley, California Award of Thanks

1965   Bismarck Junior College, Bismarck, North Dakota
              Award in Appreciation of Contribution to North
                  Dakota Through Welk's National Acclaim in
                  the World of Music

1965   Harrah's Club—South Shore Room, Lake
              Tahoe, Nevada
              Wall Plaque in Remembrance of 1965 Engagement

1965   Lions Club, Bismarck, North Dakota
              In Appreciation of Lawrence Welk's Loyalty to
                  His Native State of North Dakota

1965   Cow Belles of North Dakota
              Award of Merit

1965   North Dakota State Council
              Award of Merit

1965   Leisure World of California
              Outstanding Contributions to Musical Entertainment

1965   Knights of Columbus, Fullerton, California
              In Recognition of Lawrence Welk's
                  Entertainment Popularity

1965   Elk's Lodge, Long Beach, California
              Appreciation of Outstanding Contribution to
                  Success of Elk's Christmas Charity Ball Raising
                  One Million Dollars for the Elk's
                  Charitable Program

1965   City of Escondido, California
              Proclamation of Lawrence Welk Day on 10th
                  Anniversary of TV Show

1965   City of Windom, Minnesota
              Certificate of Citizenship

1965   Department of Corrections, Huntsville, Texas
              Honorary Convict

1965   Legislature, State of California
              Official Custodian of the Seal of the
                  State of California

1965   Long Beach Arena, Long Beach, California
              Promotional Achievement Award for
                  17,123 attendance

1966	City of Great Falls, Montana
	Key to the City
1966	City of St. Louis
	Key to the City
1966	City of Des Moines, Iowa
	Key to the City
1966	Blackfoot Tribe of Montana
	Honorary Chief "Chief Singing Eagle"
1966	Crippled Children's School, Jamestown, North Dakota
	Appreciation as Honorary Chairman of 25th Anniversary Appeal
1966	North American Air Defense Command
	Award for Helping Create and Sustain Better Public Understanding of Its Mission and Objectives
1966	Boys Club of Escondido, California
	For Helpful Assistance to the Boys Club Movement
1966	City of South Gate, California
	Plaque Honoring Lawrence Welk
1966	Jinniston Grotto of Los Angeles
	Award of Merit
1966	Polka Dancers Association
	For Outstanding Contributions to Polka Dancing
1966	American Legion Junior Auxiliary
	Award of Thanks
1966	Knights of Columbus
	The Supreme Knight's Certificate of Commendation for Exercise of Charity, Unity and Patriotism as a True Catholic
1966	Federation of Women's Clubs of California
	Certificate of Merit
1966	American Legion
	For Participation in World-Wide Broadcasts to Our Armed Forces
1966	State of Montana
	Honorary Secretary of State

1966   Shut-ins Entertainment Service
                Des Moines, Iowa
             In Recognition of Kindness, Generosity, and
                Charity Shown to Shut-Ins
1966   State of Kentucky
             Honorary Kentucky Colonel
1966   State Fair, Des Moines, Iowa
             Certificate for Breaking All Attendance and
                Gross Receipts in the 108 Years' History
                of the Iowa State Fair
1966   American Legion Auxiliary
             Certificate for "World-Round Radio Program"
                from the Hollywood Palladium
1966   State of Indiana
             Appointment by Governor with Rank and Title
                of Sagamore of the Wabash
1966   Harrah's Club—South Shore Room, Lake
                Tahoe, Nevada
             Plaque in Remembrance of 1966 Engagement
1967   New Orleans Jazz Club
             Honorary Membership
1967   City of New Orleans
             Honorary Police Chief
1967   San Fernando Woman's Club,
                Sierra-Caheunga District
             Musical Ambassador for a Better America
1967   University of San Francisco, Institute of
                Lay Theology
             For Generous Help to Students Training for
                Adult Christian Education
1967   St. John's Hospital, Santa Monica, California
             In Appreciation for "Music '67," a Fund-Raising
                Concert for the Hospital
1967   Legislature, State of North Dakota
             Named to North Dakota Hall of Fame as North
                Dakota's Favorite Son
1967   City of Bessemer, Alabama
             Honorary Mayor

1967	Chamber of Commerce, Clearwater, Florida
	Ambassador of Good Will
1967	National Association of Record Merchandisers
	Best-Selling Orchestra for the Year 1966
1967	Y.M.C.A. Century Club
	Appreciation for Welk's Support to Young
	People During the Year 1966
1967	American Legion Auxiliary
	Recognition of Outstanding Service,
	Golden Mike Award
1967	Boys Club of Santa Monica, California
	In Grateful Appreciation
1967	City of Escondido, California
	Honorary Mayor
1967	State of Nebraska
	Honorary Centennial Governor and
	Grand Marshal
1967	Association of American Schools and Colleges
	Horatio Alger Award Towards the Enhancing of
	the American Tradition of Overcoming
	Obstacles to Achieve Success Through Diligence,
	Industry and Perseverance
1967	Ursuline Sisters
	For Outstanding Contribution to the Entertainment
	World as a Former Ursuline Student
1967	American Legion Post 201, Minot, North Dakota
	For Service to God and Country as
	a Patriotic American
1967	Strasburg, North Dakota, Civic Club
	Life Membership
1968	American Cancer Society
	National Crusade Chairman
1968	City of Miami
	Key to the City
1968	Boy Scouts of America, Crescent Bay
	Area Council
	In Recognition of Service to the Boy
	Scouts of America

1968   Milledgeville, Georgia
        Honorary Fire Marshall
1968   Escondido, California, Boys Club
        For Many Years Helping Boys Become
            Better Men
1968   American Cancer Society, Maryland Division
        For Unselfish Leadership and Support in the
            Fight Against Cancer
1968   American Cancer Society, Philadelphia Division
        For Outstanding Leadership as 1968 National
            Crusade Chairman
1968   Knights of Columbus, Dakota Territory
        For Promoting Principles of Decency and
            Morality in Music and Song
1968   Santa Claus Lane Parade of Stars
        Certificate of Appreciation
1968   American Legion Post, New Rochelle, New York
        Americanism Award for Patriotism, Devotion,
            Dedication to Country
1968   Hollywood Visitors and Convention Bureau
        Tribute of Esteem: Official Host of Hollywood
1968   State of Illinois
        Sesquicentennial Medal
1968   State of North Dakota
        Theodore Roosevelt Award for
            Outstanding Achievement
1968   Harrah's Club—South Shore Room, Lake
            Tahoe, Nevada
        In Remembrance of 1968 Engagement at
            Lake Tahoe
1968   Brigham Young University
        Citation for Service to Millions of Americans
            through Popular Music
1968   American Cancer Society, Mayor of
            Colton, California
        Commendation for work in behalf of the
            American Cancer Society
1968   Mayor of Fontana, California
        Commendation for work in behalf of the
            American Cancer Society

1968   Mayor of Rialto, California
        Commendation for work in behalf of the
          American Cancer Society

1968   Mayor of Barstow, California
        Commendation for work in behalf of the
          American Cancer Society

1968   Mayor of Upland, California
        Commendation for work in behalf of the
          American Cancer Society

1968   Mayor of Chino, California
        Commendation for work in behalf of the
          American Cancer Society

1968   Mayor of Ontario, California
        Commendation for work in behalf of the
          American Cancer Society

1968   State of California, Legislative Assembly
        Resolution of Congratulations upon Appointment
          as National Crusade Chairman, American
          Cancer Society

1968   Pope Paul VI
        Papal Knight of Malta

1968   State of Maryland
        Appointment and Commission as Admiral
          of the Chesapeake

1968   United States Navy
        Recruiting Service Award

1968   United States Army
        Honorary Recruiter, Women's Army Corps

1968   Santa Ana, California, Chamber of Commerce
        Membership, Ambassador's Club

1968   Minot State College, Minot, North Dakota
        Honorary Member, Beaver Band

1968   Catholic Kolping Society of America
        The Kolping Award

1968   Commonwealth of Kentucky, Department of
          Natural Resources
        Commissioned as Admiral

1968   Congressional Record
        Commendation for National Crusade Chairman,
          American Cancer Society

1968	City of Needles, California
	Commendation for National Crusade Chairman,
	American Cancer Society
1968	City of San Bernardino, California
	Commendation for National Crusade Chairman,
	American Cancer Society
1968	City of San Diego
	Commendation for National Crusade Chairman,
	American Cancer Society
1968	Illinois Sesquicentennial
	Abraham Lincoln Plaque for Friendship and
	Affection for Illinois
1968	City of Madison, Wisconsin
	Key to the City
1968	Police Department, Reno, Nevada
	Honorary Chief of Police
1968	Santa Ana, California
	Key to the City
1968	City of Memphis, Tennessee
	Key to the City
1968	City of Charleston, West Virginia
	Key to the City
1968	U.S.S. *Olympia*
	Medal
1968	Freedoms Foundation, Valley Forge, Pennsylvania
	Award for Creating Better Understanding of the
	American Way of Life
1968	Arizona Cancer Crusaders, Phoenix
	Indian Statue
1968	National Secretaries' Association
	Honorary Membership
1968	American Cancer Society, New Jersey Division
	With Grateful Appreciation
1968–71	National Foundation of the March of Dimes
	Meritorious Service Awards
1968	State of Louisiana
	Honorary Deputy
1968	State of Mississippi
	Honorary Colonel, Governor's Staff

1968	State of Tennessee
	Proclamation of Lawrence Welk Day
1968	American Cancer Society, Los Angeles Division
	Award for Personal and Dedicated Effort
1968	City of San Antonio
	Official Appointment to the Office of Alcalde (Mayor)
1969	Operation Moral Upgrade
	For Artistic Contribution to Pleasurable and Wholesome Entertainment
1969	Hollywood, California, Chamber of Commerce
	For Contributing to Spirit of Peace and Happiness
1969	Congress of Freedom
	Liberty Award
1969	Long Beach, California, Elks
	Appreciation of Contribution for 8 Years to the Success of Christmas Charity Ball
1969	Santa Monica Sports and Arts Festival
	Sponsor Award
1969	American Cancer Society, Arnie's Crusade Army
	Recognition for Outstanding Service and Contributions
1969	Armed Forces Radio and Television Service
	For 1000th Broadcast for Armed Forces Radio 1947–1969
1969	American Legion
	Citation for Meritorious Service
1969	National Tuberculosis and Respiratory Disease Association
	Award for Outstanding Participation
1969	American Legion Auxiliary
	Appreciation for Outstanding Service and Assistance—Junior Activities
1969	American Mothers Committee
	Appreciation for Outstanding Contribution
1969	Station KOCO-TV, Oklahoma City
	Good Luck Plaque

1969   Commonwealth of Pennsylvania,
              Governor's Office
              Proclamation of Thanks for Dedication to
              Fine Music
1969   The Kids from Wisconsin
              Honorary "Kid"
1969   Association of Commerce, Ocean
              Park, California
              Recognition as Music Master of the World
1969   City of Allentown, Pennsylvania
              Key to the City
1969   The Thomas Organ Company
              The Ring Award
1969   The State of Texas
              Honorary Citizen of Texas
1969   Leland Powers School, Boston
              Honorary Diploma
1969   March of Dimes
              Award of Appreciation
1969   North Dakota Library Association
              Honorary Life Membership
1969   State of Texas
              Honorary Admiral in the Texas Navy
1969   City of Duluth, Minnesota
              Honorary Citizen
1969   The Ambassadors, Duluth, Minnesota
              Honorary Member, Ambassador Extraordinary,
              Duchy of Duluth
1969   City of Fredericksburg, Texas
              Honorary Citizen
1969   Country Music Association
              Appreciation for the Broader Acceptance and
              Progress of Country Music
1969   Thomas Organ Company
              Outstanding Achievement Award
1969   Kiwanis International
              The Kaydee Award

1969	The Nugget Club, Sparks, Nevada
	The Nugget Classic
1969	Community Chest, Santa Monica, California
	Leadership Club Member
1969	Freedoms Foundation, Valley Forge, Pennsylvania
	Award for Article entitled: "Guaranteed Wage"
1969	Freedoms Foundation, Valley Forge, Pennsylvania
	Award for Special Program on ABC
1969	Isabella Geriatric Center, New York City
	Hall of Fame; Senior Citizen Award
1970	Cadillac Crest Club
	Honorary Member
1970	County of San Bernardino, California
	Chairman of Cancer Month
1970	National Conference of Christians and Jews
	Brotherhood Award
1970	City of Tucson, Arizona
	Honorary Citizen
1970	Fraternal Order of Eagles
	Sullivan-Considine Award
1970	National Society of Sons of the American Revolution
	Good Citizenship Medal
1970	City of Chattanooga, Tennessee
	Ambassador of Good Will
1970	National Red Cross, Santa Monica, California
	American Red Cross Leader
1970	Santa Monica Pony-Colt League
	For Support of Teenage Baseball Program
1970	Congregation Mishkan Yicheskel, Los Angeles
	God and Country Award
1970	Dakota Tribe Friends
	Outstanding Service
1970	National Council for the Encouragement of Patriotism
	Recognition for Family Programming
1971	City of Los Angeles
	Certificate of Commendation for Wholesome Entertainment

1971	Xavier University, Cincinnati, Ohio
	Xavier Medal for Wholesome Entertainment
1972	California State Assembly
	Resolution
1972	Tournament of Roses Parade
	Grand Marshal
1972	The Academy of Country and Western Music
	Plaque for Man of the Year
1972	University of North Dakota
	Lux et Lux Award
1972	United States Military Chaplains
	National Citizenship Award
1973	Girl Scouts of America
	For Years of Support
1973	Order of Elks, Grand Lodge, Chicago, Illinois
	Recognition for Music and Inspiration
1973	University of North Dakota
	Doctor of Music, *honoris causa*
1973	American Heart Association
	Heart and Torch Award
1973	University of North Dakota
	Visiting Professor of History and Popular Arts
1973	WTVJ, Miami
	Citation and Plaque
1973	American Cancer Society
	National Co-Chairman
1974	Tournament of Roses Parade
	President's Trophy Winner
1974	State of Washington
	Ambassador of Good Will
1974	State of Washington
	Commissioned a Washington General
1974	Daughters of the American Revolution
	DAR Honor Medal
1975	Interstate Business and Professional Association of Los Angeles
	Certificate of Appreciation
1976	Boys Club of Escondido, California
	Special Award

1977   American Institute of Fine Arts
Footprints-on-the-Sands-of-Time Award

1979   Pepperdine University, Frank R. Seaver College
Doctor of Laws, *honoris causa*

Notes

Chapter 1

1. Quoted by J. L. Kaufman from a telephone conversation with Walter Winchell, December 1, 1955.
2. From a personal interview with Sam J. Lutz, February 14, 1979.
3. Excerpt from a news release by the Associated Press, September 30, 1971.
4. Russ Leadabrand, "Welk Chosen by Tournament," *Pasadena Star-News,* September 10, 1971, p. 1.
5. From a personal interview with Don Fedderson, March 15, 1970.
6. John Keasler, "Ford Should Have Picked Lawrence Welk," *Santa Monica Evening Outlook,* August 30, 1975, p. 19.
7. Louis B. Mayer, quoted by Paul Mayersberg, "Passage to Hollywood," *The Listener,* 1966, p. 924.

Chapter 2

1. Quoted from a personal conversation with Lawrence Welk, January 22, 1979.
2. Ibid.

3. Quoted from a personal conversation with Lawrence Welk, April 15, 1970.
4. Ibid.
5. Quoted from a personal conversation with Fern Welk, March 10, 1979.
6. Ibid.
7. Quoted from a personal conversation with Lawrence Welk, March 10, 1970.
8. Quoted from a personal conversation with Lawrence Welk, March 1, 1979.
9. Quoted from a personal conversation with Fern Welk, March 10, 1979.
10. Quoted from a personal conversation with Lawrence Welk, March 1, 1979.
11. Quoted from a personal conversation with Fern Welk, March 10, 1979.
12. Ibid.
13. Cf. Appendix, "Awards, Trophies, Certificates, Medals Presented to Lawrence Welk."
14. Quoted from a personal conversation with Lawrence Welk, March 1, 1979.

Chapter 3

1. Lawrence Welk, *Guidelines for Successful Living*, (Minneapolis: T. B. Dennison & Co., 1968), p. 14.
2. Quoted from a personal conversation with Lawrence Welk, January 23, 1979.
3. Welk, *Guidelines for Successful Living*, pp. 24–25.
4. *Congressional Record*, "Address by Lawrence Welk," Introduced by Senator Milton R. Young (Washington, D.C.: U.S. Government Printing Office, September 16, 1968), v. 114, pt. 20, p. 26884.
5. Quoted from a personal conversation with Lawrence Welk, January 23, 1979.
6. Matt. 7: 12 (Revised Standard Version).
7. Quoted from a personal interview with Jack Minor, February 22, 1970.

8. Quoted from a personal conversation with Lawrence Welk, January 23, 1979.
9. Ibid.
10. Ibid.
11. Ibid.
12. Ibid.
13. Welk, *Guidelines for Successful Living*, p. 50.
14. Ibid.
15. Welk, *Guidelines for Successful Living*, p. 101.
16. Lawrence Welk, "Free Enterprise and Personal Responsibility," *Christian Economics*, August 5, 1969, p. 1.

Chapter 4

1. Quoted from an interview with Sam J. Lutz, February 10, 1979.
2. Ibid.
3. Quoted from an interview with Don Fedderson, February 28, 1970.
4. Quoted from an interview with James Hobson, March 13, 1979.
5. Quoted from an interview with George Cates, April 10, 1970.
6. Quoted from an interview with J. L. Kaufman, March 4, 1979.
7. Quoted from an interview with Curt Ramsey, April 10, 1970.
8. Quoted from an interview with Jack Imel, April 10, 1970.

Chapter 5

1. Quoted from an interview with Bert Carter, January 18, 1979.
2. Quoted from an interview with Jack Minor, February 21, 1970.
3. Quoted from an interview with Matthew Rosenhaus, Feb. 23, 1970.
4. Quoted from an interview with Irving Ross, February 19, 1979.

Chapter 6

1. Quoted from an interview with Barbara Curtiss, January 30, 1979.
2. "Still a Mystery of Missing Audiences," *Broadcasting,* February 16, 1970, p. 24.
3. "Rambling Reporter," *Hollywood Reporter,* August 31, 1978, p. 4.
4. Data condensed from two publications, *The Nielsen Ratings in Perspective* and *NTI in Instantaneous Action* (Northbrook, Illinois: A.C. Nielsen Company, 1978 and 1974).

Chapter 7

1. Morton Moss, "He Just Keeps Bubbling Along," *Los Angeles Herald-Examiner,* May 31, 1970, p. 4.
2. Terrance O'Flaherty, "Free Advice from the Stars," *New York World-Telegram,* December 14, 1959, p. 14.
3. Larry Wolters, "The Man Who Killed Caesar," *Chicago Tribune,* May 14, 1956, p. 43.
4. Hal Humphrey, "Welk's Image Changing," *Los Angeles Times,* March 7, 1966, p. 24.
5. Bill Esposito, "Why Lawrence Welk? Here's Why," *The Transcript-Telegram* (Holyoke, Mass.), August 3, 1963, p. 23.
6. Martin Hogan, "Who Is This Lawrence Welk?" *Cincinnati Enquirer,* November 25, 1967, p. 43.
7. Dick Helm, *Variety,* September 30, 1968, p. 2.
8. Bob Rose, *Indianapolis Star,* November 27, 1968, p. 14.
9. P. F. Kluge, "The Then Generation," *Wall Street Journal,* June 15, 1970, p. 1.
10. Tony Lioce, *Evening Bulletin* (Providence, R. I.), August 25, 1975, TV p. 1.
11. Bill Granger, *Chicago Sun-Times,* September 2, 1976, TV p. 2.
12. Hal Humphrey, "Why Critics Dislike Lawrence Welk," *Detroit Free Press,* May 26, 1955, p. 11.
13. *Charlotte* (N.C.) *News,* April 2, 1963, p. 17.

14. Jack Wasserman, "Welk Packs the Forum," *Vancouver* (B.C.) *Sun,* July 27, 1967, p. 2.
15. Gary Stevens, "The Era of the Big Dance Bands," *Variety,* January 5, 1966, p. 4.
16. Edgar Penton, "Welk Fans Help Make His Career a Bubbling Success Story," *Showtime,* July 10, 1965, p. 14.
17. Jack O'Brien, "A-One A-Two-500," *New York Journal American,* January 20, 1965, p. 28.
18. Janet Kern, *The Chicago American,* June 10, 1960, p. 43.
19. Thomas E. Murphy, "The Teeth," *Hartford* (Conn.) *Courant,* December 9, 1964, p. 14. (Reprinted with permission.)
20. Thomas E. Murphy, "Hello Larry," *Hartford* (Conn.) *Courant,* February 24, 1965, p. 12. (Reprinted with permission.)
21. *Television-Radio Age,* June 19, 1967, p. 3.
22. John Hartl, *Seattle Times,* July 29, 1967, p. 1.
23. Alfred G. Aronowitz, "A Nice Old Man," *New York Post,* September 3, 1971, TV p. 1.
24. Larry Wolters, "Welk's Corn Still Is Champagne to Many," *Chicago Tribune,* June 17, 1960, p. 32.
25. Hank Grant, *Miami Herald,* April 19, 1962, p. 22.
26. Rex Polier, "Lawrence Welk Shuns Big Beat for Bubbles," *The Philadelphia Inquirer,* January 20, 1965, p. 13.
27. Lorne Parton, "Lovely, Lovely Lawrence," *Vancouver* (B.C.) *Sun,* July 27, 1967, p. 23.
28. Bob Hull, "Welk's Merry, Merry-Go-Round," *Los Angeles Herald-Examiner,* July 21, 1963, p. 4.
29. P. F. Kluge, "The Then Generation," *Wall Street Journal,* June 15, 1970, p. 1.
30. Bruce Blackadar, "The Sounds of Cocker and Welk: A Report from Different Worlds," *Toronto Sun,* August 22, 1974, TV p. 1.
31. John V. R. Bull, *The Philadelphia Inquirer,* August 13, 1975, TV p. 1.
32. John V. R. Bull, *The Philadelphia Inquirer,* August 17, 1975, TV p. 1.
33. Lawrence Maddry, *The* (Norfolk) *Virginian Pilot,* September 7, 1971, TV p. 1. (Reprinted with permission).

34. Lawrence Maddry, *The* (Norfolk) *Virginian Pilot,* September 12, 1971, TV p. 1. (Reprinted with permission).
35. Lawrence Maddry, *The* (Norfolk) *Virginian Pilot,* September 14, 1971, TV p. 1. (Reprinted with permission).
36. Clarke Williamson, "Welk Waning Even with the Oldsters," (Phoenix) *Arizona Republic,* April 25, 1968, p. 42.
37. Lawrence Laurent, "Welk and Sullivan Seen at End of Line," *Chicago Sun-Times,* April 9, 1970, p. 54.
38. P. F. Kluge, "The Then Generation," *Wall Street Journal,* June 15, 1970, p. 1.
39. Paul Jones, "Six Stars Have Quit in a Huff at Welk," *Atlanta Constitution,* March 13, 1962, p. 13.
40. P. F. Kluge, "The Then Generation," *Wall Street Journal,* June 15, 1970, p. 1.
41. Bob Rose, *Indianapolis Star,* November 27, 1968, p. 14.
42. *TV Mailbag* (a nationally syndicated feature appearing in Sunday newspaper magazine sections) (San Diego: Copley News Service), February 22, 1976.
43. John Wendeborn, (Portland) *Oregonian,* June 5, 1974, TV p. 1.
44. Charles Hanna, *Detroit Free Press,* February 20, 1971, TV p. 1.
45. Victor P. Hass, *The Omaha World-Herald,* July 20, 1975, TV p. 1.
46. Quoted from an interview with Vincent DiBari, April 15, 1970.
47. These criticisms were offered by persons who wished to remain anonymous.

Chapter 8

1. Harry Skornia, *Television and Society* (New York: McGraw-Hill, 1965); Robert Lewis Shayon, *Saturday Review,* September 12, 1970, pp. 78–79.
2. Gary A. Steiner, *The People Look at Television* (New York: Alfred A. Knopf, 1963), p. 226.
3. Kurt Lang and Gladys Lang, *MacArthur Day in Chicago, Politics and Television* (Chicago: University of Chicago Press, 1952), p. 11.

4. These data were updated from statistics given by David M. White and Richard Averson, eds., *Sight, Sound and Society* (Boston: Beacon Press, 1968), p. 240, using *Television Factbook* (Washington D.C.: Television Digest, 1979).

5. A. William Bluem, *Television: The Creative Experience* (New York: Hastings House, 1967), p. 10.

6. David M. Potter, *People of Plenty: Economic Abundance and the American Character* (Chicago: University of Chicago Press, 1954), p. 188.

7. Nicholas Johnson, *How to Talk Back to Your Television Set* (Boston: Little, Brown), 1970.

8. Norbert Wiener, *The Human Use of Human Beings* (Boston: Houghton Mifflin, 1950), p. 71.

9. Quoted from a conversation with Lawrence Welk, March 15, 1979.

Chapter 9

1. Data contained in this chapter were gathered from interviews with Ted R. Lennon, February 10, 1979.

2. Quoted from an interview with Paul Ryan, March 12, 1979.

Chapter 10

1. Quoted from a personal conversation with Lawrence Welk, March 13, 1979.

2. Quoted from an interview with Sam J. Lutz, February 14, 1979.

3. Quoted from an interview with Bert Carter, January 18, 1979.

4. Quoted from a personal conversation with Lawrence Welk, March 13, 1979.

5. Ibid.

Bibliography

Books

Barnouw, Erik. *Mass Communications.* New York: Rinehart and Company, 1956.

Bluem, A. William. *Documentary in American Television.* New York: Hastings House, 1968.

Coakley, Mary Lewis. *Mister Music Maker Lawrence Welk.* Garden City, N.Y.: Doubleday, 1958.

Dexter, Lewis A., and White, David Manning. *People, Society and Mass Communications.* New York: The Free Press, 1964.

Diserens, Charles M. *The Influence of Music on Behavior.* Princeton, N.J.: Princeton University Press, 1926.

Doob, Leonard W. *Public Opinion and Propaganda.* New York: Henry Holt & Co., 1948.

Ewen, David. *History of Popular Music.* New York: Barnes and Noble, 1961.

Farnsworth, P. R. *The Social Psychology of Music.* New York: Dryden & Co., 1958.

Govani, Albert. *The Lawrence Welk Story.* New York: Simon & Schuster, 1961.

Head, Sidney. *Broadcasting in America.* Boston: Houghton Mifflin, 1956.

271

Katz, Elihu, and Lazarsfeld, Paul. *Personal Influence.* New York: The Free Press, 1955.

Kinkle, Roger D. *The Complete Encyclopedia of Popular Music.* New Rochelle, N.Y.: Arlington House, 1948.

Klapper, Joseph. *The Effects of Mass Communications.* Glencoe Ill.: The Free Press, 1960.

Lang, Kurt, and Lang, Gladys, *MacArthur Day in Chicago, Politics and Television.* Chicago: University of Chicago Press, 1952.

Lynch, William F. *The Image Industries.* New York: Sheed and Ward, 1959.

Meyer, Hazel. *The Gold in Tin Pan Alley.* New York: J. B. Lippincott, 1958.

Nettl, Bruno. *Folk and Traditional Music of the Western Continents.* Englewood Cliffs, N.J.: Prentice-Hall, 1965.

Parr, A. H. *The Lennon Sisters.* Garden City, N.Y.: Doubleday 1960.

Potter, David M. *People of Plenty: Economic Abundance and the American Character.* Chicago: University of Chicago Press, 1954.

Rosenberg, Bernard, and White, David Manning, eds. *Mass Culture: The Popular Arts in America.* Glencoe, Ill.: The Free Press, 1957.

Schramm, Wilbur. *The Processes and Effects of Mass Communications.* Urbana: University of Illinois Press, 1954.

Silberman, Alphons. *Musik, Rundfunk und Hörer: die Soziologischen Aspekte der Musik am Rundfunk.* Cologne: Westdeutscher Verlag, 1959.

Silberman, Alphons. *The Sociology of Music.* Translated by Corbert Stewart. London: Routledge and Kegan Paul, 1963.

Simon, George T. *The Big Bands.* New York: Macmillan, 1967.

Skornia, Harry K. *Television and Society.* New York: McGraw-Hill, 1965.

Smith, Cecil. *Worlds of Music.* New York: J. B. Lippincott, 1952.

Steiner, Gary A. *The People Look at Television.* New York: Alfred A. Knopf, 1963.

Weber, Max. *The Rational and Social Foundations of Music.* Carbondale: Southern Illinois University Press, 1958.

Welk, Lawrence. *Guidelines for Successful Living*. Minneapolis: T. S. Denison & Co., 1968.

Welk, Lawrence, and McGeehan, Bernice. *Wunnerful, Wunnerful*. Englewood Cliffs, N.J.: Prentice-Hall, 1971.

Welk, Lawrence, and McGeehan, Bernice. *Ah One, Ah Two!* Englewood Cliffs, N.J.: Prentice-Hall, 1974.

Welk, Lawrence, and McGeehan, Bernice. *My America, Your America*. Englewood Cliffs, N.J.: Prentice-Hall, 1976.

White, David M., and Averson, Richard, eds. *Sight, Sound and Society*. Boston: The Beacon Press, 1968.

White, David M., and Rosenberg, Bernard. *Mass Culture: The Popular Arts in America*. New York: The Free Press, 1967.

Wiener, Norbert. *The Human Use of Human Beings*. Boston: Houghton Mifflin, 1950.

Wright, Charles. *Mass Communications*. New York: Random House, 1959.

Zehnpfennig, Gladys. *Lawrence Welk: Champagne Music Man*. Minneapolis: Denison & Co., 1968.

Articles and Dissertations

Adorno, Theodore W. "On Popular Music." *Studies in Philosophy and Social Science* 9 (1941) : 17–49.

Archer, W. K. "On the Ecology of Music." *The World of Music* 5 (1963) : 13.

Cady, H. L. "The Sociology of Music: A Perspective." *Music Educators Journal* 50 (1963) : 25–27.

Etzkorn, K. Peter. "Musical and Social Patterns of Songwriters: An Exploratory Sociological Study." *Dissertation Abstracts* 21 (1960) : 1281.

Etzkorn, K. Peter. "The Social Context of Songwriting in the United States." *Ethnomusicology* 7 (1963) : 96–106.

Etzkorn, K. Peter. "The Relationship Between Musical and Social Patterns in American Popular Music." *Journal of Research in Music Education* 12 (1964) : 279–86.

Hughes, J. M. "Fifty-Nine Case Studies on the Effects of Musical Participation on Social Development." *Music Educators Journal* 41 (February-March 1955) : p. 41.

Jarvis, D. "Music and Leisure." *Choir* 54 (July, 1963) : 126.

Kaplan, M. "Music and Mass Culture." *The Music Journal* 18 (March, 1960) : 20.

Merriam, Alan P. "Music in American Culture." *American Anthropologist* 57 (1955) : 1173–1181.

Mueller, J. H. "The Social Nature of Musical Taste." *Journal of Research in Music Education* 4, (Fall, 1956) : 113–22.

Mueller, J. H. "A Sociological Approach to Musical Behavior." *Ethnomusicology* 7 (1963) : 216–20.

Nash, Dennison. "The American Composer: A Study in Social Psychology." Doctoral dissertation, University of Pennsylvania, 1954.

Riedel, J. "The Sociology of Music." *Music Educators Journal* 49 (1962) : 39–42.

Riedel, J. "The Function of Sociability in the Sociology of Music and Music Education." *Journal of Research in Music Education* 12 (1964) : 279–86.

Schwienher, William K. "A Descriptive Analysis of the Lawrence Welk Show as a Unique Sociological Phenomenon." Doctoral dissertation, Northwestern University, 1971.

Seeger, C. "Music as a Tradition of Communication, Discipline, and Play." *Ethnomusicology* 6 (1962) : 156–63.

Weston, Paul "The Forgotten Art: Music for Television" in *Television, the Creative Experience,* edited by A. William Bluem, New York: Hastings House, 1967, 298.

Principal Articles on Lawrence Welk

Aldridge, Ron. "Bubbling On . . . Lawrence Welk Keeps Defying the Odds." *Charlotte Observer,* December 19, 1977, p. 21A.

Anderson, Jack E. "Lawrence Welk." *Miami Herald,* January 6, 1963, TV p. 12.

Atkinson, Brooks. "Welk Flows On, Miller Dries Up in Survival War." *Toronto Globe and Mail,* July 3, 1964, TV p. 1.

Atkinson, Brooks. "It's Goodby Miller, Hello Welk for Music Lovers Next Season." *New York Times,* July 18, 1964, p. 64.

Avins, Mimi. "A One An' A Two. . . .": *St. Louis Post-Dispatch,* May 18, 1975, sec. 1-10G.

Bacon, James. "Welk Sets the World Agog." *Sioux Falls Argus Leader,* January 27, 1957, p. 1C.

Ballard, Delores. "Old Welk Magic Held Audience Spellbound." *Jackson* (Tenn.) *Sun.* April 1, 1974, TV p. 1.

Banks, Harold. "Welk Wins in a Waltz." *Boston Herald American,* September 23, 1975, p. 26.

Beck, Marilyn. "What It's Like to Work for Lawrence Welk." *Chicago American,* May 14, 1967, p. 1.

Beck, Marilyn. "Welk: His Music Changes Over the Years." *Chicago American,* March 25, 1969, p. 14.

Blackadar, Bruce. "The Sounds of Cocker and Welk: A Report from Different Worlds." *Toronto Sun,* August 22, 1974, p. 23.

Blanchard, Douglas. "Lawrence Welk and the Band That Bubbles." *Toronto Star Weekly,* September 22, 1956, p. 14.

Bogert, John M. "The Lord Has Been So Very, Very Good to Us." *Glendale News Press,* March 8, 1977, p. 1.

Bull, John V. R. "Welk Brings Aura of Sweetness and Light to Spectrum." *Philadelphia Inquirer,* August 23, 1975 and August 30, 1975, TV p. 1.

Caldon, Susan. "Welk: A Sincere Man Who Makes Music for His People." (Augusta, Maine) *Kennebec Journal,* August 22, 1974, p. 6.

Coakley, Mary Lewis. "Mister Music Maker Lawrence Welk." *Philadelphia Inquirer,* September 14, 1958, pp. 1–3.

Condon, Maurice. "They Remember Lawrence Welk." *TV Guide,* April 29, 1967, p. 11.

Currier, Win. "Currier's Comments." *Oakland Morning News,* September 2, 1970, TV p. 1.

Dance, Stanley. "Johnny Hodges Meets Lawrence Welk." *Jazz,* March, 1966, p. 1.

Davidson, William. "Lawrence Welk." *Look,* June 25, 1957, p. 115.

Davis, Paul. "Man of the Year." *TV Annual,* 1956, p. 1.

Dawn, Charles. "Lawrence Welk's Music on Edgewater Beach Walk." *Chicago American,* June 14, 1939, p. 14C.

Denton, Charles. "Lawrence Welk's Champagne Music Story." *San Francisco Call-Bulletin,* June 25, 1956, p. 31.

Dornbrook, Don. "Lawrence Welk's Home Stand." *Milwaukee Journal,* March 2, 1958, p. 12.

Drew, Michael H. "Arena Bubbles with Welk Music." *Milwaukee Journal,* August 31, 1970, TV p. 1.

Emge, C. "How Welk Brought Fresh Sound from North Dakota Called Dance Music." *Down Beat,* February 9, 1955, p. 3.

Fedderson, Don. "Welk and His Public Trade Friendships." *Billboard,* Oct. 6, 1956, p. 26.

Frather, Leonard. "Hodges, Welk: Jazz Syrup on the Corn." *Los Angeles Times,* May 15, 1966, p. 11.

Freeman, D. "Welk Remembers Almost Missing the Big Harvest." *Down Beat,* April 6, 1955 p. 3.

Gehman, Richard. "For Forty Years a Happy Square." *TV Guide,* March 28, 1964, p. 23.

Govani, Albert. "The Story of Lawrence Welk." *Philadelphia Daily News,* April 24—May 6, 1967 (12 installments).

Gowran, Clay. "Welk Expected Short TV Run; Lasts 14 Years." *Chicago Tribune,* June 29, 1969, TV p. 1.

Griffith, Carolanne. "Welk Recalls Rough Road, Seeks to Help Others." *Fort Lauderdale News and Sun Sentinel,* April 13, 1974, p. 6B.

Gross, Ben. "Clean Family Shows Win on TV." *New York Sunday News,* July 20, 1969, p. 27S.

Guy, Gov. William L. "Lawrence Welk to Honor State." *Bismarck* (N.D.) *Tribune,* October 29, 1971, p. 1.

Guzzo, Louis R. "Welk's Versatile Musicians, Singers Win Him Ovation." *Seattle Times,* June 6, 1956 p. 14.

Hanna, Charles. "Lawrence of Bubbleland—Smiling Though It All." *Detroit Free Press,* February 20, 1971, TV p. 1.

Hay, Jacob. "Lawrence Welk at 68 Retains Loyalty of Tasteful Music Devotees." *Detroit News American,* May 14, 1971, TV p. 2.

Heffernan, Harold. "Welk's Coming Back and Ladies Love It." *New York Morning Call,* September 29, 1964, p. 28.

Hickey, William. "Champagne Music Man, a Vintage Rare." *Cleveland Plain Dealer,* July 25, 1969, TV p. 2.

Hilgenstuler, Ted. "Is Lawrence Welk's Music Corny?" *TV Radio Life,* April 1, 1953, p. 3.

Hill, Bob. "How to Succeed on TV." *Los Angeles Herald-Examiner,* July 21, 1963, TV p. 5.

Hilliard, Bob. "15,000 Hail Welk." *Manchester* (N.H.) *Union Leader,* August 24, 1974, TV p. 1.

Honigsberg Sam. "Lawrence Welk." *Billboard,* August 12, 1939. p. 2.

Honigsberg, Sam. "Chicago, Chicago." *Billboard,* September 16, 1939, p. 14.

Honigsberg, Sam. "Heavy Demand for Welk in Chicago." *Billboard,* September 23, 1939, p. 12.

Houston, Robert. "Lawrence Welk—a True Alger Type." *Omaha World-Herald,* August 20, 1967, p. 11.

Hruby, Frank. "Welk Brings Back Memories." *Cleveland Press,* August 22, 1972, p. 14.

Hurst, Margaret M. "Lawrence Welk." *World of Music,* December, 1964, p. 14.

Hyde, Jack. "Just Color It Champagne." *Los Angeles Times,* June 10, 1968, p. 1.

Jewett, Dave. "Welk Gives Sellout Crowd a Fun Time." *Portland* (Ore.) *Columbian,* June 6, 1974, TV p. 1.

Johnson, Erskine. "Lawrence Welk." *Los Angeles Mirror-News,* April 2, 1957, p. 2.

Jones, Will. "Dakotan Who Made Good." *Minneapolis Tribune,* May 20, 1956, p. 6.

Jones, Will. "Welk's Adverse Press Treatment." *Down Beat,* March 21, 1957, p. 37.

Joslyn, Jay. "Now They're Screaming for Welk." *Milwaukee Sentinel,* August 31, 1970, TV p. 1.

Judge, Frank. "Welk's Wise Way." *Detroit News TV Magazine,* July 10, 1966, p. 3.

Kaufman, J. L. "The Big Break." *School Music,* November, 1956, p. 20.

Klein, John. "How the Lawrence Welk Show is Formulated." *The School Musician,* September, 1956, p. 36.

Kluge, P. F. "Welk Has Fame, Fortune." *Wall Street Journal,* reprinted in *Aberdeen American News,* June 28, 1970, p. 34.

Kozak, Joseph J. "A Saturday with Lawrence Welk." *Extension,* January, 1952, p. 13.

LaCamera, Anthony. "King Midas of Music." *Boston Sunday Advertiser,* October 28, 1962, p. 12.

Laurent, Lawrence. "Welk Still Bubbling at 67, Scorns Stories of Retirement." *Denver Post,* April 2, 1970, TV p. 17.

Leadabrand, Russ. "Hats Off to Lawrence W." *Pasadena Star-News,* September 10, 1971, TV p. 1.

Leathers, Tom, "Wonderful, Wonderful?" *Kansas City Squire,* September 17, 1970, p. 7.

Lioce, Tony, "Let the Welkin Ring for This Audience." *Providence Evening Bulletin,* August 25, 1975, TV p. 1.

Lowry, Cynthia. "Success Hasn't Spoiled Our Man Mr. Welk." (Portland) *Oregonian,* June 28, 1964, TV p. 7.

Lutz, Sam. "Personality with Zingggg." *Billboard,* October 6, 1956, p. 20.

Mabley, Jack. "Bubblin' Welk's TV Secret—The People." *Chicago Daily News,* March 31, 1956, p. C26.

Mabley, Jack. "Bubbles, Polkas—Virtues of a Leader?" *Chicago Tribune,* January 20, 1975, p. 4.

Maddry, Lawrence. "Another Welk-Done Concert." (Norfolk) *Virginian Pilot,* September 9, 1971, TV p. 1.

Marlowe, Jon. "Ah-One, Ah-Two!" *Miami News,* March 11, 1977, p. 3.

Marne, Geoffrey. "Lawrence Welk: The Corn is Green." *International Musician,* March, 1971, p. 4.

Martin, P. "I Call on Lawrence Welk." *Saturday Evening Post,* June 21, 1958, 36–37, and June 28, 1958, 25–26.

McManus, Margaret. "Lawrence Welk, the Phenomenon of Television." *Des Moines Register,* April 15, 1956, p. 1.

Mercer, Charles. "Soft Smooth Music Pays for Welk." *Kansas City Star,* February 19, 1956, p. B8.

Miller, Donald. "Champagne for 40 Million." *Liguorian,* June, 1966, p. 13.

Miller, Donald. "Welk, Entertainers Draw 14,617 to Arena." *Pittsburgh Post-Gazette,* August 26, 1974, TV p. 1.

Miller, Jack. "Lawrence Welk's Bubble Machine Goes On Forever." *Windsor* (Ont.) *Star,* February 5, 1977, p. 41.

Minihan, Denise. "Lawrence Welk & Co.—It's an 'Ideal' Group." *Lawrence* (Mass.) *Eagle-Tribune,* August 23, 1974, TV p. 1.

Moffitt, Allene. "Farm Boy Lawrence Welk Traded Hoe for Accordion." (Fayetteville, N.C.) *TV Observer,* January 11, 1969, p. 3.

Morison, Elting E. "Wunnerful, Wunnerful!" *New York Times* (Book Review), October 17, 1971, p. 8.

Morrissey, Jim. "Swinging with Welk." *Louisville Courier-Journal*, April 12, 1964, p. 11M.

Murphy, Bob. "From Chewing Gum to Champagne." *Minneapolis Tribune*, March 1, 1953, p. 2.

Nachman, Gerald. "Conductor Gives Upbeat, Lays Out Welkome Mat." *New York Daily News*, January 19, 1973, p. 68.

Noonan, T. "Fans Flip at Carnegie Under Welk's Charm." *Billboard*, August 11, 1958, p. 5.

O'Brien, Jack. "A-one A-two-500!" *New York Journal American*, January 20, 1965, p. 28.

O'Haire, Patricia. "In 2 Nites, Led Zeppelin and Welk—Help, Help!" *New York Times*, September 4, 1971, TV p. 1.

Price, Paul. "Why the Lawrence Welk Show Is Most Popular in Los Angeles." *Los Angeles Daily News*, January 28, 1953, p. C11.

Rahn, Pete. "Red, White and Blue Special—Welk's 'Thank You, America'." *St. Louis Globe-Democrat*, November 20, 1970, p. 13C.

Reichman, Theda Kleinhans. "Lawrence Welk's Secret Formula for Enjoying Life." (Los Angeles) *Twin Circle*, December 3, 1978, p. 3.

Rodenbach, Clark. "Makes Welk-in Ring." *Chicago Daily News*, September 13, 1939, p. 21.

Rose, Bob. "Welk Keeps Bubble Soaring with Elixir of Familiarity." *Chicago Daily News*, December 11, 1968, p. 14.

Rose, Bob. "Lawrence Welk." *Des Moines Register*, January 19, 1969, p. M1.

Rose, Bob. "Lawrence Welk." *Des Moines Register*, January 19, 1969, TV p. 3.

Rummel, Larry. "No More Jokes Aimed at Welk." *Phoenix Gazette*, December 4, 1970, p. 90.

Sancton, Tom. "Lawrence Welk Reunited with Pete Fountain Here." *New Orleans Times-Picayune*, August 8, 1969, p. 14.

Santosuosso, Ernie. "15,000 Effervesce as Welk Previews New TV Series." *Boston Globe*, September 6, 1971, TV p. 1.

Sasso, Arthur J. "Bubbles, Bounce and Buffoonery." *Escapade*, April, 1957, p. 55.

Satchell, Michael J. "Welk Waltzes On and On and On." *Kansas City Star,* September 1, 1970, TV p. 1.

Saunders, Walter. "Lawrence Welk Has Every Move Mapped." *Rocky Mountain News,* August 27, 1975, TV p. 50.

Schlaerth, J. Don. "Hard Work Led to Success." *Buffalo Courier-Express,* January 27, 1957, p. 12B.

Schumacher, M. "Fifth Anniversary for Welkism on ABC." *New York Times,* June 12, 1960, p. 13.

Scott, Vernon. "Lawrence Welk Champagne Music but No Swearing." *St. Petersburg Times,* August 6, 1969, p. 6D.

Selvin, B. "Speed and Quality on RCA Thesaurus." *Billboard,* October 6, 1956, p. 26.

Shearer, Lloyd. "Television's Two Big Surprises: Lawrence Welk and Ernie Ford." *Parade,* May 26, 1957, p. 1.

Silva, Phyllis. "Maestro Lawrence Welk, Television Phenomenon." *Brockton* (Mass.) *Daily Enterprise,* February 28, 1973, p. 43.

Sippel, John. "Welk Aragon Stint Tops Decade Score." *Billboard,* January 10, 1962, p. 1.

Smith, Helen C. "The Welk Mystique." *Atlanta Constitution,* March 12, 1975, p. 5–1.

Tanguay, Kerwin. "Champagne Music." *The Marianist,* June, 1956, p. 9.

Tanguay, Kerwin. "Lawrence Welk and His Champagne Music." *St. Anthony Messenger,* September, 1956, p. 1.

Tanguay, Kerwin. "Welk." *The Apostle,* May, 1966, p. 12.

Telpner, Gene. "Welk's Sparkle Attracts Crowds to City Show." *Winnipeg Tribune,* August 28, 1974, p. 25.

Trauber, Leonard. "Lawrence Welk Rings Welk-in for All." *Variety,* June 6, 1956, p. 21.

Walls, Gloria. "Stays Happy with a Song in His Heart." *Los Angeles Herald-Examiner,* July 16, 1968, p. C1.

Walters, Larry. "He Serves Champagne Hot." *Chicago Tribune,* April 28, 1957, p. 32.

Walters, Larry. "The Man Who Killed Caesar." *Chicago Tribune,* May 5, 1957, p. 52.

Walters, Larry. "The Square of Tigertail Road." *Chicago Tribune Magazine,* August 4, 1963, p. 1.

Weaver, Emmett. "Welk Fans Respond Warmly to the Music of the Maestro." *Birmingham Post-Herald,* March 7, 1977, p. A6.

Welk, Lawrence. "Champagne Music." *Billboard,* August 26, 1939, p. 3.

Welk, Lawrence. "Television Places Unique Burden on Bands." *Down Beat,* April 18, 1956, p. 3.

Welk, Lawrence. "In Back of the Star, the Helping Hand." *Billboard,* October 6, 1956, p. 19.

Welk, Lawrence. "An Important Pastime." *Padre,* February, 1957, p. 1.

Welk, Lawrence. "What to Play?" *Down Beat,* April 18, 1957, p. 22.

Welk, Lawrence. "Music Fine but Talk Brought Success." *Hollywood Record,* August 9, 1967, p. 14.

Welk, Lawrence. "Work, Hardship and Fear." *Pittsburgh Press,* February 8, 1970, p. 31.

Wendeborn, John. "Music Critic Gains Respect for Welk." (Portland) *Oregonian,* June 5, 1974, TV p. 1.

Williams, Robert J. "Lawrence Welk, A Self-Appraisal." *Philadelphia Sunday Bulletin,* September 16, 1962, p. 2TV.

Wooten, Dick. "Here Come the Bubbles." *Cleveland Press,* July 26, 1969, p. 34.

Index